M000169093

Laruelle

Laruelle
A Stranger Thought

Anthony Paul Smith

polity

Copyright © Anthony Paul Smith 2016

The right of Anthony Paul Smith to be identified as Author of this Work has been asserted in accordance with the UK Copyright, Designs and Patents Act 1988.

First published in 2016 by Polity Press

Polity Press
65 Bridge Street
Cambridge CB2 1UR, UK

Polity Press
350 Main Street
Malden, MA 02148, USA

All rights reserved. Except for the quotation of short passages for the purpose of criticism and review, no part of this publication may be reproduced, stored in a retrieval system, or transmitted, in any form or by any means, electronic, mechanical, photocopying, recording or otherwise, without the prior permission of the publisher.

ISBN-13: 978-0-7456-7122-2
ISBN-13: 978-0-7456-7123-9 (pb)

A catalogue record for this book is available from the British Library.

Library of Congress Cataloging-in-Publication Data

Names: Smith, Anthony Paul, 1982-
Title: Laruelle : a stranger thought / Anthony Paul Smith.
Description: Malden, MA : Polity Press, 2016. | Includes bibliographical references and index.
Identifiers: LCCN 2015037053| ISBN 9780745671222 (hardback : alk. paper) | ISBN 9780745671239 (pbk. : alk. paper)
Subjects: LCSH: Laruelle, François.
Classification: LCC B2433.L374 S65 2106 | DDC 194–dc23 LC record available at http://lccn.loc.gov/2015037053

Typeset in 10.5 on 12 pt Palatino
by Toppan Best-set Premedia Limited
Printed and bound in the UK by CPI Group (UK) Ltd, Croydon, CRO 4YY

The publisher has used its best endeavors to ensure that the URLs for external websites referred to in this book are correct and active at the time of going to press. However, the publisher has no responsibility for the websites and can make no guarantee that a site will remain live or that the content is or will remain appropriate.

Every effort has been made to trace all copyright holders, but if any have been inadvertently overlooked the publisher will be pleased to include any necessary credits in any subsequent reprint or edition.

For further information on Polity, visit our website: politybooks.com

J'éclate. Je suis le feu. Je suis la mer.
Le monde se défait. Mais je suis le monde.

La fin, la fin disions-nous.
Aimé Césaire, "Les armes miraculeuses"

Aimer un étranger comme soi-même implique comme contrepartie:
s'aimer soi-même comme un étranger.
Simone Weil, *La Pesanteur et la grâce*

Contents

Acknowledgments

First I want to acknowledge Alexander R. Galloway for recommending this project to Polity, and John B. Thompson for commissioning it. This book is the result of a number of years of research and writing, and John has been supportive and patient throughout the process. Toward the end of the writing of this book, Alex's own book engaging with Laruelle was published, and thinking alongside of his reading helped me to get clarity on a number of important issues. My sincere gratitude also goes to Elliott Karstadt, editorial assistant at Polity, who guided me throughout the process in what is mostly a thankless task, and to George Owers who took over that task after Elliott's departure. Thank you to Leigh Mueller for her work as copyeditor. She has improved the text greatly.

This book was written concurrently with *François Laruelle's Principles of Non-Philosophy: A Critical Introduction and Guide*, a study of one of Laruelle's most important works. As with that book, I am thankful to the readers of drafts: Alice Rekab, Michael O'Neill Burns, and Marika Rose. My gratitude also goes to my colleagues in the Department of Religion at La Salle University, especially the support of the chair, Maureen O'Connell, and the encouragement of Jack Downey and Jordan Copeland. I acknowledge the financial support provided by Tom Keagy, Dean of the School of Arts and Sciences at La Salle University, which allowed me to participate in the colloquium held at Cerisy in September of 2014 on Laruelle's non-standard philosophy, where I presented aspects of chapter 5. There I benefited from conversations with Ian James, John Ó Maoilearca, Joshua Ramey, Rocco Gangle, Drew S. Burk,

Katerina Kolozova, and others. Further elements of chapter 5 were presented at "Superpositions: A Symposium on Laruelle and the Humanities," held at The New School in New York. I am thankful for the invitation to speak from Rocco, Julius Greve, and Ed Keller, and for comments from Dave Mesing, Ed Kazarian, and Benjamin Norris. Elements of chapter 6 were presented in 2012 at the Leeds Art Gallery at the invitation of Anne Reid, for "Abandoned Projectors: A Pavilion Forum." Parts of chapter 7 were presented in Dublin at the 2013 Mystical Theology Network conference "Mystical Theology: Eruptions from France," and I benefitted from the comments of Louise Sullivan, Marika Rose, and Kate Tomas there. Earlier versions of chapter 7 appeared in *Postmodern Saints of France: Refiguring "the Holy" in Contemporary French Philosophy*, ed. Colby Dickinson (New York and London: Bloomsbury, 2013) as "Laruelle and the Messiah before the Saints," and in *Analecta Hermeneutica* 4 (2013) as "'Who do you say that I am?': Secular Christologies in Contemporary French Philosophy," and I gratefully acknowledge the permission of the publishers of these titles to reproduce in full. Parts of chapter 3 were presented in New York at the 2014 "Derrida Today" conference, and I am thankful to Michael Naas for his comments and provocations. Alex Dubilet was also present at many of these events and I am thankful for the discussions we had in New York over trips to pizza parlors. These were but continuations of the many discussions we have had about Laruelle and related problems as we work along parallel but distinct paths.

This book is dedicated to Daniel Colucciello Barber. His intellectual creativity and insights are only matched by the loyalty and care he shows in friendship. Everything I have written feels indelibly marked by his thought, and even where we may differ it nonetheless feels like grace: a grace without any hope of achievement.

Abbreviations of Works by François Laruelle

TE   *Théorie des etrangers. Science des hommes, démocratie, non-psychanalyse*

TI   *Théorie des identités. Fractalité généralisée et philosophie artificielle*

Introduction: What Is to Be Done with Philosophy?

A certain desire for the end is endemic to twentieth-century philosophy. This is true of both the so-called Continental and analytic varieties. That end may take the form of the end of philosophy itself as it diffuses into a thousand other scientific disciplines claiming to be able to answer the old questions more concretely. Or that end may only be the end of metaphysics or history, the end of phenomenology, the end of language, or the death of God or Man, just the small death of the author – one may even look forward to the grand death of everything in the solar catastrophe, or perhaps one simply wants to be done with judgment. It seems that most philosophers want something in the end, while perhaps most readers just want to be done. "Are we done?" This is perhaps a familiar question at the end of an introduction to philosophy lecture by some bored undergraduate forced to take it as part of their core courses. Setting aside the source, the question remains in the desire of so many philosophers: are we done with philosophy?

The question arises because philosophy is in the midst of an identity crisis. This is nothing particularly new. If we go back, all the way back to the beginning of institutionalized philosophy in Plato's Academy, then we might read his acceptance of the impossibility of a philosopher-king at the helm of an ideal republic after the death of Dion of Syracuse as the first major crisis of philosophy.[1] For the identity crisis of philosophy is a crisis over the point of philosophy and the ability of philosophy to affect the so-called "real world." For Laruelle, philosophy desires to affect the Real itself, and it cannot because the Real is always already indifferent to it. Since philosophy cannot affect the Real it desires to affect, it must then settle for second-best, which is affecting the world, just as Plato settles for advising the new rulers of Syracuse after the death of Dion. And yet philosophy cannot even live up to second-best.

The non-philosophy of François Laruelle suggests that this is the wrong question to ask: it is a false question. Bergson defined this kind of question as being one that leads us to a false answer. The true question is not "Are we done with philosophy?", but "What is to be done with philosophy?"[2]

This book explores the answer to this question that Laruelle provides in his non-philosophy. The point of non-philosophy is not a different philosophical analysis of the traditional materials that philosophy has tended to dominate, but a mutation or recoding of the machinery of philosophy itself in order to create a new practice of thought. Non-Philosophy is not simply a "new philosophy."[3] It does not add yet another voice to interminable debates, but at its best aims for something different, something strange and alien to standard philosophy. Non-Philosophy is stranger than philosophy. And this hitherto untold strangeness lies behind the two-fold purpose of this book. The first part of the book provides a generic introduction to non-philosophy, tracing its most general structures. In this part of the book, the reader will be introduced to the fundamental inquiry into the essence of philosophy that Laruelle's method of "dualysis" constitutes. In Chapter 1, I explicate Laruelle's theory and analysis of what he calls the "Philosophical Decision." This is a constant theme throughout Laruelle's oeuvre, though most clearly laid out in *Philosophies of Difference* (1986, and 2010 in English translation) and *Principles of Non-Philosophy* (1996, and 2013 in English translation). The theory of the Philosophical Decision requires that we also investigate Laruelle's theory of the One, which allows Philosophical Decision to emerge from the background noise of philosophical machinery acting upon various fields. Chapter 2 turns to the methods employed by Laruelle to mutate and make a new use out of the Philosophical Decision. Laruelle himself calls these methods a "style" and "syntax" and so this chapter surveys and explains this style and syntax. It explains the sometimes mystifying aspects of Laruelle's written style as part and parcel of the practice of non-philosophy, as his syntax is constructed in such a way as to address philosophy's underlying self-sufficiency. Therefore the intentionally difficult syntax aims not at confusion but at a reorganization of thought itself. Part I of the text gives the reader a synthetic view of non-philosophy that prepares them for the specificity of Laruelle's engagement with the other materials that populate Part II of the book.

Part II is organized into five chapters to evoke the five waves of non-philosophy. These waves are Laruelle's own division of his work into five distinct periods that remain largely consistent over time, but with new materials and focus in each period. However, I do not present here a simple history of non-philosophy, as I have elsewhere presented such a history by focusing on either the change in axioms that guide each wave or the history of the conjugation of science and philosophy.[4] Instead I have picked five significant thematics running throughout each of the five waves and show how these thematics are engaged with from his early work to his most contemporary, and in turn how they help to develop the practice of non-philosophy.

I have chosen this structure in part to address a criticism by Ray Brassier, one of the early Anglophone readers of Laruelle and translator of some of his essays. It was Brassier's work, alongside John Ó Maoilearca's, that introduced me to non-philosophy. And while I have learned a great deal from both of them, it was a certain annoyance (philosophy does not only begin in wonder!) at the criticism Brassier makes in *Nihil Unbound* that spurred me to undertake this book in this particular way. He claims that Laruelle's work is always focused simply on the machinery of non-philosophy, writing:

> one cannot but be struck by the formalism and the paucity of detail in his handling of these topics, which seems cursory even in comparison with orthodox philosophical treatments of the same themes. Indeed, the brunt of the conceptual labour in these confrontations with ethics, Marxism, and mysticism is devoted to refining or fine-tuning his own non-philosophical machinery, while actual engagement with the specifics of the subject matter is confined to discussions of more or less arbitrarily selected philosophemes on the topic in question. The results are texts in which descriptions of the workings of Laruelle's non-philosophical apparatus continue to occupy centre-stage while the philosophical material which is ostensibly the focus of analysis is relegated to a perfunctory supporting role.... Thus in his book on ethics (*Éthique de l'étranger*) Laruelle does not actually provide anything like a substantive conceptual analysis of ethical tropes in contemporary philosophy; he simply uses potted versions of Plato, Kant, and Levinas to sketch what a non-philosophical theory of 'the ethical' would look like. Similarly, in his

Introduction to Non-Marxism he does not actually engage in an analysis of Marxist theory and practice; he simply uses two idiosyncratic philosophical readings of Marx, those of Althusser and Henry, as the basis for outlining what a non-philosophical theory of Marxism would look like.[5]

It appears that, for Brassier, non-philosophy has not delivered on any of its perceived promises. He even states in his characteristically harsh style that "Laruelle's writings have yet to inspire anything beyond uncritical emulation or exasperated dismissal."[6] On this reading, non-philosophy would remain an ultimately fruitless bootstrapping that, aside from the machinery itself, offers nothing new to philosophy as such.

Brassier's criticism hinges on what I see as a fundamental misunderstanding of Laruelle's non-philosophy. He confuses the philosophical material that Laruelle pulls from standard philosophy with material that Laruelle aims to analyze. But Laruelle does not want to provide us with another philosophical analysis. Instead he wants to use the different philosophical analyses to do something with philosophy, without making any claim about the Real that conditions every theoretical project. To show how Laruelle does this, I engage with his corpus generically (or synthetically in the standard philosophical idiom) rather than linearly. This means that I do not present a developmental reading of non-philosophy. Laruelle himself says that such a reading of non-philosophy as a linear evolution would be artificial: "It is more a question of kaleidoscopic views, all similar yet rearranged each time...Each book in a sense reprises the same problems 'from zero', again throwing the dice or reshuffling the cards of science, philosophy, Marxism, gnosis, man as Stranger and Christ. The essence of non-philosophy would be, let's say, fractal and fictioned."[7]

This also means that I really do aim here at a general introduction to non-philosophy. While at times I mark certain differences in my understanding of non-philosophy from others who have engaged with Laruelle's large body of work, this is not a book aiming to mark out a certain space or assuming major familiarity with the specific debates amongst Francophone and Anglophone non-philosophers. Instead, I firstly hope to help new readers of Laruelle to gain a foothold in his own texts, rather than this text alone, by explicating some of the main concepts and questions that non-philosophy engages with. I then turn to helping new readers situate non-philosophy in relation to some other debates in various areas of philosophy and theory more generally, through creative readings of those concepts and questions alongside other forms of thought that I take to be radical. The radical nature of these other discourses is assessed on the basis of their incisiveness and rigor in their understanding of the world as well as their strangeness according to the norms of the standard model of philosophy and various forms of theory produced by that model.

I attempt to model the fractal nature of non-philosophy in the structure of the book. Fractals are complex patterns that remain self-similar across different scales. This means that ultimately there is a single overarching shape to the book that is found in each chapter. So, Part I of the text scales out to consider non-philosophy generally as a theory and practice. Chapter 1 presents Laruelle's theory of the Philosophical Decision, which is often taken to be the critical aspect of non-philosophy. Laruelle, however, presents this theory as a diagnostic of philosophy, an act of identifying what it is that makes philosophy in general. The purpose of this is not to destroy philosophy, but to disempower it so that it loses its self-sufficiency, or at least has its authoritarian impulses much weakened. Chapter 2 then turns to the style of non-philosophy. Here we look at the way non-philosophy works with philosophy as a material, the syntax it deploys, and some of the concepts that operate on philosophical material. If the theory of Philosophical Decision is the negative and critical move of non-philosophy, then its style is its constructive mode. The two ultimately cannot be separated since the negation of philosophy allows for philosophy to be used in the production or fabulation of new forms of theory.

After this general introduction to non-philosophy, we then move to Part II of the book in which we look at how it operates on the different scales imposed by specific domains of knowledge. We begin with politics in chapter 3, where we see an equivocation of politics and philosophy. Here we look at the way that politics and philosophy mirror one another in their decisional structure through an investigation of Laruelle's early works in political philosophy. We then turn to his later conception of a "democracy (of) thought" as the model that non-philosophy attempts to follow in thinking various theoretical materials together. This moves us from politics to science in chapter 4, since it is science that allows Laruelle to think otherwise than philosophically. Here we look at the way that science enacts a very different kind of relationship regarding the thinking of an object and the real object. We see here the beginnings of Laruelle's focus upon the human in the way in which he sees

science as a fundamentally humane form of thinking that blocks
the possibility of presenting a singular essence of the human. This
evocation of the human moves us then to the question of ethics in
chapter 5. Here we investigate Laruelle's attempt to create a new
kind of humanism, or non-humanism, by putting him in dialogue
with important critical theorists on the question of race. This helps
to elucidate Laruelle's thinking, but also puts him in dialogue with
those outside of the mainstream of philosophy who are engaged in
projects more like non-philosophy than those within the discipline
of philosophy proper. Here we begin to see the importance of
certain kinds of fictions in his theory as he develops the importance
of names like "victim" and "stranger" for his ethical theory. And
so, in chapter 6, we turn to his conception of philo-fiction to investigate further his theory of fiction and the ways in which non-
philosophy acts as a kind of philo-fiction or "science-phiction." As
we see there, this notion of philo-fiction speaks to the general shape
of non-philosophy as it again posits a radically foreclosed Real-One
untouched and unrepresentable by philosophy, but also posits that
we may write stories regarding, that we may fabulate, rigorous
fictions that speak to our unlearned knowledge about the radical
immanence of this Real. This emphasis on fabulation or the fictive
aspects of naming in non-philosophy opens us to a discussion of
religion in chapter 7. Here we investigate the importance of messianism and mysticism to Laruelle's work, not as an escape from
reality, but as human fictions that express demands regarding the
salvation of human beings as well as the need for something
beyond worldly forms of thought to think through what such a
salvation would be. This connection of religion and science fiction
through their fictive elements is made by Laruelle himself as he
claims that religion, in the form of a gnosticism that runs throughout the institutional forms of religion, poses the same question as
science fiction: *"should we save humanity? and What do we mean by
humanity?"*[8] I then conclude the book by examining what possible
future there may be for non-philosophy. I do not argue that the
future will be Laruellean or make any grandiose claims about the
power of non-philosophy to change the world. As we may come
to see in our living it, there is nothing particularly laudable about
the future. Yet the future comes regardless, and it may be that non-
philosophy offers tools for doing something with the future in the
now.

I have my criticisms of Laruelle's project, but its supposed fruitlessness is not one of them.[9] I have almost entirely left my criticisms

of Laruelle to the side, seeing my role in writing this introduction as being to balance the scales somewhat and present the strengths of Laruelle's project. To do so I have put Laruelle in creative dialogue with other thinkers, though not often ones in the mainstream of philosophy in either its Continental or analytic modes, as I have already said. From my limited perspective, analytic philosophy appears to still be conditioned largely by a hegemonic Liberal political project and is in many ways moribund as it works out increasingly self-referential and self-limiting problems. At the same time, Continental philosophy has largely continued to focus on explicating its own history or moving toward new forms of metaphysics. One could introduce Laruelle in this standard way, comparing him to this analytic philosopher or placing him in this Continental history.[10] I could also simply give the facts regarding Laruelle's development; I could place him in his historical context (he was born in France in 1937 and has lived out most of his adult life in Paris), list his books (he has written over 25 books, with his first appearing in 1971), detail and assess his debates with Derrida, Luc Ferry (former French Minister for Youth, National Education, and Research), Badiou, and others. Such an approach has merits, but it does not show the power and potential of non-philosophy. Non-Philosophy provides resources for carrying out radically creative work that can take traditional tropes in standard philosophical discourse and combine them with exciting forms of thought taking place without regard for that tradition. In being stranger than philosophy, it allows one steeped in the history of philosophy to radically refuse the borders of philosophy and other forms of human knowledge. More importantly, it breaks down the frame imposed by that history of philosophy when considering questions of identity, universality, ethics, knowledge, science, faith, art, and other traditional themes of philosophy.

I have elsewhere tried to show how Laruelle's non-philosophy may help to dissolve certain problems in environmental philosophy and may fruitfully engage with the science of ecology. Philosophers often ignore ecology as a science, even if it has become somewhat in vogue to give attention to certain environmental issues or to borrow some concepts from the wider field of environmental studies – like the anthropocene. While the science of ecology may not have the cachet of neuroscience or cosmology, it is already doing rich philosophical work and the method of non-philosophy draws that out. That text, *A Non-Philosophical Theory of Nature*, does more to show the creative possibility for Laruelle's non-philosophy of science (he calls this both a non-epistemology and a unified theory of science and philosophy) than does my chapter on science in this text. Instead, here I have tried to show the importance of science for the project of non-philosophy and how Laruelle in general understands the relationship, creating a kind of introduction that may be supplemented by my earlier text and Laruelle's own many books on the topic. In this book, I focus most on the overarching politico-ethical arc of non-philosophy, specifically by showing how Laruelle's project may join with the critical theory of race in an attempt to create a humanism made to the measure of the Human-in-Human rather than the measure of the world or a bleak cosmos.[11] These fields are not normally respected by institutional philosophers, and undoubtedly many of the thinkers referenced alongside of Laruelle are unconcerned about the proliferation and reproduction of institutional philosophy. Insofar as institutional philosophy fails to respect these fields and thinkers, it does so because those thinkers dare to consider problems that are much harder to think through than an Anglo-pessimism I regard as cheap in its talk of a cold world or the ultimate heat death of the universe. We are here, fragile creatures that we are, and, regardless of any future death, that fact of existing matters in both the physical and moral sense, regardless of how finite or limited that mattering is.

The two-fold purpose of this book really flows from one underlying drive: to show what can be done with non-philosophy and let that doing speak for itself. Many readers have come to Laruelle and felt exasperated at the strangeness of it, overwhelmed by how painful it was to work through the texts. And, for all that pain, what does the reader get? Detractors and even early adaptors have sat in judgment upon Laruelle's project and ruled it fruitless. I embrace Laruelle's fruitlessness, unlike these detractors, as a kind of anti-natalism regarding philosophy (though likely not an anti-natalism regarding human beings), precisely because it may join with projects on the fringes of institutional philosophy and theory more generally. I have no desire to have this judgment overturned on appeal – no desire for a debate on whether or not Laruelle's non-philosophy is truly fruitful. Like many works and methods of theory, it has already gone forth and multiplied in ways unrecognizable to philosophy's reproductive regime. Thought always multiplies. Only a naturalist version of theodicy – a "naturdicy" or "biodicy" – would look to the number of intellectual offspring or to successful grant applications in order to declare that this truly is the best of all possible intellectual worlds. Intellectual brilliance is fragile and it dies and passes from the earth. Perhaps it does so everyday with every lost language and every doctoral graduate who remains unemployed.

One of the reasons I was first drawn to Laruelle's non-philosophy was precisely because of its rejection of theodicy in every form, even those that persist after the death of God. So to those who sat in judgment, not only of Laruelle but of those who have tried to take up the method and project it in their own way, I can only respond, "You say so" (Matt 27:11).[12] That non-philosophy is *philosophically* fruitless is indeed the good news proclaimed here. As this is not a book of mystagogy, at least not in any straightforwardly derogatory sense, the drive behind it is to show the ways in which non-philosophy allows us to enter into traditional or standard philosophical material and do something with it. For better or for worse, we are not done with philosophy, but we may be able to do something with it. For, however fragile and finite that doing is, it will always be real.

Part I

A Generic Introduction

1

Theory of the Philosophical Decision

"Choose this day whom you will serve": non-philosophical indifference to philosophical faith

Philosophy has a faith that is particular to it. Laruelle claims that everything we call philosophy shares the same invariant structure as what he calls "decision." The particularity of this faith is revealed by theorizing this decision and tracing the general practice of philosophy in its unrecognized piety. As we move toward a purely abstract or generic presentation of Philosophical Decision, I will introduce increasingly technical language before responding to some criticisms of Laruelle's theory. But before we descend into the technical details it may be useful to first anchor ourselves in the model that Laruelle uses when he presents the work of non-philosophy, claiming that it may be thought of as an apparatus or a machine, which in his latest work Laruelle compares to a particle collider.[1] Standard philosophy is inserted into this apparatus and is worked upon. This processing of philosophy through the apparatus is what allows for the identity of philosophy to emerge or be seen. We shall start at the end and travel backwards. First we will turn to the summary of the results this apparatus provided and then look at the formal or generic structure which Laruelle constructed from this theoretical collider.

While each of Laruelle texts essentially starts from zero, there are certain texts where the greater emphasis is given to the identification of philosophical decision. Our main reference points will be *Philosophies of Difference* and *Principles of Non-Philosophy*, with supplements from other texts, like the *Dictionary of Non-Philosophy* (1998, and 2013 in English translation) which provides for us a summary of the findings of the theoretical inquiry into philosophy's identity:

> Philosophy's principal and formalized invariant or structure: in accordance with philosophy, which does not indicate it without also simultaneously auto-affecting philosophy and affecting its own identity; in accordance with non-philosophy which this time gives Philosophical Decision a radical identity (of) structure or that determines it in-the-last-instance. Its synonyms: dyad and unity, amphibology, unity-of-contraries, mixture, blending – they are even likely to have a double usage, intra-philosophical and non-philosophical, which changes its sense. Philosophical Decision is a mixture of indecision and decision, never pure decision.[2]

Even in this general definition we see that Laruelle is attentive to the ways in which this decisional structure may manifest in a variety of ways, as he lists the various synonyms and recognizes that this decisional structure relies on a certain "amphibology" or structural inconsistency. We also see in this definition a recognition that there are at least two ways of reading the meaning of this structure, much in the way classical economics and Marxist economics are able to recognize the underlying structure of economics while their presentation of that structure varies greatly. For philosophy this recognition of a structure is a matter of speaking to philosophy's power, what it does, and why it matters that it does it. Whether it is an eliminativist philosophy that aims to cull certain manifest mythologies from the way in which we think, or it is a matter of a productive philosophy aiming to change the world, each philosopher finds a sufficient reason for their existence as a philosopher.

The supreme example of this confidence in philosophy is given voice perhaps most forcefully by Laruelle's contemporary, Alain Badiou. When asked about Laruelle's non-philosophy Badiou responded, "I have difficulty in understanding Laruelle [laughs] especially regarding the question of the Real. The strength of philosophy is its decisions in regards to the Real."[3] There is in that moment of laughter an expression of philosophy's supreme confidence, even if only in the promise of philosophy rather than its actuality since we know many philosophers are disillusioned with their work and the work of their colleagues, but still await something like a philosophical messiah (to bring to mind that double "end of philosophy" referenced in our introduction, according to which this messiah could be the fulfillment of philosophy's promise within philosophy itself or through a proliferation of other disciplines). Decision, with regard to philosophy, names the *agon* or contest of philosophy. It names the belief that there could emerge from the history of philosophical battle the *right* philosophy, and that philosophy may access this Real or what we might more colloquially refer to in English as *the* truth.

Non-Philosophy may be bold in its claim to have identified something invariant to philosophy, but its boldness comes from a refusal to attempt a circumscription of the Real or to provide any end or goal for thought at all. Non-Philosophy is in this way a kind of sobering up from philosophical drunkenness and its attendant harassment of the Real. Laruelle continues in the *Dictionary of Non-Philosophy* with his intervention, repeating to philosophy what it said the night before:

> The Philosophical Decision is an operation of transcendence that believes (in a naive and hallucinatory way) in the possibility of a unitary discourse of the Real.... To philosophize is to decide on the Real and on thought, which ensues from it, that is to philosophize is to believe philosophy is able to align the Real and thought with the universal order of the Principle of Sufficient Reason (the Logos), but also more generally in accordance with the "total" or unitary order of the Principle of Sufficient Philosophy.[4]

Philosophy has a faith in itself, it has its own driving myth.[5] In relation to philosophical faith, non-philosophy acts similarly to the field of religious studies, especially as it emerged in the seventeenth and eighteenth centuries through the scientific study of the bible. Scholars like Ernest Renan and Ferdinand Christian Baur, building off the work of Spinoza and Erasmus, began to use new techniques in the study of Christian scriptures. In so doing they treated that scripture like one object among others, equal in the sense that it too could be subjected to this sort of critical inquiry. Non-Philosophy comes to philosophy – every philosophy – as something that claims a certain sufficiency, much like some religious communities look to scriptures or dogmas as having sufficiency in their disclosure of truth, and non-philosophy then treats that philosophy as something subject to critical inquiry.

The unity given to the world by either Christian scripture/dogma or philosophy is not truly sufficient. It is not rooted in some timeless essence. But, as those scholars of biblical literature showed with regard to scripture and as Laruelle shows with regard to philosophy, they developed contingently and did so radically. Everything that takes place in philosophy is grounded upon radical contingency.[6] It could be otherwise. The committed biblical inerrantist counts his blessings that he was not born an aboriginal, and the philosopher praises the achievement of Plato. But it would be absurd, it would be pure theodicy or naturdicy, to think there was a reason the Christian was born in Indianapolis or Sheffield or that the name of Plato survived but that of some forgotten African thinker did not. And so, when the philosopher comes along and declares to the neophyte, "choose this day whom you will serve" (Joshua 24:15), the non-philosopher refuses for there is simply no sufficient reason to choose: "there is no reason to 'choose' Heidegger rather than Nietzsche or vice versa."[7] To continue with the example of Heidegger(–Derrida) and Nietzsche(–Deleuze) that Laruelle explores at length in his *Philosophies of Difference*, there is no reason to choose because it is already a forced choice. It all depends from the start how difference is posed (in the case of these philosophies of difference), for in that initial posing or positioning by the philosopher the choice is already made.

The choice does not need to be made, however, when one realizes that there is no reason to absolutely pose or position difference or any other philosophical elemental as "everything" or "the All": "To perceive the sheer expanse of this model [the invariant structure of philosophy], one must go back to the canonical enunciation: *Everything is (Water Earth, Fire, etc.).*"[8] The history of philosophy is the history of the debates over such choices because philosophy is itself rooted in absolute contingency (a rejection of the principle of sufficient reason made by Laruelle decades before Meillassoux made such a move popular amongst some in Continental philosophy). It is because of this absolute contingency that philosophy turns to decision.[9] Absolute contingency is as close as Laruelle comes to a positive description of the One, which often appears to take the form of a kind of apophaticism or "un-saying," but the One is not the object of his analysis. Indeed, his point will be that philosophizing about the One (or Real, as he uses these terms largely interchangeably, depending upon context) is precisely what philosophy does. Since non-philosophy is a science of philosophy, it wants to investigate that act of philosophizing rather than the One itself (which is un-representable and thus foreclosed to such speculation). Laruelle then looks to what lies beneath philosophy's choice itself, the choice that allows for the manifestation of all philosophy's positions and, ultimately, the way in which both forms of philosophy work in terms of continuing to be productive of thought despite their seemingly mutually exclusive claims.[10] What underlies it is what Laruelle calls the One in its radical immanence – no reflection need be done and no choice can be made, for the One is indifferent to all of its effects, to all the various philosophies that manifest from it. Thus the point is to model thought from the One, rather than aiming to think the One. The point is simply not to play the philosophical game at all, not to suspend some decision in favor of another, but to be indifferent to every form of the decision.

Here we come to an element of non-philosophy not often acknowledged in its early Anglophone reception – and when it was acknowledged it was often denigrated. For what underlies all philosophical decisions, claims Laruelle, is the human in its finitude and radical immanence. This is the abyssal ground of all philosophy for Laruelle: the human. It is important that we understand this is not a philosophy of the human, nor a denial that intelligence is found elsewhere (as he also explores animal life and artificial intelligence), but that the lived (reality) of the human is purely contingent and it is out of the human contingency that human thought comes:[11]

> But measured against the finite or "individual" man who precedes philosophical decision, who affects it with stronger contingency, there is neither more nor less absurdity in one choice than in another, but an equal absurdity, an equal absence of sufficient reason for the choice, an "absence" that is the true "sufficient reason" of philosophical decision and of the war philosophical decision wages against itself. *We must posit the equivalence of philosophical decisions.*[12]

As we can see here, the human is indeed the measure of philosophy for Laruelle, but it would be a mistake to confuse this with anthropocentrism. The radical immanence of the human takes the same status as the radical immanence of the Real and the One (equivalent terms in Laruelle's work). As such there can be no philosophy of the human, or even from the human, that would provide the measure of *all* things. Anthropocentrism is yet another philosophical decision that must be made equivalent to others and which finds its very ground in the human.

This is not a moralism, either. Making these philosophical decisions equivalent is not simply making them equivalent as "bad" or "evil." The point of offering this critique of philosophy is not to finally indict philosophy, to bring it to trial for some crime against humanity that arises out of its invariant structure. They are made equivalent simply as relative – or, to speak more precisely, they are made equivalent as *material*. Laruelle wants to *do something* with philosophy, not choose one philosophy over the other. Non-Philosophy is therefore not a moralism, but a pragmatic.

Tracing the structure

Any attempt to do something with some material requires that we develop some kind of general understanding of that material. And crucially – and this bears repeating because of its importance – philosophy is cast as material by non-philosophy. We have already followed much of the shape of that general understanding in this chapter through a discussion of philosophy as having a faith that is particular to it – a faith that says it can affect everything through its particularity. Like most faiths, this particular philosophical faith is rooted in a practice. That practice is the focus of this section, as we trace the structure of Philosophical Decision.

The most technical explication in English of Laruelle's theory of the Philosophical Decision has been Brassier's in *Nihil Unbound*. There he presents a largely synthetic reconstruction of Laruelle's understanding of Decision. Brassier focuses on the mixture of transcendence and immanence in philosophy. In this mixture there is an initial separation of the empirical/immanent and a priori/transcendent, of datum and factum, that are then "gathered together" and united again under some absolute transcendental authority (Descartes' "I think," Kant's faculties, Husserl's ego). This transcendental authority is ultimately thought as some reified empirical thing and so the final moment of unification is one where the conditioned and the unconditioned are "mixed" and shown to co-constitute one another. This final moment, in Brassier's reconstruction, is said to be a second form of immanence, but one that is transcendentally represented. It is this whole process, taken to expose the transcendental conditions for being, that is coextensive with philosophy and leads to the delusion that philosophy is thereby co-constituting of the Real. For Brassier this means that Laruelle understands every philosophical decision to be recapitulation of the formal structure of Kant's transcendental deduction.[13]

Brassier's reading, as has already been said, is a very powerful reconstruction of Laruelle's theory of Philosophical Decision, which is presented in a number of places in different ways according to the philosophical material that is at play. However, Brassier's focus on the Kantian form of Decision allows him to overstate certain elements and thereby present a *less formal* understanding of the structure than he could. This is because his reading depends in large part upon Laruelle's essay "The Transcendental Method," which focuses on this Kantian element and the post-Kantian trajectory of the German Idealists and phenomenologists (Hegel, Fichte, Husserl, and Michel Henry in particular). The essay is particularly useful for Brassier's reading since he presents Laruelle as a corrective to certain problems he finds in Meillassoux's project while wanting to retain certain elements of his philosophy. Laruelle appears to have a certain fit with Meillassoux as he appears to diagnose correlationism in this 1989 essay.[14] And, indeed, in that essay Laruelle marks an equivalence between transcendence and decision writing: "not every philosophy can be called transcendental, but the transcendental inheres in every philosophy...For philosophy is always a *decision* or a transcendence."[15] Brassier's reading is largely faithful to Laruelle's own theory and should remain useful for students attempting to work through the difficulty of that theory. However, Brassier's engagement with Laruelle was always in the service of Brassier's own project (and rightly so, since Brassier was not producing a history of philosophy or a secondary work on Laruelle) and so his presentation of the theory of Decision leaves out aspects that may also be important and useful for other projects.

With regard to "The Transcendental Method," this general form of philosophy plays out specifically with regard to factum and datum. This specificity makes sense when Laruelle is focusing upon the transcendental form of European philosophy, though conceivably other terms may be inserted into the general protocol and produce a different analysis of the actuality of that particular philosophical form. Laruelle suggests this plasticity in the same essay. "The Transcendental Method" largely focuses on the way the transcendental plays out in Kant and Husserl (these being names that index what he calls the "major tradition"), but also explores the way in which this major tradition contains elements exploited by a "minor tradition" (indexed by the names of Fichte, the early Schelling, and Henry). This minor tradition is also said to push the boundaries or functioning of decision itself, again suggesting a certain plasticity not emphasized in Brassier's reading.

Laruelle is more general than Brassier when he writes: "To philosophize is thus to circulate, or to circulate-in-half: 'to turn.'... Always the same mechanism: first the dyad or decision that divides/doubles – with more or less undivided distance and positivity in distance – then its reprise and reposition in a synthetic and systematic unity, and finally the 'transcendental' return to the empirical dyad."[16] And Laruelle shows later on in *Principles of Non-Philosophy* how this general shape may be given precise shape by different determining materials. As *Principles of Non-Philosophy* focuses upon post-Kantian idealism and phenomenology (whose proponents, following the argument of Jean-Luc Marion, include Descartes), we find him again using the material of Kant here as he sketches out five layers of determination whereby Philosophical Decision may be seen as akin to Kant's table of judgments in the *Critique of Pure Reason*.[17] These five determinations are: essence of the form of Philosophical Decision; essence of the contents of Philosophical Decision; the two possible conditions for the existence of Philosophical Decision; the specific *a prioris* that arise from these two dimensions; the terms that individuate these essences and exist with the *a prioris* he identifies.[18] These are presented as material or "layers" from which Philosophical Decision emerges and we will now examine each in turn.

1 *Essence of the form of Philosophical Decision*. The essence of Philosophical Decision is taken in part from philosophy's own projection of certain transcendences – foremost amongst them Being – which are taken to be the fundamental structure for forms of understanding reality that are autonomous from that reality. Laruelle reads these projections into philosophy itself, claiming that the essence of Philosophical Decision is this *auto*, "that is to say the idea of an absolute autonomy of *Philosophy*."[19] In less abstract terms, the essence of the form of Philosophical Decision is the philosophical faith already discussed. The primary philosophical act persists in the belief that philosophy is autonomous, that it can do what it says.

2 *Essence of the contents of Philosophical Decision*. If the essence of the form relates to how philosophy really acts in the world (or what it takes to be its real or in-itself character), then the essence of the contents refers to what is taken to be transcendental within that practice. These are the concepts which philosophy causes to circulate within its structure. These contents are always the concepts

that are divided in Decision and Laruelle names "identity and difference" amongst them, but we could also place here factum and
datum, immanence and transcendence, the empirical and the transcendental, and so on.

3 *Dimensions of and conditions for the existence of Philosophical Decision.* From these two different forms of essence we come to the
ground necessary for the general practice of Decision. Decision
cannot merely claim an essence, but must find a field upon which
that essence will act. We see already the dyadic structure of philosophy emerges here, for there is a difference between the essence
and the field upon which that essence may emerge through practice. Laruelle writes, "Here again is a dyad of determinations: the
givenness of Decision determined by itself as a result of Auto-
Givenness; its position determined by itself or Auto-Position.
Givenness and position are as though two dimensions of PhD
[Philosophical Decision]; they are not dissociable or exclusive
except by means of abstraction."[20] These two terms, givenness and
position, are akin to my use of essence and field here. In Laruelle's
teasing out of the structure of philosophy, he claims that something
may be given, but it must be posited in order to create a connection
between its being and our thought of it. These two dimensions
(givenness and position) are central to his explication in *Principles
of Non-Philosophy* and arise specifically from the history of German
idealism and phenomenology. But they map onto the general philosophical drive to correlate being and thought, to position what is
given and thereby take something as given through its position
upon a field.

4 *Specific a prioris.* At this point Laruelle begins to mimic Kant's
table of judgments more specifically, mapping out three forms for
each of givenness and position and then their three respective *a
prioris.*[21] The way in which an individual instance of Decision plays
out can be mapped onto this table, which suggests something akin
to Lacan's cartography of the psychoanalytic subject playing out
between the four discourses of the master, the university, the hys-
teric, and the analyst.[22] Here the object is not the subject, but rather
the entire discourse of philosophy, and so it is a matter of modeling
the various instantiations that discourse may take. Before turning
to explain the modifiers of this model it is necessary to be clear
about Laruelle's use of the term *a prioris.*

The singular use of the term is of course familiar to readers of
Kant and post-Kantian philosophy as referring to what comes
before experience in the structure of rational thought. Laruelle's

own plural use of the term is derived in part from this use, but also derives from Foucault's own pluralizing in *The Order of Things* where these *a prioris* are not taken to be ahistorical, but structure certain historical epistemological stances. Foucault summarizes this understanding of *a prioris* clearly when he writes:

> all [inquiries of a philosophical and scientific nature] rested upon a sort of historical *a priori*, which authorized them in their dispersion and in their singular and divergent projects, and rendered equally possible all the differences of opinion of which they were the source....This *a priori* is what, in a given period, delimits in the totality of experience a field of knowledge, defines the mode of being of the objects that appear in that field, provides man's everyday perception with theoretical powers, and defines the conditions in which he can sustain a discourse about things that is recognized to be true.[23]

While Laruelle's non-philosophical analysis does not historicize philosophy, it does relativize it and so is able to identify the elements of philosophy that must structure it prior to the philosophical act in a way parallel to Foucault's own historicizing.

Returning then to Kant's table of judgments, let us unpack these *a prioris* before then developing how they help us to see philosophy in this newly relativized way. We see in Laruelle's sketching of the table that auto- or self-givenness and auto- or self-position each has three *a prioris* that correspond to three different forms of givenness. These three forms of givenness may circulate amongst one another in various ways in the works of various philosophers. The first form of givenness is what Laruelle calls an "empirico-regional" sort. This refers to a term like "life" raised to the status of a "real transcendence" that philosophy identifies with, as is the case of Henry in his phenomenology of life. The *a priori* attached to this form of givenness is "affection." The second form of givenness is that of the discourse of philosophy itself in relation to all possible experience. Philosophy here is an ahistorical Idea that is receptive to all possible experience, and accordingly the *a priori* attached to it is given the name "reception." The third form of givenness emerges from the divided nature of the preceding two, where some givenness is needed to unify the philosophical act, and the *a priori* attached is called "intuition." Students of the history of European philosophy will be familiar with these terms as they circulate in German Idealism and phenomenology, and Laruelle explicitly draws upon these traditions here.

Since Decision is always structured by a dyad, the three *a prioris* of auto-givenness find a second corollary set of three *a prioris* attached to auto-position. For Laruelle, position is simply "the objectification of philosophy itself"[24] – that is, the way in which philosophy understands philosophy to be positioned in the world and with regard to itself. He identifies three moments attached to the three *a prioris*. The first moment of position is to locate philosophy as exterior to its object, and the *a priori* attached here is "transcendence." The second moment of position is that of philosophy's foundation or basis, and the attached *a priori* takes the name of "plane." The third moment of position is again the dyad produced by the preceding two, and it takes the *a priori* name of "unity." Laruelle's claim is that these *a prioris* can be located in individual philosophies as structuring their work. In his examinations of those philosophies these *a prioris* are surfaced and shown to be operative.

5 *Individuating terms.* The terms that Laruelle takes to individuate the forms of Philosophical Decision's essence may find an analogue with his notion of material. That is, these terms are the elements that philosophy takes as its object, but after being over-determined by philosophy through its practice of Decision they become "representational invariants, quasi-'symbols' that function throughout a system or tradition."[25] Such terms may exist at various levels of philosophical practice, like the regional (for example within the specific form of philosophy that exists in relation to a discipline outside of it, like philosophy of science or philosophy of religion), the categorical (the terms that index the unambiguous principles of philosophical practice and are then projected upon fields that are not philosophical), and the transcendental (the structures produced by philosophy that are taken by philosophy to structure thought and experience). These individuating terms enter into a kind of feedback loop within the machine of Philosophical Decision, for they are produced by that decision and at the same time may then come to be acted upon in a decisional way: "They [the terms] are in turn always philosophizable; the machine of Decision is always able *de jure* to be recast in their name, and to produce in and with them a new specifically philosophical *sense* intended to 'fulfill' them more or less intuitively."[26]

The reader may indeed be a bit bewildered by the abstraction of Laruelle's sketching of his theory here, but the phenomenological detail with which he unpacks his theory witnesses to a genuinely rigorous theory. This theory is beyond its caricature as something akin to a moral condemnation of philosophy or a declaration of the end of philosophy. The style that Laruelle pursues in developing this theory in *Principles of Non-Philosophy* is borrowed from Kant and phenomenology, though now the object under consideration is not cognition or Being, but philosophy itself. Each layer of Philosophical Decision developed is a tracing of the structure out of which philosophy emerges. If philosophy is, as Brassier claims, "an intellectual practice with a complex material history" and simply "what philosophers do," then the layers of Philosophical Decision are the structure of that practice, history, and doing.[27] While each individual practice of philosophy, each historical instantiation of philosophy, and each particular philosopher may be different, that difference is caught and constrained by the structure of Decision, according to Laruelle. Take, for example, the difference between philosophies of transcendence or philosophies of immanence, which in recent decades have been the focus of a seemingly grounding antagonism within the history of philosophy due in part to the important influence of Gilles Deleuze. Laruelle sees the difference between these to be minimal. Concerning this difference he writes:

> The most universal invariant trait of philosophy is a fractional matrix in 2/3 terms: it gives itself an interiority and an exteriority, an immanence and a transcendence *simultaneously*, in a synthetic or hierarchal structure, the one overcoming the other in turn. This matrix of "Philosophical Decision" can be read as the identity of a double relation of philosophy to itself. First, an identity of 2/3 (insofar as the third term, synthesis, is immanent to the dyad, philosophy being in need of itself). Second, a 3/2 identity (insofar as the term of synthesis is transcendent to the dyad, philosophy being in excess of itself).[28]

This minimal difference means that *within* philosophy and even from a relative distance *outside* philosophy, the difference matters a great deal, but from a stance of *indifference* toward philosophy (within or outside) the difference is still constrained by the general structure. Regarding this indifference, remember that Laruelle locates a major and minor tradition in transcendental philosophy whereby the minor tradition constitutes a philosophy that pushes the structure to its limit. This matters in terms of the forms of philosophy that non-philosophy will take as useful for its own practice. If non-philosophy aims to produce a radical form of thought, then it will need to do so using tools amenable to such retrofitting.

Returning to the general structure from which individual philosophies emerge, we see that it is a structure of circulation of philosophy itself. From the layers discussed above come three major terms that circulate. These terms may be beings, Being, and *Dasein*, where *Dasein* comes to be dominated by the Being that exceeds it as in Heidegger, or the actual, virtual, and real as in Deleuze. The process of dualysis that Laruelle develops as a way of analyzing various instances of Philosophical Decision is a method of untangling these terms and specifying their function within each instance. We can see how that dualysis may play out using these two examples, though we will use them only in an extremely abbreviated way. The purpose here is simply to point toward examples of what this may look like, while fully developing such a dualysis would require delving into their texts with more depth and rigor. In Heidegger, there is a scission between beings (empirical) and Being itself (transcendent) that is synthesized in an immanent way by *Dasein*, as the being that has Being as its fundamental concern. In Deleuze, the virtual and the actual are both held together within the real (breaking the old dualism of the possible and the real), but the actual emerges from the process of virtualization that forms the plane of immanence.

Scholars of Heidegger and scholars of Deleuze undoubtedly would quibble with the terms "empirical" or "transcendental" applied to Heidegger's and Deleuze's specific terms, especially since Laruelle's non-philosophy may be understood as challenging or moving outside of these historical philosophical positions, but these terms still serve to loosely map their work into the general structure of philosophy. Thus the point is not to denigrate their work or to show that Heidegger or Deleuze is really an empiricist or a transcendental philosopher. That sort of counter-reading is the typical philosophical move made by philosophers in their readings of the history of philosophy, including Heidegger and Deleuze when they write on their forebears. Rather the purpose of mapping them using these terms is to identify the internal functioning of their philosophy as philosophy and to rework its functioning or connect up its functioning with other disciplinary functions to produce different theoretical results rather than another instance of Decision.

Turning to another summary of Philosophical Decision, we can begin to see how non-philosophy's own practice emerges from a mutation of this decisional structure in an analogous way to the emergence of non-Euclidean geometry. Non-Euclidean geometry does not emerge from a negation of Euclidean geometry, but it emerges from a generalization of Euclidean geometry. We can see this generalization of philosophy's decisional structure when Laruelle writes, "We will say that Philosophical Decision is the Idea of *a relative-absolute whole*. Its most encompassing and least detailed mechanism can in effect be described – and we have done so here and there – as a structure in 2/3 terms, as a Dyad + One, as an empirico-transcendental mixture, a quasi-circular and topological doublet, etc."[29] Here the meaning of the 2/3 or 3/2 becomes clearer. In the structure of Philosophical Decision there is always a dyad – like the beings/Being dyad in Heidegger – and some kind of synthesis taken as One. In the case of Heidegger, it is *Dasein*, the lived (reality) of the human that carries forth both its existence as an empirical human being and concern or awareness of transcendent Being. Following in part Michel Henry's reading and redirection of Heidegger's fundamental ontology, we may see in *Dasein* not simply a synthesis that would be dividable again so that *Dasein* comes ultimately to be subject to the Being that exceeds *Dasein*, but a radical immanence of being/Beings. Laruelle thus shifts philosophy to non-philosophy by thinking from these instances of the One, with a studied indifference to the dyads of philosophy, treating these instead as effects of the One that may be useful but are not determinant of the One.

Can there be a philosophy in general?

In order to truly understand Laruelle's theory of Philosophical Decision, we must also consider a major criticism of it that has been presented. In a debate between Laruelle and Derrida, it was claimed that there is a reductive violence done to philosophy in Laruelle's theory of philosophical decision, a kind of terrorism practiced upon its body.[30] This view is shared by Brassier. For Brassier the claim to have uncovered the invariant structure of philosophy is the source of non-philosophy's fruitlessness and its inability to spawn anything but mystagogy. For his part, Brassier attempts to recast Laruelle's non-philosophy in the mold of philosophy through a focus on determination-in-the-last-instance as a powerful form of philosophical negation, while excising the tumor of Laruelle's theory of Philosophical Decision.[31] Yet, as Part I will show in outline, Laruelle's project is both a "science of philosophy" (its critical and negative mode as found in the theory of Philosophical Decision) and a "philo-fiction" (its constructive mode as found in the construction of various new theories). The theory of Philosophical Decision is the science of philosophy in condensed form. To excise it is to mutilate the body of non-philosophy beyond recognition and to break the very apparatus that allows Laruelle to construct a concept like determination-in-the-last-instance. For, ultimately, the two aspects of non-philosophy are one. They are not separated in any meaningful sense. Non-Philosophy is generic in this way.

To help us unpack this generic nature of non-philosophy, let us look more closely at Brassier's criticism so as to have it as a background from which our image of non-philosophy may emerge. Brassier begins with a criticism of Laruelle's insistence that when one writes of philosophy one does so with the definite article: *la philosophie*. Thus every philosophy is a Philosophy-with-a-capital-P, as we might emphasize it in English, following Robin Mackay's translation. This is how we may speak of philosophy "in general" – or, as Alexander Galloway calls it, the standard model of philosophy.[32] However, Brassier seems to think that this single remark is the same as Laruelle's entire argument regarding the invariant structure of philosophy. In my estimation Brassier is wrong. While in English we do not need the definite article to speak of philosophy, there is still a sense that to discuss philosophy generally is to discuss philosophy as such. It would then have some kind of identity. For Brassier, though, this identity (which has a technical sense for Laruelle) is a search for an ideal essence: "Thus Laruelle's insistence on identifying the essence of *la philosophie* over and above any listing of all those things which are named 'philosophy' seems as misguided as would be the attempt to define the essence of *le sport* over and above a list of all those activities which we happen to call 'sport.' "[33]

This is a weak criticism, since even what gets defined as sport would indeed take on a certain identity. Outside the deployment of metaphor, one would not call the writing activity I am currently engaged with "sport." To invoke the phenomenological tradition that Brassier utterly maligns, we get to the identity of sport through what Husserl called "eidetic variation" or getting to the essence of a thing by allowing its many ways of appearing to appear.[34] Sport may appear in many ways, but for Husserl one may get to the invariant essence or idea of sport through the perception of that variation and, perhaps more importantly, its limits. Thus, there may be some structural overlap between *Halo* (the popular first-person shooter video game) and football, but there is enough of a structural difference that the way in which they appear is different enough for us to need to distinguish them if we hope to provide any kind of meaningful analysis. Husserl's concept of "eidetic variation" is a familiar phenomenological tool that shares much in common with the way in which Laruelle's own science of philosophy works. While Brassier asserts that "the claim decisional auto-position embodies the essence of philosophy saddles Laruelle with an intolerable burden" of going, philosophy by philosophy, and showing its structure, the claim is actually ridiculous as it would imply that in order to speak of sport one would have to go, individual player by individual player, to show that there was something called "sport."[35] Laruelle and Brassier are not playing out the usual realist versus nominalist game here: for Laruelle the existence of transcendentals and particulars that are so important in those philosophical debates is a simple material with which to do something. Thus, while our earlier reference to Husserl might suggest to some readers that Laruelle is a kind of Platonist in the way Husserl was (and so anti-nominalist), it is rather that, in taking on the posture of science (to be explained in more detail in chapter 4), Laruelle acts pragmatically in his identifications, rather than with a concern for metaphysical sufficiency or determination.

Brassier, despite attempting to create a materialist and realist philosophy, deploys his nominalist argument when he writes, "What we call 'philosophy' is an intellectual practice with a complex material history, and even though its register of abstraction distinguishes it from others, only idealists like Heidegger have sought to exalt it above all other activities by imbuing it with a perennial and abyssal 'essence' whose epochal unfolding is deemed capable of determining the course of history."[36] The claims here are difficult to parse, since on the one hand philosophy is beyond the sort of identification Laruelle claims to perform, and yet Brassier still is willing to distinguish it from other intellectual practices on the basis of its "register of abstraction." Assumedly such a register would be invariant in some sense, even if only temporally local to some particular philosophical epoch. But this is merely a continuation of the obfuscation of what Laruelle is doing in his identification of philosophy, and the attempt to associate him with the idealist philosophy of someone like Heidegger, thereby sullying him, does not cover that obfuscation. For Laruelle the invariant character of decision does not determine history in any straightforward sense. This would be to assume that history is real in the sense that Laruelle intends this term (a theme we will turn to in chapter 6). Rather, the focus on the identity of philosophy is precisely attuned to the material structure of its practice, which in turn precisely *impoverishes* and *brings low* Philosophy-with-a-capital-P rather than exulting it in some Heideggerian salute to authenticity.

Laruelle clearly derives some of his understanding of the history of philosophy from Heidegger's own. However, Laruelle's relationship to Heidegger's philosophy is almost uniformly antagonistic from his earliest writing. Heidegger develops a Eurocentric vision of philosophy as being born in Greece and coming to adulthood in Germany. The political and ethical consequences of this narrative are not inconsequential and should not be downplayed as some readers have tried to do regarding his allegiance to Nazism and anti-Semitism. Laruelle's understanding of this history differs greatly from Heidegger's. While Heidegger remains Eurocentric and while Laruelle refers to the "Occidental" character of philosophy, the overall framework and evaluation diverge completely. Heidegger sees philosophy as a universal element of human life and, by virtue of its being born in Europe, he values the human life of Europeans more for carrying the child of philosophy into the future. Insofar as philosophy may spread throughout the world – to Japan, for example (the site where some of his work was taken up in serious ways by the Kyoto School) – it does so through a kind of transcendental form of Europe that spreads to other cultures and changes them.[37] In his transformation of philosophy into simple material, Laruelle does not understand philosophy as "universal" in the usual sense. When he speaks to the Occidental character of philosophy, he speaks to the particularity of philosophy, the recognition that (European) philosophers' claims to universality in their philosophy are false and constitute a kind of harassment of human beings denied the status of "human." To generalize philosophy is then to disempower its internal Eurocentrism and to make it a material that can be taken up outside of the European colonialism that philosophy has served for centuries, even in its radical forms.[38]

Some readers could accuse me here of misunderstanding Brassier's criticism, since he in fact goes on to claim that Laruelle conflates this invariant identity of philosophy with the idea that it can be embodied by individual philosophers:

> Thus Laruelle conflates the defensible claim that Plato, Leibniz, Kant, Hegel, and Nietzsche exemplify what is most profound in philosophy with the indefensible idealist claim that they embody its

essence. This is like claiming that great sportsmen [*sic*] not only exemplify certain physical and mental prowess, but also embody the essence of sport. So when Laruelle declares that "philosophy itself" has told him that it is an auto-affecting whole, one can only respond that "philosophy itself" never speaks, since it is a figment; only philosophers speak – even and especially those philosophers who claim philosophy itself speaks through them.[39]

It is difficult to adjudicate Brassier's claims here, since in the midst of this accusation he cites no text that would show Laruelle making this claim that "philosophy itself" speaks in some particularly egregious way. As when certain commentators *do* claim that a particular athlete embodies the essence of sport, it seems perfectly reasonable that Laruelle would make such a poetic use of language.

At the same time, to understand Laruelle on individual philosophers requires that we concede that certain names index the constellation of texts, claims, and indeed material practices of the individual philosopher and those who may attempt to expand their work. Thus we may speak of Marx-the-philosopher, but the name-of-Marx also indexes a number of texts and readings of texts that are simply not reducible to the individual life of Karl Marx as he lived it. We will explore this question of subjectivity throughout the book, but this further probing into Brassier's criticism and the demonstration of its ultimate confusion should be enough for us to begin to see the reasonableness behind claiming that there is something like philosophy as a kind of infrastructure for thinking that determines – or, more accurately, "overdetermines," in the usual and technical sense we will explore later – the human practice of thought as such.

Understanding this – human thought – as the scope of the project of non-philosophy may open Laruelle to charges of hubris, but it is the very hubris of philosophy that Laruelle aims to disempower and weaken with his theory of Philosophical Decision. For while non-philosophy aims to be a science of philosophy, and thus of those bordering regional knowledges infected and modified by their spontaneous forms of philosophy, philosophy itself claims to provide the very conditions for thinking the Real as such. Since the reader may not yet be familiar with the meaning behind this term for Laruelle, we may state the claim in this way: philosophy believes itself to be sufficient unto itself to know and change whatever it comes into contact with. While this aspect of decision runs deep through the practices of every aspect of Western philosophy, this identification akin to eidetic variation does not claim that every individual work of the philosopher = X (Plato, Descartes, Hume, Kant, Hegel, Nietzsche, Heidegger, Russell, Derrida, Deleuze, or even the Churchlands) manifests the essence of philosophy, but that when those philosophers act in ways that are non-philosophical those acts are overdetermined by that overarching philosophical structure of decision and they are alienated from those intellectual products by that overdetermining decisional structure. Laruelle himself indicates as much in his own attempt at a succinct definition of Philosophical Decision: "Philosophical Decision is a mixture of indecision and decision, never pure decision."[40]

Allow me to summarize then the argument against the criticism voiced by Brassier (it is a criticism shared by others, but Brassier presents it the most seriously and fully, and so we index it generally with his name). Brassier's main claim is that Laruelle's theory of Philosophical Decision is too broad, and this broadness commits him to either an idealism (the ultimate sin for a materialist philosopher) or an infinite task of demonstrating this decisional structure within each person who takes the title "philosopher." This infinite task would be required if Brassier is correct in his claim that there is no essence of philosophy, and that philosophy is only what emerges from a complex material history. There is thus no invariant philosophy, only certain ways of doing philosophy and we may follow Brassier in adjudicating which are true and which are not through deference and compliance to what the sciences tell us the nature of reality is.

This is not the place to present criticism of Brassier's scientistic ideology that underpins the quasi-religious nihilism of *Nihil Unbound*. But it is necessary for our response to this criticism to point out that Laruelle and Brassier have wildly different understandings of science and the importance of science for any theoretical undertaking. Brassier makes special reference to the empirical findings of a particular science – namely cosmology and its prophetic modeling of the heat death of the universe – which he takes to act as a universal acid for any philosophy of meaning. Brassier also makes reference to other particular sciences, specifically in their eliminativist and deflationary modes as what might challenge philosophies of subjectivity or mind, since some scientists claim there is no evidence for a substantial self underlying processes of the brain and other biological processes. The point here is not that such appeals are wrong, but that the appeal is to the *empirical* aspect of the sciences and not their essence of identity as identical with the "immanental" practice of science.[41]

It is too easy to point out that there is a contradiction in Brassier's reasoning here – because, on the one hand, appeals to particular empirical claims by particular sciences manifest universal validity in philosophical claims like "we are dead already"; and, on the other hand, Brassier claims that Laruelle goes too far when he argues that there is something generic to philosophy's practice. Furthermore, from the philosophical perspective of materialism, it is true of everything, including the sciences, that they are produced by complex material histories. Even from the non-philosophical perspective, it would be true that there is no sufficient reason for something to be what it is, as Laruelle affirms the radical finitude and contingency of the emergence of philosophy. This philosophical claim that everything develops (either in itself or in the way it is understood) is true of all objects of scientific inquiry. Science, like philosophy, has an essence or identity that is also radically contingent and but an effect of the One (explored in the next chapter).[42] Insofar as non-philosophy aims to be a science of philosophy and takes the same scientific posture or stance toward philosophy as other sciences do for their particular objects, then non-philosophy is able to model a structure or tendency within those material processes.

The power of science is that it is able to model these generic structures, without any necessary claim to determination, structure, or mixture with that object. In those cases where the subject observing does impact understanding of the object or the object itself, the particular science takes this as a single phenomenon – or as at least a single material problem – to engage.[43] It does not in either case claim final sufficiency of its knowledge over the unrepresentable (the One or the Real) but only claims to be a particular practice. Those well-known examples when a particular scientist does begin to claim sufficiency – as in the case of some popular science or those scientists acting as public intellectuals – begin to embody a certain philosophical subject position as they pass from the actual practice of their science to (often disappointingly weak) philosophical practice. Laruelle has simply taken the common scientific practice of speaking about something in general and attempted to sketch out the actual structure of that generic nature, which we will now turn to.

Many may reasonably approach Laruelle's non-philosophy with suspicion, wondering how in fact he supports the broad claim that there is an identity to philosophy that non-philosophy uncovers as the science of philosophy. However, hopefully the preceding at least opens up the possibility of such an identification akin to the ways in which science, in neither a philosophically realist nor nominalist way, pragmatically identifies and distinguishes all manner of things without thereby claiming to have destroyed them, negated them, or even spoken the final word regarding them (in this way phenomenology, for all the ways in which it is maligned, is closer to science than contemporary "speculative realists"). With that openness in place, we will turn now to tracing the actual conception of decision as Laruelle lays it out in his work. As Laruelle "reprises the same problems 'from zero,'" we do not focus on a single text, but construct a kind of kaleidoscopic view by engaging with a range of texts on the decision. Readers should understand that, while non-philosophy certainly can be cast linearly, there is a remarkable consistency to the way in which the theory is presented.[44]

If we now see Brassier oscillating between realism and nominalism, the purpose is not to show how Laruelle decides finally on the correct way forward.[45] Laruelle flat out refuses to play the game of asking whether the true philosophy is philosophy X or philosophy Y. That game is all too typical of philosophy as such. The aim of non-philosophy is instead to locate what is generic to both realism and nominalism (and any philosophy = X). Being made equivalent, in the sense of expressing the identity of philosophy, is what transforms the hallucinated vision of philosophy into a simple material, one thing amongst others liable to be used by human beings.

Now, at the end of our exploration of the Philosophical Decision, we can see the ways in which it allows one to cast philosophy as material that may be worked with, rather than a kind of quasi-divine discipline of knowledge. Marking one last return to Brassier's criticism, we can certainly admit that Laruelle's description of this structure owes much to the tradition of philosophy running from Plato through Kant, Nietzsche, and Heidegger, to contemporary French philosophers like Derrida and Deleuze. We have also seen, however, that while the overall sense of decision remains consistent, there is a multitude of ways for that consistency to manifest itself. So if someone wanted to use the non-philosophical method to investigate the practice of the neurophilosophers Paul and Patricia Churchland, to take the case that Brassier identifies as a limit to non-philosophy, its description would necessarily change due to the change in particularity. Laruelle's point regarding this structure of philosophy is not to negate philosophy, but to relativize it. Laruelle does not deny in his work that there are philosophical elements running throughout other regional knowledges. This is in part an example of the power of philosophy. Laruelle's critique of philosophy is carried out so as to disempower certain authoritarian aspects of philosophy in favor of unleashing and recasting philosophical concepts in new ways. This positive project is what we now turn to.

2

The Style of Non-Philosophy

No philosophy in the wild

If, in the previous chapter, non-philosophy was presented in its negative, deconstructive form, then what might the positive form look like? Laruelle makes the seemingly damning claim in *Philosophies of Difference* that:

> [Thinking] is no longer a matter, as in Husserl or Nietzsche, of suspending all transcendent philosophical positions, but of indifferentiating, one might say, every operation of suspension, of rendering useless the reduction itself by rejecting it, together with the thesis of the word, gregariousness, etc., outside of the essence of the *veritas transcendentalis*. To presuppose them in order to differentiate them, deconstruct them, analyze them, precisely this is the essential presupposition of philosophical decision as such, and it is from this that we discover it is a matter for a different logic than that of philosophy's interminable auto/hetero-affection.[1]

So what does that logic look like if we are to be concerned with *doing* something, even if it is not a practice organized or structured by standard philosophical logic? This chapter attempts to answer that question.

Throughout this book, we have used the term "non-philosophy" to refer to Laruelle's project, and readers of Laruelle's texts cannot fail to see the proliferation of various uses of the "non" throughout his work (non-epistemology, non-Marxism, non-psychoanalysis, non-Christianity, non-photography, etc.). There is undeniably

something comical in this constant use, though we would be wrong
⌜to think that Laruelle wasn't in on this joke. By entering into some
field, the limits of which are delineated by philosophy, and proclaiming that his use of that field will be a non-X he already frus-
trates the philosophers who might demand he play by the rules set
by philosophy. Laruelle's critics take the ease with which "non"
comes to the tips of Laruelle's fingers as he writes to be a sign that
non-philosophy does not have anything to add to philosophical
⌞ discourse. I am not interested here in arguing for Laruelle's place
in the parliament of philosophy, where he can join with this or that
party in the interminable debates of parliamentary philosophy. For,
to stick with this metaphor of a parliament, such debates are always
framed by rules taken to externally structure those parties. If one
wants to be an *authentic* politician, then one follows these rules, one
allows them to structure the debates, and, except in very rare cases
of revolution, the structure for those debates is never up for debate.
The logic of the "non" includes a refusal of such a desire for authenticity. It is a refusal of the frame as frame, instead treating that
frame as entirely a part of the material and actors that the frame
claims to condition.

The positive project of non-philosophy is the non-Hobbesian
answer to the question Frank Ocean sings on "No Church in the
Wild":

> What's a mob to a king?
> What's a king to a god?
> What's a god to a non-believer who don't believe in anything?
> Will he make it out alive?
> No church in the wild.

While the line "Will he make it out alive?" suggests some anxiety
regarding potential violence once we see the removal of hierarchy,
we still see a fundamental truth illustrated in the song: that such
hierarchies, regardless of usefulness, depend upon some differential relation and are ultimately fictional or constructed. This truth
is repeated within the positive project of non-philosophy and is
what lies behind Laruelle's location of Philosophical Decision. The
style of non-philosophy is not differential in this way, though it is
also not a rejection of difference or the philosophies of difference.
While such differential structures are indeed helpful for tracing the
shape of the world, precisely because these differential structures
produce the world – in Laruelle's sense of the term, which refers

to a closed and self-sufficient whole – they also create a duplicity in which thought is taken as representational, as always differing from what it does in what it says.

Laruelle's project aims to be unilateral in approach, not to think from difference but to think from identity or radical immanence. What does it mean to say that there is no church in the wild? At a fundamental level, it is to say that all such institutions of authority have some cause outside of those institutions which does not recognize those institutions' authority. The effects of this cause (the institutions, but other forms of identity as well) do not form a relationship with this cause. From the perspective of the cause, there is no effect. This cause, which Laruelle will signify with the names "the One" or "the Real" and sometimes simply "Real-One," has no relation, not even to itself. In a sense this is what is meant by the term "wild" as when we think of a wild animal. Georges Bataille perhaps summarizes this sense of wildness in terms familiar to readers of French philosophy when he writes, "every animal is *in the world like water in water*."[2] While Laruelle remains somewhat anthropocentric and has marked a distinction between the human and non-human animals, such a distinction is not located at the level of immanence. The human is "wild," it is prior-to-first in his terminology. The human in its radical immanence does what it says and says what it does. It is this form of radical immanence that Laruelle locates as performed within the sciences, and this form that he makes manifest in his own practice. As Laruelle writes, "the transcendental nature of non-philosophy demands" that it function "without distinction of what it says and what it does."[3]

Rocco Gangle claims that Laruelle's aversion to examples arises in part from this principle of unilaterality. Philosophers use such particular examples to illustrate some general or universal structure and yet those universal structures are claimed to govern those very examples.[4] In non-philosophy, the example is the very practice contained in the text, and it is in this claim about non-philosophy's style that one can see clearly how Laruelle models his project on the sciences.[5] Practice in the sciences (and by this term we do not mean the ersatz-philosophies of "popular science") finds the scientist engaged with thinking in a directly realist mode. When she considers the gene or the ecosystem, she engages with the identity or radical immanence of that object. While scientists may then move to a form of philosophical distancing or transcendence through a reduction of some other object to another (say the life of a human to their genes), that is a move outside of the direct practice of science.

As a positive project non-philosophy has two aspects. The first has already been discussed through what is often taken to be the negative aspect of non-philosophy, its theory of Philosophical Decision. Such a project models itself upon science by casting itself as a science of philosophy. It does not aim to be a philosophy upon philosophy, but to model the stance or posture taken by science toward its objects. The second aspect of non-philosophy's project is the development of various conjugations and unified theories. These may take the form of two philosophies brought together in interesting ways. Laruelle commented on this aspect of his thought in an interview from 2012 saying:

> I had the feeling that in order to completely change the concept of philosophy, two philosophies were always necessary, as if each of the philosophers represented half of philosophy, basically, which I felt to be the non-completeness of a particular philosophy; this problem would have to be resolved each time by the combination of two philosophers. I have followed this way of doing things, a little bit in spite of myself, always combining two philosophies as if each of them was lacking what the other had. You could think that this is a dialectical relation. But in fact that was not that at all, because it was, each time, two philosophies and not one philosophy and the entire history of philosophy in addition. Thus, I am part of a *conjugation*, I like this term a lot, of philosophies which replaced the missing concept.[6]

Laruelle's attraction to bringing together different philosophical systems was evident in his early work, which he claims was undertaken prior to the project of non-philosophy proper. For instance, in his *Machines textuelles*, he brings together Derrida and Deleuze in ways that prefigured very recent projects by decades. This conjugation is repeated during the development of non-philosophy proper as it is seen in his major work *Philosophies of Difference*, where he presents a threefold conjugation of Heidegger to Derrida and Nietzsche to Deleuze, and Heidegger–Derrida to Nietzsche–Deleuze, which allows him to think a complete theory of philosophical attempts to construe difference.

The second aspect of the positive project of non-philosophy is often referred to as a unified theory of philosophy and some other regional knowledge, which may be understood as an extension of the conjugation of philosophies. In *Principles of Non-Philosophy*, we find Laruelle claiming generally that non-philosophy is a unified theory of philosophy and science, while he claims that *Future Christ* (2001, and 2010 in English translation) is an example of a unified theory of philosophy and Christianity, or in *Photo-Fiction, a Non-Standard Aesthetics* (2012 in bilingual edition) he claims that his thinking through art should be understood as a unified theory of philosophy and photography – or aesthetics more generally. In each case it is a matter of a mutual mutating of philosophy and the other material into a distinctly new practice whereby what is thought is practiced at the same time. Therefore *Future Christ* is not simply a reflection upon religion, or (Gnostic) Christianity more specifically, but the attempt to allow the materials of a particular religious tradition to mutate philosophical practice while also mutating that religious material as well (hence its "heretical" nature). All the phases of non-philosophy are, as Laruelle says, "defined by the conjugation of a problem and a method of solution."[7]

In the chapters to follow, we will see what these unified theories look like and what they produce, and so in a sense this chapter on the positive project of non-philosophy is only a prelude to the development of that positive project to follow. The focus then of this chapter will be on the overarching style and syntax of non-philosophy that manifests in particular ways through the different materials engaged with. This style may be thought of as a kind of software that allows the hardware of philosophy to do new things. Laruelle himself uses the term "quantware" to describe his engagement with quantum theory.[8] This use of the term "quantware" speaks to the way that Laruelle seeks to recode philosophy according to concepts derived from quantum theory. It is not a matter of providing quantum theory with a philosophy, but of creating a discontinuous or non-identical thought. This means a thought that is thinking in a quantum way, but without regard for any positive statements akin to popular science texts. Thus, we have "non-identical" in the sense that Laruelle has given to the "non," meaning there is no difference between this philosophical fiction and quantum theory for they are "superposed." Quantum superposition is interesting for Laruelle in part because it allows for a discontinuity that does not require a thinking of some transcendental form of difference. The philo-fiction created by Laruelle's engagement with quantum theory may have the added benefit of addressing some of the spontaneous philosophical positions found in quantum theory, but the goal is always to think philosophically under the conditions or determinations of a stranger theory. Those who think of Laruelle as a kind of pure rebel forever sneering at philosophy might be confused by this move since there is a philosophical precedent in Kant. Kant's *Critique of Pure Reason* may be thought of as responding to the new physics developed by Newton without necessarily providing simply a philosophical commentary upon that physics. Laruelle would argue that Kant remains determined by the decisional structure of philosophy in that response to Newton, but he also thinks quantum physics provides a more fecund ground from which to cultivate new forms of thought and lends itself to less decisional philosophical practice. The point, which must be belabored because of the pervasive misunderstanding of Laruelle's critique, is not to negate philosophy but to pick it up and recast it on a new trajectory.[9]

Tracing that trajectory will be the focus of the rest of this chapter. There are major concepts that structure the practice of non-philosophy in each of its domains including determination-in-the-last-instance, unilateral duality, and force-(of)-thought. These are explored in detail in my *François Laruelle's Principles of Non-Philosophy*, which is (somewhat obviously) the companion I have written to Laruelle's *Principles of Non-Philosophy*. Instead of a deep exploration of those concepts here I have instead provided a brief synopsis of the concept of the One and relate these other concepts briefly to that central and guiding concept.[10] We will then turn to a short overview of some of the conventions found in Laruelle's writing and see how they seek to express non-philosophical thought without any distance between the expression and the expressed thought, between what it does and what it says.

Thinking in-One and its effects

Laruelle is consistent in his claim that what drives non-philosophical practice is the place of the One within it: "The non-philosophical practice of philosophy rests upon a single theorem: *The One understood as vision-in-One or as transcendental experience non-thetic (of) itself, is what determines philosophical decision in the last instance as non-philosophy or in view of it.*"[11] But what is the One for Laruelle? To give a succinct answer to this question is a challenge, for the One is the heart and soul and the flesh and blood of non-philosophy. Like all such things that lie beyond full representation, the term "the One" is an expression of something it will never capture, as a piece of erotic poetry is to the lived act of two lovers. Yet, despite this romanticism, it is also what grounds the rigorously abstract practice of non-philosophy: the One is what gives non-philosophy its scientific character.

Laruelle begins with the One because philosophy is unable to. Laruelle writes a response to Heidegger's claim that Western philosophy has been the history of the forgetting of Being: "The forgetting of the One is the condition for the thought of Being, but also for the thought of the forgetting of Being."[12] The decisional nature of (European) philosophy guides it toward its objects of Being and Alterity, for these lend themselves to philosophical manipulation in ways that the austere abstraction of the One does not. The One may not be split if it is to be taken as One, whereas Being is defined by the difference between its coming and passing away, and Alterity is defined by its difference from the Same. The One remains forgotten by philosophy precisely because to be remembered would require that it be cut up and dismembered first, and thereby it would be lost.

A student of the history of philosophy may object that the One is an important concept for a number of philosophers in history. Foremost amongst these philosophers would be the Neo-Platonists. Laruelle is, of course, aware of Neo-Platonists and credits them, along with a "school of psychoanalysts skilled in the most esoteric thoughts" (likely a reference to Lacanian psychoanalysis), for distinguishing themselves from other philosophies in their having "seemingly distinguished [the One] from Being."[13] While Laruelle is clearly influenced by Neo-Platonism in his centering of the One, he seeks in a number of works to describe the essence of the One from the perspective of the One rather than to trace its figure from outside of the One.[14] With regard to the One what differentiates Laruelle from Neo-Platonism and psychoanalysis is that Laruelle's vision-in-One does not require the creation of "assemblages with Being" or "arrangements with the Unconscious" that rely on a certain distance between the One and thought.[15] Such distance is endemic to Philosophical Decision and thus we still have not entered into the essence of the One, but seek only to think the One, to grasp it as a desired object. This is ultimately the meaning of his concept "vision-in-One." The point is not to think the One at all, but to think Philosophy and the World created by decision as if they were in-One – to think Philosophy and the World through what is unthought within them, upon which they depend for consistency without being able to affect that One.

This conception of the One requires a different practice of thought from that required by the standard philosophical concept of Being. As Laruelle writes in *Philosophies of Difference*, "There is a typology of Being; there is no typology of the One."[16] Instead of propositional philosophy, thinking One requires the formulation of axioms. The axiomatic style is important for Laruelle's setting-up of the mechanisms of non-philosophy, for axioms are not representational. They may be thought of as expressive of some principle. However, the truth of that principle is not something that can be demonstrated; instead, an axiom organizes how thinking will take place. If the thought does not work, then axioms may be reevaluated or modified, but the evaluation of the axioms only happens through setting them and watching how they function. In other words, the axioms are evaluated by what they allow to manifest through them, not by the strength of their ability to represent something beyond them.

Laruelle's description of the essence of the One then takes the form of an axiomatic. We may find two systematic instances of this axiomatization. The first is adapted from Brassier's summary of Laruelle's longer axiomatic descriptions in *Philosophy and Non-Philosophy*, and reads:

> 1. [The One] is phenomenon-in-itself, the phenomenon as *already*-given or given-*without*-givenness, rather than constituted as given via the transcendental synthesis of empirical and a priori, given and givenness.
> 2. [The One] is the phenomenon as *already*-manifest or manifest-*without*-manifestation, the phenomenon-without-phenomenality, rather than the phenomenon which is posited and presupposed as manifest in accordance with the transcendental synthesis of the manifest and manifestation.
> 3. [The One] is that in and through which we have been *already*-gripped rather than any originary factum or datum by which we suppose ourselves to be gripped.
> 4. [The One] is *already*-acquired prior to all cognitive or intuitive acquisition, rather than that which is merely posited and presupposed as acquired through the a priori forms of cognition and intuition.
> 5. [The One] is *already*-inherent prior to all the substantialist forcings of inherence, conditioning all those supposedly inherent models of identity, be they analytic, synthetic, or differential.[17]

The second instance is found in the *Dictionary of Non-Philosophy* and is a truncated version of the above:

Non-Philosophy formulates an open series of axioms on the One understood as vision-in-One and no longer as the desired One:

1) The One is radical immanence, identity-without-transcendence, not associated with a transcendence or a division.

2) The One is in-One or vision-in-One and not in-Being or in-Difference.

3) The One is the Real insofar as it is foreclosed to all symbolization (thought, knowledge, etc.).

4) The One is the given-without-givenness and separated-without-separation – of givenness.

5) The One is that which determines or gives in-the-last-instance the thought-world as a given (object of a givenness).[18]

These lists are both helpful, and together form the most complete summary of Laruelle's presentation of the essence of the One. In sum, they present a concept that may not be thought in a representational way, but which nonetheless underlies all representational thought. We might say that One can be evoked, but it may not be grasped, and that in its being evoked what is manifest is what has already been evoked in the act of evocation.

The One evokes the sense of radical immanence and does so immediately in Laruelle's work. From the start, the impossibility of thinking the One becomes apparent and so what is called for is a thinking from the One or in-One, as has already been claimed. What Laruelle has thus come into contact with here is what Daniel Colucciello Barber has identified as the dual demands of thinking from the namelessness of immanence and the necessity of signification for thought.[19] The One is simply a signification for what cannot be signified, it is already a name pulled from the history of philosophy to evoke what is already-manifest for philosophy to even act. As Laruelle writes, "The Manifest is the absolute requirement of manifestation; it must be accepted that it precedes manifestation and that it is, as One, already manifest before any 'philosophical aid to manifestation.' Man does not have to assist the One – as philosophy believes – for it is the One that assists Philosophy and the World."[20] That is, the One is a recognition that radical immanence remains properly nameless, and yet this name, "the One," follows from the necessity of signification within philosophy and the world. What is signified is philosophy and the world's relativity and contingency. This axiomatic description of the already-manifest unthought of philosophy and the world carries with it certain consequences and effects that Laruelle crafts into operations of non-philosophical thought. These take the names of determina-tion-in-the-last-instance, unilateral duality, and force-(of)-thought. We will quickly summarize these effects and what they do for Laruelle before turning to a discussion of his syntax and writing conventions.

Determination-in-the-last-instance

The first consequence of this axiomatic of the One is a recognition of its unilateral character. If the One is unrepresentable and prior to all manifestations, then the One is unaffected by the representa-tions and manifestations that proceed from it. In *Principles of Non-Philosophy*, Laruelle presents a formalism of the One in which this unilateral One or One in-itself is presented as One-in-One. The effects of this One witnessed to by philosophy are called non(-One) to signify their resistance to the One. Amongst these instances of non(-One) may be found thought and Being. There also exists the (non-)One which refers to the positive attempts to work with the already-manifest and unrepresentable character of the One. While (non-)One is a name that serves to place it within this simple schematism of the One and its effects, it takes more specific names in Laruelle's work as "cloning" and "force-(of)-thought."[21]

Determination-in-the-last-instance (DLI) is the name given to the causality of the One upon the various instances of non(-One).[22] Traditional philosophical explanations of causality always begin with a division between two terms (cause and effect) and this divi-sion is found even in radical explanations such as Spinoza's con-ception of immanent causality, just where one of the terms is taken now as passive.[23] This separation, in both strong and weak forms, reduces the moment to a relation and that relation will determine the two identities in a reciprocal or dialectical way. DLI refuses the initial division between cause and effect because such a division is unthinkable from the radical immanence of the One. Insofar as there are instances of the non(-One) or things like thought and Being that lend themselves to traditional accounts of causality and dialectical philosophy, from the perspective of the radically imma-nent One these effects come after the One and do not form a premise of the One.[24] In other words, the One experiences no alien-ation, it is beyond being affected by the play of forces and appear-ances, but such play proceeds from the One.

As Laruelle summarizes it, "'Last-instance' means that the One
is the real unique cause, whatever the distance of the effect or the
mediations that separate it from the One might be... The cause is
always-already experienced through the One or 'in-One' – this is
the radical performativity of immanence – or has always-already
sustained its efficacy."[25] In-the-last-instance there is no difference
between the One and its effects, there is no cause and effect except
from a local perspective. This raises certain problems. How does
this avoid a dualism or correlationism akin to that of post-Kantian
philosophy's problem of knowledge of the thing-in-itself and the
appearance of a thing, or the phenomenological correlation of
noesis and noema? Secondly, what kind of understanding are we
given of thought and theory generally, including that of non-philosophy, if the One is unrepresentable? Does thought think anything real or is all thought simply a form of belief and opinion
without support or ground? Laruelle's response to such questions
may be summarized by the concepts of unilateral duality and force-
(of)-thought, respectively.

Unilateral duality

"The dualism that analyzes Being or Difference is still the philosophy of Being, while the One for its account has neither a
monist philosophy nor a dualist philosophy, nor probably any
philosophy 'at all'"[26] Non-Philosophy nevertheless retains a sense
of the dual and duality even as it rejects dualism. This will be,
however, a duality that is unilateral, in distinction to a mixed,
equally weighty, or substantial dualism. From the perspective of
the One the usual terms found in dualistic philosophies, like
thought and Being, are only local effects of a greater dual relation
or what Laruelle refers to as a "uni-lation."[27] Dualism is founded
or determined in the last instance by the immanence of the One,
such that, from the perspective of the One, there is no dualism.
Laruelle summarizes the relationship of the One to the non-(One)
in *Introduction to Non-Marxism* (2000, and 2015 in English translation) writing, "So [this relation] is not a matter of "difference," of
the co-extension of the One and the Two, of the One that is Two
and of the Two which is One in some reversible way. It seems,
instead, that DLI must be irreversible, the One is only One, even
with the Two, and the Two forms a Two with the One only from
its point of view as the Two."[28]

Unilateral duality is one way of understanding the field upon which philosophical forces and appearances play. The problem of the relation between thought and Being has recurred throughout Western philosophy's history. In recent years, Continental philosophers have returned to this problem and couched it under the label of "correlationism."[29] The "problem of correlation" at one level simply refers to the question regarding the relationship of thought to Being, though many of these philosophers are clearly aggregating Being and the Real in their posing of this question, in a way that would imply there is a traditional decisional apparatus at work. "Correlationists" is the name given by Meillassoux to those philosophers who presume, explicitly or implicitly, that Being cannot be thought apart from some subjective content.[30]

Laruelle's unilateral duality offers an account of the correlation of thought and Being, or the thing-in-itself and appearance, or what Husserl called more rigorously the noetic and the noema as well as the noetic–noema correlate (here we again see the triadic nature of philosophy). Laruelle's account, however, differs significantly from that of Speculative Realism and in part that difference arises from a more subtle reading of the phenomenological tradition that remains critical in the best sense of the word. What unilateral duality does is allow for a strict duality between One and its effects, while still allowing those affects to relate in dialectical or reciprocal ways at the local level. In a sense what Laruelle does here is "provincialize" philosophy. Whereas philosophy has tended to take its dualisms as absolute or even taken its absolutes to be absolute while retaining a mixed character, non-philosophy's axiomatics of the One says that these various philosophies are at play in a determinate field, a determine time, and that their play depends upon something unthought and beyond their ability to affect. This has the effect of providing an account of philosophy's substantial character – that is, philosophy does do something, and when one does philosophy one may be productive. But unilateral duality also undercuts philosophy's faith in itself or its claims to dominate other discourses.

An example of this may be seen with regard to phenomenology, when Laruelle writes, "This sense of philosophy-form as grasped in-identity takes on different forms according to the levels or moments considered in the philosophy-form. DLI does not, for example, exclude noetico-noematic duality, but simply its origin in consciousness or Being and its aspect of infinitely reversible bi-lateral correlation."[31] In making philosophical thought relative or provincial, Laruelle both limits the self-aggrandizement of human thought, and dignifies and makes equal the varieties of human thought within those limits. What, then, is the relation of this thought to the Real? Is thought of any kind, or even in its generality, able to think something true? To respond to these questions, we turn finally to the force-(of)-thought.

Force-(of)-thought

From a non-philosophical perspective, the questions above are badly posed and so may constitute false problems, because an answer to the question of the relation of thought to the One (or Real) is already found in DLI and unilateral duality. Laruelle summarizes this as follows: "When the One is taken as a point of view for a thought that can only emanate or proceed from it, then this thought is posited after the One as its material and as what has already supported the efficacy of the One."[32] Thought is an effect of the One that does not in turn affect the Real. Thought is never able to grasp the One, but it may think from it and may produce certain axiomatic statements regarding the One. Furthermore, these thoughts may be true, but they are true without a determining transcendent mixture with what might be named "Truth." This transcendent name might alienate thought in relation to something transcendentally dominant but reversible with thought.

Force-(of)-thought (FT) then comes to name an understanding of thought as an effect of the One.[33] Laruelle claims that FT is "the first possible experience of thought – after vision-in-One, which is not itself a thought – and it is a defetishizing experience."[34] Insofar as the vision-in-One is another name for DLI we already have an understanding of part of this claim. Thought is produced and determined-in-the-last-instance by the One, which is not a thought. This relation to the One is what defetishizes thought, marking it as relative and limited. Yet thought also does something as an effect of the One and this productive power of thought will be deployed in non-philosophy.

In forming the concept of FT (*force (de) pensée* in French), Laruelle draws on Marxist theories of labor power (*force de travail* in French) as well as Nietzschean and Deleuzian theories of thought as the product of forces.[35] Laruelle claims to radicalize these theories by subjecting them to the vision-in-One, by thinking their theories under the consequences derived from the axiomatics of the One.

What is retained is a sense that thought is the relative productive force within philosophy and that even though this productive force is subject to certain real limitations, it is also the means of changing the world. Importantly, the world is a construction according to Laruelle, and there is a strict separation of the One and the world. But, nonetheless, even though the world is relative, it has real effects upon human beings as subjects. Entering into the world that is formed by thought – philosophy in particular – may also produce real but relative effects.

What does this then mean in terms of the various forms of thought and their hierarchal competition? To bring forth the anxiety of modern, secular individuals, we may ask: would Laruelle's theory leave one unable to differentiate between the claims of religion and those of science? Is Laruelle's philosophy another instance of "flat ontologies" which are currently *en vogue* amongst other Continental philosophers and theorists? Laruelle's theory does not fit easily into prepackaged debates regarding threats to the (European) Enlightenment project or the equal reality of entities (from unicorns to numbers to quasars to imaginary friends) in a "Latour litany." In his recent work Laruelle has privileged a particular science, quantum physics, though he has continued to produce works on messianism and investigations into Christian and Gnostic theology. One will not find in these works instances of new-age syncretism or attempts to show how ancient religious wisdom is repeated in new scientific forms. Instead, there is a rigorous but wild experimentalism of engaging with thought. In provincializing (European) philosophy, Laruelle frees thought from such bizarrely paternalistic questions as: "Does this philosophy let *those people* off the hook? Does it help educate the ignorant?" The non-philosopher is not an educator in the traditional sense and the concept of FT instead recognizes that the evaluation of thought is carried out through engagement with the particular principles and products of a specific form of thought. Each form of thought has a region and its own scientific character and must be evaluated according to its effects in that region. When Laruelle forms unified theories, he does so by unifying regions or forms of knowledge, not by subjecting a region to another's dominance.

These preceding concepts are the most general of those found in non-philosophy. They form the limits and conditions of the non-philosophical project, but also show what non-philosophy may do in terms of moving between various domains and forms of knowledge. These concepts produce different effects depending on what fields non-philosophy attempts to conjugate, but the radical equality and finitude before the One structures all such conjugations. Laruelle also deploys certain forms of syntax and writing conventions throughout his work that flow from the principle that non-philosophy does what it says and says what it does – or, in other words, that what non-philosophy produces is what is before the reader. These conventions are sometimes halting to a reader as they may appear esoteric. However, they are simple operations meant to manifest non-philosophical practice in a graphical way, and are meant to elucidate more than obscure.

Rules for writing non-philosophy

Readers of Laruelle's work often remark that his style is very difficult. There continues to be hostility in mainstream Anglophone philosophy regarding the difficulty and extensive technical language of French and German philosophy (at least in translation) and the ways these get taken up by Anglophone philosophers writing in the tradition of French, German, and other Continental traditions. Even in Anglophone Continental philosophy, there has been something of a backlash against difficult prose, with one of the declared laudable aspects of Speculative Realism being its attempt to adopt analytic and scientific clarity in its prose. Undoubtedly, Laruelle's work is difficult at first glance, and yet his writing is also littered with concepts and conventions that will be familiar to readers of Continental philosophy and the history of Western philosophy generally.

This is part of what makes his thought so strange. What makes someone a stranger is not a totally unrecognizable nature, but a commonality that yet does not quite fit into one's own framework for making sense of a certain field of experience. One only needs to consider popular and proliferating xenophobic, anti-immigration screeds written by right-wing nationalists to understand this feeling of strangeness. For in those texts there is a palpable sense of anxiety that a stranger may have already penetrated their borders and threatens their own supposed integrity. The emphasis on differences, often simply the product of stereotypes, in these discourses is meant to shore up defenses so that one is aware of the "stranger danger" of an "enemy within," able to make that stranger recognizable as "not from around here." The practice of non-philosophy is not concerned with bringing down philosophy from the inside, so to speak, but it does accept a certain homelessness, a perpetual status as a foreigner within the intellectual field. The style of non-philosophy carries something of a fugitive practice about it, akin to George Jackson's line, "I may run, but all the time that I am, I'll be looking for a stick."[36] This line is the source of Gilles Deleuze and Félix Guattari's conception of a "line of flight," whereby one deterritorializes objects on the run and turns them into weapons.[37] Laruelle has a similar sense of deterritoralization in the way he engages with the "toolbox" of philosophy: "Non-Philosophy's vocabulary is mainly that of philosophy, but each term is constantly reworked in its sense, in its figure, and sometimes in its signifier. This language is taken from anywhere in the tradition – a toolbox, no doubt, *but where the box itself is a tool*, where every tool is inseparable from the box."[38] His writing does not aim for something outside of itself, but attempts to think all at once, as if the sober analysis of philosophy and the wild experimentalism were inseparable.

In this way Laruelle's writing is both conservative and experimental, traditional and heretical. One of the issues that consistently plagues readers of European philosophy (and presumably an issue for any kind of engagement with a literature written in a language that is not one's own) is the dependence upon translations unless one is a specialist who has dedicated years of their life to language study. There are aspects of Laruelle's writing that are lost in translation – probably inevitably so. This is akin to the way in which Heidegger's original German exploits the range of meaning present in everyday German by turning simple words into technical terms, *Dasein* perhaps being the most obvious case as it could simply refer to an "existence" or "presence" in a simple, non-technical way. His translators have had to decide whether to emphasize that technicality or their everyday character. This is a choice that simply doesn't exist in the original. French philosophy generally suffers from this problem as well, since in English we tend to use Latinate terms for technical, academic language that lends translations of French an academic air that is often not there in the original. The French language does not have the same split between abstract terms and everyday terms (which in English are often of Saxon origin), and its source of origin is simpler than the origins of English words and thus French relies on other ways to differentiate formal versus informal use of language. Laruelle's writing carries with it a great deal of formality, but also contains literary and even poetic elements. And to further complicate the issue, the reader should also note that non-philosophy's fugitive status with regard to philosophy lends itself to a practice of sampling, such that Laruelle will often imitate the style of other philosophers in his writing as well.

All of this is important to the practice of non-philosophy, because it speaks to the kind of freedom that the non-philosophical project engenders. Yet such a freedom could turn into its own kind of harassment if it were simply a puerile form of play (which is not to denigrate play in general). Many of us are familiar with poor attempts at shock art that simply bore and say nothing of interest, regardless of whether they take the form of "high art" or an episode of *Family Guy*. So non-philosophical freedom comes with certain guidelines for its writing, with a certain recognition of the limits imposed by the material it is working with, even as it stretches these limits. Non-Philosophy is like the freest form of musical improvization in this way. In free jazz and other forms of improvisation, there is still a valuing of technique and an understanding of certain limits that frame and are exploited in the improvization. An understanding of these rules will help the reader see the purpose behind seemingly obscure conventions. We will begin with the way major concepts or "first names" are formed in non-philosophy and then turn to the more specific syntax of operators and other graphical conventions used to make non-philosophical sense of these names.

First names

What are often thought of as concepts in standard philosophical discourse are described by Laruelle as "first names." This is a response to the problem described above by Barber as the properly nameless character of radical immanence and the necessity of signification. If the One is unrepresentable or nameless, then there can be no true concept of the One, but only a proliferation of different forms of signifying the One which never fully capture the One (including the very term "the One"). Instead, these are simply names that "symbolize the Real [One] and its modes according to its radical immanence or its identity."[39] This conception of naming arises from Aristotelian philosophy in which first terms (like "first philosophy") resist any regress and may break a viciously circular form of thinking that would not allow for any particular thought.

Laruelle differs from Aristotle in that first names are not "proper names" – that is, they do not guarantee anything sufficiently and only perform what they are upon the local field of a specific non-philosophical intervention. One first name developed within a certain philosophical or other regional field (say the *cogito* or unconscious) may not be a productive name in another field.[40]

This local character of first names is determined by how they are formed, since these first names (which include the Real, immanence, One, identity, Man-in-person, Man-in-Man, and Humans) become first names by taking a "philosophical concept and entering into the constitution of the axioms that describe the One."[41] This is a process referred to as the "axiomatized abstraction" of philosophical material. In the preceding quote, the material used was referred to as a "philosophical concept."[42] Philosophies and other aspects of regional forms of knowing (the other disciplines and sciences) are treated by Laruelle as simple material after they have been made relative or been deprived of their sufficiency in the theory of Philosophical Decision. Axiomatized abstraction treats this material under the conditions imposed by the axiomatic of the One, but may be expressed by certain operators – naming being one of those operators, but also certain adjectives like "radical" and prepositions like "in-," "without-," and "non-."[43]

Operators

Certain operators refer to the radical nature of immanence, as the three listed above do. To think "in" something is to think without separation, to think non-philosophically. But even these operators are derived from philosophical material as Laruelle explains with regard to the "without" in his *Introduction to Non-Marxism*: "The 'without', an operator for materialism, is now utilized as an axiomatic operator. The first is an auto-division, an auto-repression of philosophy, and so its conservation. The second signifies the separated-without-separation proper to the Real or to the infrastructure. It is about moving from the usage of philosophy's faith to its usage as material and model."[44] One way to think of this "without" then is as the radically immanent or radically lived form of the concept without any transcendent idea separate from and determining of that lived content.

We also see here the use of a past participle in the term "separated." This use of the past participle is also common in non-philosophical writing, often but not always in conjunction with the "without" operator. Laruelle explains that "the past participle [is] not indicating here the result of action but the phenomenal state of things immanent (to) itself."[45] Thus, again, the past participle expresses the radical immanence of a concept from the One, rather than attempting to think a range of relations that produce some identity reversible with those relations. We also see in the quote above that certain propositions have been placed in parentheses. This acts to suspend the relational aspect of the term, while also allowing for such a suspension of distance to be viewed, since this distance has an effect within the philosophy-world. Relatedly, Laruelle often uses hyphens to create a graphical expression of the undivided-in-the-last-instance character of a concept – that is, he wants to eliminate philosophical distance even at the level of the grapheme in his writing.

There are other operators in non-philosophical syntax that do not have positive meanings. One such group of negative hyphenated words in non-philosophy is the combination of a definite article and a term, as in *la-philosophie*. For positive terms, like One-in-One, these hyphens speak to the radical character of the terms' immanence, while with regard to negative terms this aggregation of the term and its article speaks to the inability to think philosophy's claimed ideal form apart from its empirical instantiations, or to separate its transcendental and empirical forms. This is difficult to translate into idiomatic English, though Robin Mackay's decision to translate instances of this as "Philosophy-with-a-capital-P" strikes me as best, and is found in translations of Lacan as well, while my earliest translations stuck to the more direct but less idiomatic "the-philosophy." Other terms are turned into suffixes and prefixes. For example when "world" is a suffix or a prefix with some other term, as in "thought-world," it indicates a sense of supposed sufficiency operative in that term.[46] This sufficiency is identified in non-philosophical analysis because it resists in a certain way the radical nature of immanence. That resistance is then taken into account through this recognition and naming, allowing it to be submitted in different ways to the axiomatics of the One.

Laruelle is largely consistent with his use of these conventions and they serve to express in truncated form the entire structure of non-philosophical practice. These conventions are often dependent upon certain specificities of the French language and those are often not able to be captured fully in translation. The plasticity of language and certain shared elements of French and English allow for certain conventions to cross over, though if non-philosophy is to become a useful practice in Anglophone philosophy and theory it must not simply remain at the level of studying Laruelle's works. Certain simple conventions particular to English could and should be developed in analogous ways to Laruelle's French creations. As a small example, I have deployed terms in parentheses throughout this text. Philosophy is often written as "(European) philosophy," to at least bring attention to an aspect of philosophical practice often ignored, as well as to suspend philosophy's authority by bringing attention to its provincial nature. At other times I use these parentheses to suspend a term that is needed according to the usage of idiomatic English, but which would run afoul of certain non-philosophical principles. For example "lived experience" will be written as "lived (experience)." Other, more creative, examples may be developed by those taking up Laruelle's work in English. Like Laruelle, those who seek to write under the conditions of radical immanence will need to develop rules for dealing with the materials of thinking, and these rules must remain plastic so as to respond in new and interesting ways to that material.

Part II

Unified Theories and the Waves of Non-Philosophy

3

Politics, or a Democracy (of) Thought

The equivocation of politics and philosophy

In his *Laruelle: Against the Digital*, Alexander R. Galloway deploys the old Maoist ideological mantra "the one divides into two" as a useful hermeneutic lens for reading the history of contemporary French philosophy. Such a digitalization of the One is for Galloway paradigmatic of the philosophical decision, but it is also paradigmatic of politics: "In the most elemental sense, *all philosophy is a form of political philosophy* ... The political is two."[1] This spontaneous alliance between philosophy and politics helps us to understand the ways in which non-philosophy engages with politics, just as it will help us in chapter 5 to understand Laruelle's relative privileging of ethics over politics.

The relationship between politics and the development of Laruelle's non-philosophy is complex because his most direct engagement with politics takes place in his early work, work that Laruelle claims was not fully non-philosophical and that yet prefigured in many ways the non-philosophical project he went on to pursue. He tells us about this period in his own truncated history of non-philosophy as separated into distinct periods labeled "Philosophy I through V" in *Principles of Non-Philosophy*:

> Philosophy I placed itself under the authority of the Principle of Sufficient Philosophy but already sought to put certain themes to work; themes that would only find their definite form, a transformed form, in Philosophy III: the individual, its identity and its

multiplicity, a transcendental and productive experience of thought, the theoretical domination of philosophy, the attempt to construct a problematic rivaling that of Marx, though mainly on Nietzschean terrain and with Nietzschean means.[2]

This early period of work is marked by four major texts published between 1976 and 1978, to which we will shortly turn our attention. But questions around politics and the political also frame the shift from Philosophy I to Philosophy II, or from standard philosophy to the non-philosophical project proper.

In this chapter, I will sketch Laruelle's standard philosophical foray into political philosophy and then turn to the ways in which his political concerns came to be thought differently under a non-philosophical paradigm. We will come to see, as Galloway's remarks prefigure, that for Laruelle politics is a continuation of philosophy by different means. As we move through the chapter, outlining the themes of materialism, power and force, and the duality of authorities and minorities, I hope to show that the meaning of this equivocation of politics and philosophy is not simply a naive idealism but a powerful statement regarding the ways in which thought may enter into what Laruelle calls "imma-nent struggle" and so bear on more intense life-and-death struggles within the world. Non-Philosophy does not promise a politics of the future, but finds a way to use politics and to struggle produc-tively within the political world for the sake of actual human beings.

Laboring under the principle of sufficient philosophy

As I said in the Introduction, I have elsewhere provided two trun-cated histories of non-philosophy and I will not repeat that history in the same way here. But in these chapters on non-philosophy's various unified theories I will occasionally survey their place in the development of Laruelle's non-philosophy. It is important though that this process of situating his thought within a broader history is not taken as sufficient or merely linear in its development. Laru-elle remarks, in an interview about the beginning of his writing process, "One day, after I had completed my studies, I sat at my desk, and I cleared away all the books, everything that had already been written. I started again with a new blank sheet of paper, and

I began to search myself."[3] This "beginning again, for the first time" is characteristic of each of Laruelle's texts as the basic material elements and the form they take are remarkably consistent, but the specific instantiations they come to take in each book depends upon the new material added to the theoretical matrix and engaged with by Laruelle and this in turn has effects on the shape they come to take in the next instantiation.

If Laruelle's engagement with politics marks Philosophy I so clearly, it is also the case that the movement to non-philosophy in Philosophy II is also marked by the political. Laruelle's first publication comes in 1971 with the appearance of his minor thesis (published as part of the process of receiving a doctorate in the French system). This text, *Phénomène et différence. Essai sur Ravaisson*, was on the work of Félix Ravaisson, and the influence of Laruelle's advisor, Paul Ricœur, can be seen on the work. But Laruelle's own work comes rushing headlong onto the scene of French philosophy with four books all comprising around 300 pages over the course of just two years. Each touched on political questions or couched their themes within what were seen at the time as political thematics: *Machines textuelles. Déconstruction et libido d'écriture* ("Textual Machines: Deconstruction and the Libido of Writing") (1976), *Nietzsche contre Heidegger. Thèses pour une politique nietzschéenne* ("Nietzsche Contra Heidegger: Theses Towards a Nietzschean Politics") (1977), *Le Déclin de l'écriture* ("The Decline of Literature) (1977), and *Au-delà du principe de pouvoir* ("Beyond the Power Principle") (1978). Each of these texts is remarkable in various ways, and there is a certain sense in which the early Laruelle was engaging very seriously with some of the more exciting projects taking place in France at the time. There was even a recognition of the quality of this early work by Derrida himself. In Derrida's major work *The Post Card: From Socrates to Freud and Beyond*, we see him paying what can only be called homage. There he first makes the claim, "Beyond the pleasure principle – power."[4] And he then goes on to credit Laruelle with potentially elaborating such a claim, writing:

> Could what I was then attempting in a seminar, on the basis of a reading and a "monographic" exercise, in the environs of a single text by Freud, join up or intersect in some way with the project that provides the title for Laruelle's latest book *Au-delà du principe de pouvoir*? I am not yet certain. Without directly treating the Freudian text, Laruelle's book refers to it and displaces it in depth, beyond the citational parody of its title. From *Machines textuelles. Déconstruction et libido d'écriture, Nietzsche contre Heidegger. Thèses pour une politique*

nietzschéenne, and *Le Déclin de l'écriture* onward, a powerful elaboration is following its course.[5]

In the 1970s, Laruelle's work could have been included amongst
that of other philosophers engaging in deconstruction, such as
Sarah Kofman, Jean-Luc Nancy, Philippe Lacoue-Labarthe, and
Derrida himself (all of whom pose questions to Laruelle in the
appendix to *Le Déclin de l'écriture*). Indeed, he was one of the early
French adopters of deconstruction, but also was part of a French
trend of crafting a literary and political reading of Nietzsche, along
the same lines as Sarah Kofman and Gilles Deleuze – all while
remaining deeply influenced by Marxism at the same time as he
saw his work to be following a certain failure of Marxism, without
abandoning it as others had done. In some ways these works could
be translated today and would find an easy home in debates around
materialist political philosophy, but they are also marked by a
strangeness that is unambiguously non-philosophical. So there is
in these early works a move away from difference as a founding
concept and a concern with the radical immanence of the human
that underlies any projected subject positions. And while Laruelle
himself claims this early work was prior to his discovery of the
Philosophical Decision, and so prior to the project of non-philosophy, these early texts were the first experiments that allowed him
to discover and identify Philosophical Decision. This is seen clearly
when one recognizes that the first two of his early texts (*Machines
textuelles* and *Nietzsche contre Heidegger*) are major engagements
with four thinkers who will come to be the focus of his first sustained investigation into the Philosophical Decision in *Philosophies
of Difference*: Nietzsche, Heidegger, Derrida, and Deleuze.

While the various interesting claims in each text may deserve
some attention, for the sake of the mandate of this book I have
limited us to a few main themes: a particular kind of materialism
related to producing texts, his theory of power, the concept of the
individual caught between minorities and authorities, and finally
the ways in which politics is taken up into non-philosophy as a
way of thinking democratically as part of a struggle that outstrips
the limits of standard political models.

A materialist reading of deconstruction

At first, Laruelle was welcomed into the den of the deconstruction-
ists, but was always kept at a distance. This situation came to a

head in the debate between Derrida and Laruelle regarding the possibility of a science of philosophy, like non-philosophy. So, while Derrida declares in 1980 that this early work is a "powerful elaboration," a short eight years later he is insinuating that Laruelle practices a kind of terroristic violence, rounding out a series of objections to his projects with the pointed question: "Ultimately, all the questions that I want to ask come down to this schema: why do you reduce – and isn't there a violence here of the type you denounce in philosophical society? – so many gestures which could accompany you along the path you wish to pursue?"[6] In short, while some of the questions Derrida asks in his litany are valid and others point toward fundamental misunderstandings, the final question points toward a kind of unelaborated critique regarding the scope of Laruelle's claim concerning the existence of an identity (in the technical language of non-philosophy) or essence (to use the standard philosophical term) of philosophy located in Philosophical Decision. Prior to this conclusion, Derrida accused Laruelle of not playing by the rules of public discourse – essentially of being anti-social: "What makes it difficult to go along with the movement I would like to accompany you in, is that it sometimes seems to me to consist in you carrying out a violent shuffling of the cards in a game whose rules are known to you alone."[7] Laruelle's response is interesting, saying to Derrida:

> your questions have a very particular style, which I found highly interesting, that of retorsion: "You're just like those you criticize"; "You're doing just what you claim to abhor." You taught me in your work that one should be wary of retorsion. So I would like to suggest that to the extent that you are making a certain use of retorsion, and this is a theme that recurred throughout, right up to the end via the accusation of socio-philosophical war, then it is necessarily the case that some of your objections in a certain way mean precisely the opposite of what I said.[8]

Laruelle is responding here to a philosopher whom he has learned a great deal from. He dedicated his early work to unfolding in interesting new dimensions Derrida's deconstruction in a materialist way that was decades ahead of its time. According to many of its proponents the emergence of a "speculative turn" marked the decline of deconstruction's erstwhile hegemony over the avant-garde of Continental philosophy and those disciplines in dialogue with it. The one Derridean dialogue partner these resurgent "realists" and "materialists" were willing to entertain was Martin Hägglund and his 2008 *Radical Atheism: Derrida and the Time of Life*. This text re-opened a debate regarding the fit – and I mean to emphasize this Darwinian notion – of materialism to Derrida's deconstruction, and vice versa. Hägglund, who of course is not the first to propose such a reading, maintains that the readings of Derrida that had become prevalent were missing what was vital in Derrida's thought. They were making pious and conservative a philosophy that stands in the tradition of the Radical Enlightenment and so firmly on the side of an atheistic, materialist philosophy. Dispensing with these readings – named by Hägglund variously as "ethicist," "religious," and so on – would allow Derrida's philosophy to enter into contemporary debates regarding materialism, realism, and the primacy of the sciences over a kind of overly sentimental ethics and religiosity.[9] We have to become sober, Hägglund's work suggests, and the path to sobriety follows the 12-step model requiring absolute abstinence. It requires a radical abstinence from religious discourses, a radical atheism that is done with a transcendent ideal guiding our political action. Now, in the light of the morning after, our political and social engagements should be conditioned by our material and real finitude as revealed by the post-Darwinian biological sciences.

My purpose here is not to quibble with Hägglund's reading of Derrida or to pick sides in the fight he has picked with other readers of Derrida like John Caputo.[10] I bring up this debate because, again judging by the amount of interest produced formally in journals as well as informally on blogs, people took Hägglund's materialist reading as largely unprecedented. It is perhaps owing to the often-referenced difficulty of Laruelle's writing and the vagaries of the academic translation industry that his early work was largely ignored in the Anglophone reception of Derrida. Laruelle's own heretical tendencies placed him as an outsider to the outsiders within the French system where Derrida's work struggled for an audience for a number of years. But Laruelle's reading of deconstruction is marked by the same inventiveness and heretical moves as his later work, and so a "materialist" reading of deconstruction marks these texts. This reading examines deconstruction, rather than pitching it into what must be something like the equivalent of the Hundred Years' War (though lasting much longer) between a materialist "radical atheism" and a religiously determined philosophy (whether within deconstruction or within the wider milieu of European and American philosophy). Soon we will look in more depth at Laruelle's conception of materialism, but here let me state what it allows Laruelle to do: deconstruction is shown to be a material, textual practice (though this isn't new, it was not often commented upon so explicitly in the 1970s) as well as being conditioned by material concerns (the meaning of the libido of writing). This means that deconstruction is not treated as a philosophy sufficient to the Real, but as itself a player within the same immanent material field.

How Laruelle does this is ingenious. He reads Derrida with a Deleuzian supplement. After asking and setting aside a question he will go on to answer in *Philosophies of Difference* – namely, "What difference can there be between two systems of difference (that of Deleuze and that of Derrida)?" – he says:

> I have only tried to make the series Delida/Derreuze resonate (these "proper" names function as libidinal intensities or burdens, they interpenetrate each other and impinge one upon the other, disappropriating one by the other, to the great displeasure, we hope, of the epigonal appropriations and hasty oppositions...) repeating deconstruction within the signs of intensive production, re-inscribing the affirmation of the Eternal Return within textuality, causing intensive difference and textual simulacrum to communicate, within a reciprocal parody that sometimes displaces deconstruction and intensifies it right up to active and affirmative difference.[11]

What this means in practice is that he takes up Derrida's work and reads it through Deleuzian concepts like the plane of immanence, desiring machines, and machinic materialism.

So what exactly is this materialism? How is it different from the materialism that figures like Hägglund have tried to align Derrida with? Like Deleuze and Guattari in *Anti-Oedipus*, which is obviously one of the main sources of Laruelle's reading even though it is only referenced once in passing, Laruelle focuses on the way in which texts are shown to couple with other texts in deconstruction. These texts function like machines that may be plugged into other machines, allowing for flows between them or for flows to be cut off from each other.[12] There is in *Anti-Oedipus* a threefold structure to machinic materialism: machines and desire are the unilateral duality of production (later this becomes the actual and the virtual) and the anti-production of the full Body without Organs.[13] Laruelle mimics this in his reading of Derrida, casting a threefold structure to deconstruction that includes: "A) *textual*, which designates the linguistic representation of the text [the actual], b) *textuel*, which designates the a-signifying functions or machines of the text, being the general textuality within its "transcendental" functioning; c) *a-textual*, which designates (against perhaps what deconstruction wants or can do?) the active indifference of the generality (of writing) in the text, indeed in the writing."[14] Again we see the triadic nature of philosophy traced by Laruelle even prior to non-philosophy proper.

This machinic materialist schema of writing allows Laruelle then to trace the ways in which the desire of deconstruction flows in the production and destruction or a-production of texts. While this doesn't mark Derrida as post-Darwinian, it does do something far closer to the sciences than simply arguing for a metaphysical view that enlarges on the empirical claims of a particular science (something Hägglund is at least tempted by, if not subject to). That is, this machinic materialism is an actual *local* analysis and modeling of writing, local analysis and modeling being what science actually does.

In modeling (or "cloning" in Laruelle's later terminology, and "parodying" in his early terminology at play here) deconstruction, he is able to both practice a non-idealist materialism and show how deconstruction itself is not an idealism. He writes:

> The textua(e)l [*textue(a)l* i.e., the productive element of writing] is not a new idealism of the text cut off from its outside-texts, but the destruction of this textual idealism, the production of general textuality effects, by working on the text and the outside-text within their co-belonging....A new concept and a new practice of reference – writing as referential – there you have what produces deconstruction, what re-produces ceaselessly with itself and within new texts, that through which it finally detaches textuality as such from old, metaphysical references, be they matter or the various practices that one claims it offers textuality so generously. The process of deconstruction produces or "engenders" its own reference, its *référance* [spelled here with an unheard and only seen "a" instead of an "e," like "*différance*"].[15]

This quote encapsulates the initial upshot of such a machinic materialism as it captures both that deconstruction is a practice and that this practice is a kind or re-production. Throughout *Machines textuelles*, Laruelle references words with the prefix "re-" to describe deconstruction, ultimately claiming that deconstruction is indelibly marked by practices of the "eternal return of the...Other." The textual material that deconstruction engages with is put into play through mimetic parody and generalized repetition, always casting the text along an arc that moves outside the text and back to it. The material reading of deconstruction shows that it is an economy, a general economy that produces past the limits thought to be outlined by either critical philosophy or structuralism and that will only come to really be thought by a science of philosophy or a non-philosophy.[16]

A materialist politics and a theory of power and force

Ultimately, the structure of *Machines textuelles* sets out the machinic materialist reading of deconstruction by tracing its general economy, meaning it traces practices of the "eternal return of the ...Other," or mimetic parody and generalized repetition, already touched on, and the way in which this shows how the practice of writing escapes or outruns the very signifier/signified structure on the order of simple Newtonian causality. This all leads to Laruelle's discussion of the libido of writing or writerly libido. As he says, "Our 'thesis' posits the subordination of textual values to libidinal values."[17] Here, to pass to another important thematic of this early work, we will examine these "libidinal values" and the meaning this reading has for deconstruction and how Laruelle's project unfolded.

Laruelle claims that Derrida's deconstruction lacks a theory of power (the reader familiar with Derrida's later explicit writings on politics should keep in mind that Laruelle is making this claim during the early phases of the development of deconstruction). Laruelle begins to provide that theory of power in *Machines textuelles* by asking, "What does the deconstructor desire?" With this question he moves from the general economy that his materialism sketches for him to the question of the subject who acts within that economy.[18] By examining the writerly libido that drives deconstruction, he asks who deconstructs, in a way that does not see any strict or real separation between libido and the writing of that libido. That is, the subject who desires deconstruction is deconstructive of the subject itself. Deconstruction begins to unravel the way in which the subject, the lived (reality) of the person who thinks and writes deconstructively, is cast in thought itself – an important prefiguring of the way in which non-philosophy does not claim to act on politics itself, but instead carries out a political act within thinking.

Libido is another name for force. With *Nietzsche contre Heidegger*, Laruelle turns to the question of power and marks out this theme of force that will be taken up as one of the main modifiers within non-philosophical practice.[19] *Nietzsche contre Heidegger* is an interesting text simply on the basis of its political reading of Nietzsche's philosophy and critique of Heidegger's reading of Nietzsche, as well as for the positive project Laruelle puts forward in parallel to other French philosophers attempting to think the meaning and possibility of cultural revolution. Foremost amongst those for Laruelle were Guy Lardreau and Christian Jambet in their work *L'Ange. Pour une cynégétique du semblant, ontologie de la révolution 1* (1976), which posits a radical dualism between master and rebel. Laruelle claims that such a simplistic Manichaeism is too narrow to produce the kind of analysis required. He instead suggests a fourfold structure within his machinic materialism that looks at the operation of thinkers as sorts of machines that operate within the parameters of Mastery, Rebellion, Fascism, and Resistance.[20] He then goes on to apply such a fourfold structure to what he calls the Nietzsche-machine ("like a computer, but a machine for politics") as the philosophy that "assumes fascism in order to vanquish it" and locates the active/resisting pole of his thought in tension with the fascistic pole.[21] This tension is found elsewhere in other thinkers but may there take on the character of duplicity (an inclusive disjunction where the Master assimilates the Rebel to himself, thus again calling for the radical break between Mastery and Rebellion).[22]

While *Nietzsche contre Heidegger* and the other works are interesting in themselves (I hope the short summaries above evidence this and will perhaps entice curious readers to track them down), their theses and concepts are not the focus of Laruelle's non-philosophical casting of political concepts. What remains in the mature work is the unexpected combination of Marx and Nietzsche, with Nietzsche's conception of power and libido being read through the Marxist distinction of the productive forces and the relations of production, while Nietzsche is proclaimed to be "the only thinker for whom, even more than for Marx, *there will be* politics (as the cause of the fascistic or rebellious subject)."[23] Laruelle, as we discussed in chapter 2, often brings together or conjugates two philosophers, and that is on display in his reading of Nietzsche with Marx. He reads Nietzsche as a machinic materialist by thinking him with Marx, with Marxist dialectical materialism and historical materialism becoming political materialism and machinic materialism.[24] More importantly, with regard to force, the means or relations of production are clarified as relations of power: "The reality of every real, the materiality of all matter (the object of the Eternal Return of the Same) is constituted by 'forces' in relation, or by hierarchies of partial organs of power. They form the Relations of Power that occupy and displace the Marxist position of the Relations of Production."[25] Laruelle goes on to clarify this understanding of force, writing: "By the ambiguous term 'force' Nietzsche designates a drive and an organ of power at the same time....So we discover that *Nietzsche, by positing every reality as relations of power, and power as (partial) drives, invents the political 'anatomy' of the unconscious.*"[26] Forces are, then, what drive forward politics or any human attempt to resist or stratify into State power. It is these forces that "in the last instance" drive production.[27] And this production is enlarged beyond the world of economics to the very domain of human thinking. This notion of force will be familiar to those who are conversant with Marxist philosophy, and it is indeed pivoting on Marx's conception of labor power that we move from these political works that labor under the domination of the principle of sufficient philosophy to Laruelle's project of non-philosophy. For, as we have already seen, non-philosophy takes as one of its guiding concepts the force-(of)-thought or *force (de) pensée*. In the same way that labor power in Marxist philosophy is the abstract name for capacities the human being *qua* worker has to produce, so is force-(of)-thought the abstract name for the capacities of the thinker.[28] These capacities are not alienated in the radical immanence of the human being and are what drives forward the theoretical project of non-philosophy in its attempt to free the force-(of)-thought crystalized in the production of philosophical works that are by their totalizing nature alienating or harassing of the lived (reality) of the human person. And, as in Marxism, these are capacities that an individual possesses but that are common to the generic character of humanity. This move to thinking in a human way is what truly begins the project of mutating politics within the parameters of non-philosophy.

Can thinking be democratic?

So we see that, from his early writings to the mature works, Laruelle is concerned with production and with the specific capacities and powers of human beings to produce without alienation. Specifically, we see, with the move from labor power (*force de travail*) to force-(of)-thought, that the project of non-philosophy carries these concerns not into the world, but into philosophy. That is, politics and political concepts are taken to be *thinking and thoughts about politics* that are liable to be recast *toward the project of producing thought*. Thus a democracy (of) thought will be concerned not with a democracy in the world – there is no promise within non-philosophy of sketching out the political program that will finally bring about revolution – but with the possibility of organizing philosophical thought to be democratic or communist in itself (Laruelle marks an equivalence between communism and democracy). While aspects of non-philosophy may bear upon concerns outside of its primary focus – that is, carrying out a science of philosophy that allows for mutations of thought via unified theories – those domains exterior to philosophy are already taken to be practicing thought. Insofar as they may lapse into fantasies of their own sufficiency – like the principle of sufficient rebellion identified in *Future Christ* – they practice a kind of philosophy that may benefit from the non-philosophical act of disempowering that sufficiency in the name of the Human-in-Human, meaning the radically immanent and unrepresentable human.

In many ways Laruelle's foray into politics carries much in common with the works of other Continental philosophers and theoreticians who aim for their thought to inform radical politics and act as an expression of that same radical politics. A focus on minorities and minoritarian thinking, as in Deleuze and Foucault, a theory that begins not from the State and its politics but instead from those whose labor the apparatus of State and Capital captures while they owe their existence to that labour, as Negri and other neo-Marxists claim: a rejection of economism and deterministic forms of thinking, but also a strong critique of the reactionary nostalgia of Heidegger's anti-science and anti-technology stances – as Badiou and others have argued for. The list could go on, but the question that arises for a reader is then: what, if anything, does Laruelle add that is distinctive? Unlike these thinkers, his later work no longer looks to produce a politics from a philosophy, or even to have philosophy act as an expression of some future politics. Politics, especially as cast by political philosophers, is a form of philosophy that believes itself able to provide the conditions for everything. And yet the reality of politics as it plays out is always fraught with structures that end up harassing everyone. There is simply no right politics in the world, no way to be political that doesn't have the potential to be drawn to the fascistic pole identified by Laruelle via Nietzsche. And on this point there is a profound pessimism regarding the world pervading Laruelle's work that is often not recognized – a true pessimism that recognizes the duplicity of political distinction. Here a reader may be tempted to quietism, to an anti-politics or an apolitical stance. What Laruelle's mutation of political philosophy gives us is not a quietism or an anti-politics, or even apolitics, but a radical separation between the human and politics. Translated into slightly more standard philosophical terms, this means that the lived immanence of the human is indifferent to politics. Politics may harass the human, may bring to bear oppression of subjects and so on, but there remains something foreclosed to politics that such harassment simply cannot reach.

Since it is largely in the realm of politics or through political readings of textuality that Laruelle labored under the principle of sufficient philosophy, it comes as no surprise that the transition from philosophy to non-philosophy takes place through a rethinking of politics and its relation to non-philosophy's guiding thread. The guiding thread is the Real-One, operating as the even more abstract name for the Human-in-Human. What Laruelle provides for us in his move from world to Human is a disempowering of politics. In the way that his early materialism allowed him to read texts as political texts, as materials in the world that were amenable to human use, so does his later vision-in-One (a privileging of matter over materialism or the Real over realism) allow him to disempower the transcendent, harassing claims of politics so as to turn what politics produces and what produces politics into simple materials. With regard to his project, this is localized to the realm of thought and the practice of thinking. Thus his mutation of politics will be with regard to how thinking may be political and how politics takes place in thinking.

This rethinking takes place in the first two works that Laruelle identifies as non-philosophical: *Le Principe de minorité* (1981), which may be translated as "The Minority Principle"; and *Une biographie de l'homme ordinaire* (1985), which may be translated as "A Biography of Ordinary Man." Both texts begin with thinking from the minority position rather than the position of authority. And, in *Une biographie*, Laruelle takes up a phrase from Mao that French Maoists and other revolutionary theorists often repeated, which in English we know as "it is right to rebel against reactionaries," and turns it against philosophy, writing: "It is right to revolt [*On a raison de se révolter*] against philosophers." The French term here is *se révolter* and, since Laruelle marks an important difference between *se révolter* and *se rebeller*, I have tended to translate these terms as "revolt" and "rebellion."[29] But, linguistic distinctions aside, Laruelle asks the question that may be on the reader's mind: "But why?"

Philosophy, like politics, does not care for the human, for the ordinary man and the ordinary woman. Non-Philosophy begins through thinking the One, the radical immanence of this ordinary human. The transition here from an authoritarian politics/philosophy to a minoritarian one is summed up succinctly by Laruelle in five theses translated and presented here:

1   man really exists and he is really distinct from the World – a thesis that contradicts nearly every philosophy;
2   man is a living mystic sentenced [*condamné*] to action, a contemplative being doomed to practice for reasons that are unknown to him;
3   as living practice, man is sentenced a second time, and for the same reasons, to philosophy;
4   this double sentence organizes his fate, and this fate is called the "World," "History," "Language," "Sexuality," "Power," etc., all of which we designate generally as the *Authorities*;
5   a rigorous science of ordinary man, which is just to say of man, is possible: a biography of the individual as Minorities and as Authorities – a theoretical description grounded upon the life man leads between these two poles and that suffices to define him.[30]

We see here the vision of a kind of moving beyond the harassment of a totalizing politics and a turn toward a deeper gnosticism that runs throughout Laruelle's work. For the world is politics – meaning it is philosophy – and while human beings may be condemned to the practice of this politics, there is something Human-in-Human that remains foreclosed to this world and that is completely distinct from the world according to the causality of unilateral duality that is so important in Laruelle's work.

Before turning again to a text by Laruelle allow me to provide a summary of the turn away from the massive, authoritarian concept of politics equivalent to the philosophy that human beings are sentenced to practice in the world. Carl Schmitt famously declared that politics is concerned with the distinction between friend and enemy.[31] Such a view of politics is not the exclusive purview of Schmitt and his incipient fascism on display in his essay. It is truly the summary of how modernity understood revolutionary politics and is therefore a part of the structure of political organizations ostensibly concerned with radical equality, like the Soviets or even liberals who hold progressive values concerning universal inclusion within a unitary democratic State politics.[32] In those instances, it still becomes a matter of recognizing the enemies of inclusion and excluding them, or recognizing the enemies of radical equality and segregating them or disempowering them. While I do not wish to reject radical equality, this does locate a certain paradox at the heart of radical politics (which remains political): in its drive to include everyone, it still must distinguish and operate by exclusion, making its task ultimately impossible.

This has consequences for political action and movements and this paradox is not unknown to political theorists and activists. There is a certain immeasurable character to this attempt to measure the friend by way of the enemy, and vice versa. Such immeasurableness is the ground of the friend/enemy distinction, the decision of friend or enemy, and so operates as the force of that very distinction. This distinction may be located within the relations of the disciplines, and from the perspective of philosophy there is a need to either make friends or enemies of the respective other domains of knowledge like science, art, ethics, politics, etc. What Laruelle thus names as the democracy (of) thought is the act of making thought itself democratic. Treating all forms of thought as equal, radically equal, in a unified theory where concepts freely mingle and conjugate into new forms. This radical equality of thought comes not from their inherent goodness, but through their being equally foreclosed ultimately to radical immanence, through their being unable to take the measure of the Human-in-Human while being equally liable to some human use.

In the style of non-philosophy, we may say that this immeasurableness is another name for radical immanence, for the indistinction in-the-last-instance of friend/enemy. But this indistinction needs to be carefully parsed so as to avoid the sorts of confusions that may cast Laruelle as a standard liberal or universalist thinker of inclusion through the subtraction of certain particularities or the exclusion of certain maligned others – for example, the notion that, to be fully included in American democracy the Black American must have her blackness subtracted so that one "only" engages with another human being, or the Muslim in French democracy must have their cultural and religious identity subtracted so that they may engage "simply" as French. This conflation of American liberalism and French universalist republicanism might strike some readers as clumsy and lacking in nuance. However, despite important differences, there is an isomorphism at work here regarding subtraction in relation to minority identities. Both claim to provide freedom for the individual, either by removing obstacles to individual freedom or by subtracting markers of identity that might mark the individual as something other than a fellow citizen. Yet, in each case, there is a figure of the free individual or a figure of the universal that is held up as the normative figure. Some individuals and citizens simply fit the figure, while others are marked by their distinction or difference from that figure. It would be too easy and clumsy to say that communist philosophers who claim that their projects are universalist projects, as Badiou and Žižek do, are then still within the frame of liberalism because of their universalism. But such attempts at radical universalism do still remain within the frame of distinction and separation that is, at the very least, haunted by the same system of excluding in order to include. The root of this system of inclusion via subtraction and exclusion can be seen in the way Badiou's and Žižek's own attempts to think universalism arise out of the Christian project put forward by St. Paul.[33] Badiou and Žižek locate the subtractive project of St. Paul in his declaration, "There is no longer Jew or Greek, there is no longer slave or free, there is no longer male or female; for all of you are one in Christ Jesus" (Galatians 3:28). While this might appear as if identities are being subtracted, what is really at play is the creation of a new substantive and exclusionary identity: one is neither Jew nor Greek because one is now a Christian. Out of this subtraction, a distinction and then an exclusion are made.[34]

Laruelle's generic identity has no figure precisely because his understanding of the generic occurs through an indistinction that is expressed but not captured through the unilateralization of the minor or oppressed name in a dyad. This unilateralization results in the unilateral Stranger, instead of the stranger/citizen dyad, the unilateral Black instead of the Black/white dyad, or – a figure Laruelle has devoted much time to in his later work – the unilateral victim instead of the victim/persecutor dyad. The full development of this indistinction will be carried out in chapter 5, but we already see that development prefigured in Laruelle's discussion of democracy when he writes: "Who is finally the 'subject' who declares the theory of democracy?...Only the Foreigner [*Étranger*] has the right [*juste*] or adequate point of view, that is democratic point of view, regarding the theory of man and, therefore, regarding political theory."[35] Here the term Laruelle uses in French is *étranger* which is variously translated as "stranger," "foreigner," or "alien" and in political discourse this term carries all the weight and prejudice in English that discussions of foreigners do, hence the decision to translate the preceding quote with "Foreigner," despite translators of Laruelle usually using the term "stranger." Laruelle's claim is, then, that democracy is only truly democratic when it is generalized, when there is no basis of identity other than the lived (reality) of the worldless Human-in-Human. Democracy is never democratic in a State, but only when it is determined by those very people who destabilize the State.

Laruelle says, "Democracy will not have taken place, if it is not the without-place of Man-in-Man."[36] The reference here to the utopian impulse of non-philosophy ("utopia" literally meaning "no-place" in the original Greek) is more than fanciful and fruitless desire for something other than this world, it is more than an ado-lescent refusal to grow up (though there is something to this desire for Laruelle). Rather, it is a fundamental truth of democracy and how democracy is normally thought. Laruelle says to think democ-racy, to perform a political philosophy of democracy, is not to practice democracy, it is not to be democratic. This is especially true for philosophy, because "To philosophize on X is to withdraw from X; to take an essential distance from the term for which we posit other terms, for example predicates of X."[37] Philosophy is not dem-ocratic, especially when it thinks democracy, because its decisional structure requires that it separate itself from democracy while also claiming to think the all that democracy names. However, this "all" (the "equality for all" fundamental to true democratic practice) is now constituted by the philosopher who takes himself to be an exception to that "all." Laruelle accuses philosophy of a fundamen-tal dishonesty when it claims to be democratic:

> The philosopher, legislating for reason, the life of the mind [*vie de la pensée*] or social life, makes an exception even of the fact that he does not do what he says or does not say what he does, but, speaking the law, he makes an exception and enjoys the privilege of speaking about it and imposing it with his authority. I speak the truth, says the liar; I speak democracy, says the anti-democrat: this is the paradox of the philosopher as thinker of All who is never short of expedients for presenting the paradox as if it were acceptable.[38]

This dishonesty, this act of lying by philosophy, has consequences for how philosophy understands democracy.

Take again, for example, the work of Badiou, who has purposely cast his philosophical work as thoroughly in the service of politics, and whose own militancy is evidenced by a number of campaigns he has supported or been a part of in France. We are not concerned here with the political work in itself, which is clearly laudable and even in some sense inspiring as an example of that of an engaged intellectual, but we are concerned here with the form of his philosophical practice. His philosophy may appear to contain a certain disempowering of philosophy akin to a withdrawal from philosophical sufficiency and authority. This appearance comes from the fact that for Badiou philosophy is concerned with truth, but produces no truths in itself.[39] Instead, philosophy only exists in service to certain truth-events in the domains of politics, science, art, and love. Yet – this is where the insidiousness of the philosopher's dishonesty comes into view – these truth-events are decided upon by philosophy – in particular, the philosophy of Badiou. The truths of these events do not speak for themselves, but require a kind of philosophical representative to speak for them. Thus even the value of "evental sites" given to one movement or practice over another (communism for all politics, set theory for science, cinema for art, and psychoanalysis for all understanding of love) is something philosophy itself decides upon.[40] While these four sites may at first glance seem as if they are sort of thought-citizens or comrades within a democracy or communism (of) thought, their separation is rigorously planned out.[41] And the exception to those who are subjected to truth-events is precisely the philosophy that sketches out the destinies and fates of the particular subjects.

Since philosophy takes itself to be exceptional with regard to democracy, democracy is then strange or foreign to it. As Laruelle says, "democracy cannot be complete because the All is composed and said by way of some exception. *Philosophically, democracy is undecidable*."[42] For a democracy – lived-out or of thought – to be truly democracy, to speak to an equality-in-the-last-instance, it must not be political, but thought from the position of radical immanence, from the Real.[43] In this way, democracy names a fundamentally unified, though not unitary, lived (reality). This unification takes on a particularly ethical form, one where the indivision, the equality of democracy, is carried out by bringing the multitude under the condition of a single generic identity. Laruelle summarizes this form of democratic thinking as *"To think in a democratic way in-the-last-instance is to make use of two approaches within the indivision of a single one.*"[44] Though we will see shortly that the way this indivision takes place matters.

Thought must be destabilized by those foreign or strange to philosophy, and in that process thought may come to offer a clearer (human) vision of revolutionary politics. I continue to use this phrase because there is something to be retained in radical politics as the minor tradition of politics. There are certain instances in radical political movements of human salvation and the possibility of an overturning of the world in Laruelle's sense. Yet, part of that clear (human) vision of politics comes from recognizing that failure is a part of the theory. This is perhaps the most important hinge-point between Laruelle's non-politics and his non-ethics (which are merely terms to index his attempts to mutate these domains of thought). For failure and victimhood, which are explored in chapters 5 and 6, are intimately connected. The failure of world communism, for example, produces victims both in the ways it continued the politics of friend and enemy within communist states, and in its failure to overturn capitalism – thus, a failure to save those who fall victim to that overwhelming thought-world. And yet, Laruelle also claims that this radical form of democracy is equivalent to communism: "The democracy of-the-last-instance could after all be called 'communism' – if subtracted from every historical instance just as much as from spontanism, if the 'common' of communism was understood as the generic, if communism was understood as the generic constant of history."[45] Laruelle's later work turns away from Nietzschean themes to more explicitly Marxist ones, but unlike some of his contemporaries he fearlessly considers thinking the failure of Marxism as part of the task of thinking Marxism. There is no need to cover over this failure with references to its true essence or to heroic figures of communism, as Badiou and Žižek do in their philosophies. Neither is there a need to abandon Marxism, as other less well-known figures like Bernard-Henry Lévi, André Glucksmann, and still others in Laruelle's generation did. That is, he rejects responding to this failure via resentment that emerges in the symptoms of hero worship or simple desertion.[46] Instead, Laruelle takes this failure to be part of Marxism and part of what needs to be mutated into a non-Marxism: "Our conjuncture and our order, we have said, is that Marxism is *inseparable* from its failure as much as it is *irreducible* to it."[47]

Treating political theory in this way has consequences. First, if failure is part of the essence of Marxism, it is not a reason to abandon Marxism, or to abandon theory more generally, since

Marx's philosophy at least aims to be a unified theory of philosophy and science in the service of human beings. Insofar as its failure is part of its essence, thinking that failure is an instance of the force-(of)-thought operating on material in order to fashion something else from it. In Laruelle's case, this is a non-Marxism that provides many of the overarching structures of his thought as surveyed in chapter 2. This could be expanded to a general understanding of how radical political movements and philosophy or theory may relate to one another. The point is to continue to think the failure, to locate where the necessary failure comes from, since anything outside of radical immanence will be riven with paradoxes and inconsistency. This inconsistency, though, carries some good news for, in the midst of our practice and theory, we are not trapped by those failures, we are not ultimately subject to them – at least not if we recognize and think through them.

And, finally, though politics always carries forth its own inconsistency, thinking remains a human act and one that is found amongst every ordinary human – which is to say, every human being. To think is part of human resistance to the very same authorities that human beings hallucinate into the world. Against these hallucinations we may continue to think and thus follow what is found amidst our foreignness to worldly domination. Laruelle makes the claim that this strangeness to the world comes with a maxim: "The maxim of the Stranger-subject, of the 'Proletariat' delivered from philosophy: 'do not give up on theory!' "[48] This democratic theory, which is an acting out of democracy/communism and a theory of democracy/communism, is carried forth through the practice of the various attempts at unified theory.

4

Science, or Philosophy's Other

From the philosophy of science to the posture of science

Non-Philosophy has a special relationship to science. One might already expect this, since Laruelle has also called his project a "science of philosophy," and the guiding models for non-philosophy are derived from scientific fields: Non-Euclidean geometry as the generalization of Euclidean geometry through the suspension of two of its fundamental axioms; and the non-standard models of logics and physics grounded in part by Gödel's incompleteness theorem and present in debates in quantum physics. Yet, this is not a standard philosophy of science. Laruelle never claims to show how science is possible or to complete science with a metaphysics. Readers will no doubt see that his approach varies a great deal from so-called analytic philosophies of science, but it also differs a great deal from those instances in Continental philosophy in which science has a privileged place.

Laruelle's understanding of science necessarily differs from the available standard forms of philosophy of science or epistemology. Laruelle's analysis of philosophy is that philosophies of X (where X may be science, art, religion, human nature, etc.) always confuse their project with the X itself. Moreover, philosophy usually does so by forcing its supposed object under something else it takes to be constitutive of the Real (Being, nothingness, language, God, or any other host of names we may give to a transcendence that philosophy always makes figure twice as we saw in his description of the decisional apparatus). Throughout Laruelle's writings, there is a certain prominence of science that suggests he thinks there is something particular in the relationship of philosophy to science. Philosophy is often hostile to other regions outside of it – like art or religion, where an antagonism to both can be seen going all the way back to Plato. Yet, the relationship to science, although philosophy sometimes antagonistically declares "science does not think," is not a case of straightforward antagonism.[1] Rather, philosophy's relationship to science is structured like a political exclusion.

To say that the relationship of philosophy to science is structured like a political exclusion means that when philosophy attempts to think science it of course does so through its decisional apparatus. This then obscures and breaks apart the identity of science and turns it into a mirror of philosophy. Any thinking of X within philosophy comes to be a thinking of philosophy. The general structure of philosophical decision may be expressed in any number of different ways, as we explored in chapter 1, but Laruelle thinks there is something particular about the way in which philosophy directs and attempts to dominate its relationship to science in this decisional structure – for philosophy uses science more explicitly to think itself: it excludes science from itself as the State excludes the foreigner to set up the differential identity of the citizen versus the foreigner, and so on. A nation-state *needs* the people who are excluded by it, and in the same way philosophy *needs* science as its excluded other in order to know itself as philosophy. Laruelle claims that in the synthetic a priori judgment, "Kant simply revealed the essence and algorithm of philosophy as a mixture of metaphysics and science."[2]

Laruelle identifies the way that philosophy casts science as the Other of thought in the paradigmatic Heideggerian declaration that "science does not think." The particulars of this declaration vary according to the philosophical system, but Laruelle's claim is that this declaration is present in scientistic forms of epistemology just as much as it is present in Heidegger's critique of science in favor of poetry.[3] In every case, science is cast as the Other to thought as ruled over by philosophy as the bureaucrat of the disciplines – a bureaucrat, even if philosophers sometimes like to think of philosophy as the King or Party Leader. Laruelle is here drawing on the work of Levinas and Derrida in an unexpected way, using their theories of the Other not to think ethics as normally conceived, but as a kind of ethics of thought. While Laruelle will ultimately not ground non-philosophy upon the Other or *différance* in the same ways as Levinas and Derrida did in their distinct approaches, he nonetheless deploys the concept at a local level: first as a diagnostic, and then as the first round of treatment.

In the political and social world, the Other is often forced to be two things at once, always torn between the dominant culture's disdain for the Other and the desire for the Other. To take a common example, consider the American discourse one finds in right-wing, anti-immigrant propaganda regarding Mexican immigrants. Mexican immigrants are accused of being lazy and untrustworthy. Yet at the same time they are accused of taking "all the jobs" and doing that work better and for less money than American "natural-born citizens." Disdain and desire; both too lazy and too hard-working. Science too is subject to this kind of othering at the level of thought:

> Science is perhaps the great unknown of Western thought [*pensée occidentale*]. Not that philosophy, under the form of epistemologies and ontological foundations, has not consecrated it. On the contrary: it is precisely because we have always had a philosophical and Greek vision that science remains unknown in its essence. Our experience of science is marked at once by a devaluation (as devoid of meaning and absolute truth) and an overvaluation (as factuality and efficacy), both are characteristics of the philosophical and "cultural" interpretation of science.[4]

Laruelle rejects this sense of science as philosophy's Other, yet he also takes something from this general structure of philosophy's thinking of science and attempts to radicalize it. For in treating science as philosophy's Other, we find ourselves also subject to an ethical demand within thought that we respond to this Other on its own terms. In this response, we find that the strictures and borders set up within philosophy are broken, that thought changes: "the cause that is unilaterally derived from thought is not the Other of thought, but transforms its thought in its Other."[5]

In order to understand the specific way that this identity of science comes to direct non-philosophical practice, we will first look at how Laruelle understands standard philosophy's splitting of the identity of science. Then we will turn to his description of science, which he calls "non-epistemological," and then to how the posture brought out by that description comes to be what non-philosophy itself practices. In summary, by taking the position of science, we take the position of the stranger in the philosopher's country, but also gain the knowledge that there are no real territories as such, despite our philosophico-statist hallucinations.[6] It is important to understand that what this non-epistemology offers is not a way of adjudicating the claims of science or of grounding scientific knowledge – science is able to think for itself – but, rather, Laruelle's attempt to draw out the identity of science will have an effect on how we understand thinking generally. What he aims to affect is not science, but the practice of thought as normally manifest in the philosophical mode. This is not fruitless, but if one looks for the fruit of the project within the standard goals of epistemology one will not find it.

The division of labor on the factory floor of theory

Fundamental to Laruelle's understanding of thought is that it is a human activity, a human practice. When human (beings) engage in theory, they are in the midst of creating something, they are in the midst of labor, and are fashioning something from the material around them. It is in many ways beautiful, and anyone may know that beauty if they have ever fallen in love with an idea, or derived pleasure from reading a book or from writing an essay exploring the theme in a movie, or, after a lot of hard work, finally gotten the quadratic formula or any number of pleasures derived from other theoretical practices. Yet, there is also a clear alienation in theory as well. We are all familiar with the tedium of forced theoretical activities as well, and how science is often divorced from the pleasures of science and sutured to techno-capitalism. But, contra Heidegger's technophobia, the fact that capitalism is so technophilic does not suggest that technology is a particularly fraught domain that is more likely to promote alienation than any other.[7] It only really tells us that the pleasure derived from technology is always blocked by the *demand* to enjoy technology. While we may love our smartphones because we are able to create a kind of intimacy never before possible with friends and loved ones from whom we are separated by thousands of miles, we are also harassed by the devices constantly and enjoined to attend to them as one might attend to a sacred object of transcendence.

One way to resist such alienation and harassment is to profane the object, to make it everyday and remove the false allure of transcendence that surrounds it. This sort of profanation is what

Laruelle carries out within theory as he provides something akin to a political economy of philosophical practice by tracing its triple division of intellectual labor imposed by philosophy with regard to science, as he explains in one of his central texts on science, *Théorie des identités* (1992). Since *Théorie des identités* is not translated, and at the time of writing I know of no plans for it to be translated in the immediate future, I will let Laruelle's own words explain this division of labor, rather than providing a summary of them:

> From Plato to Heidegger there reigns a triple *division of intellectual labor*: 1) They accept that science produces forms of knowledge [*connaissances*], but they refuse it thought. For science there are forms of knowledge without thought; for philosophy there is authentic thought, which by necessity needs these forms of knowledge, but which, on the other hand, grounds those forms of knowledge, legitimates them and provides them with a genealogy and critique all at once. 2) There is an absolute science, unique and self-grounded – a first philosophy as ontology or logic – and the empirical sciences, which are multiple, are contingent according to their object and only produce forms of knowledge that are relative. Philosophy divides the concept of science after it has separated knowledge and thought. 3) For philosophy there is Being as authentic and totally real; for science there are not even beings, but the properties of beings or the facts; the object of knowledge is now what is divided.[8]

In other words, general to philosophy's approach to science is an approach that might be thought of this way. First, science produces certain forms of understanding or knowledge, but does not perform the deeper task of thinking. From the perspective of philosophy, particular "empirical" sciences do not provide the transcendental conditions for their own undertaking, for example, and do not provide the unity of their own practice with that of others. In a certain way, science does not think because it does not produce sense, but only produces nonsense that require meta-scientific, i.e. philosophical, statements to unearth their meaning.

Of course, when philosophy makes such claims it is being disingenuous. For the tripartite structure of philosophical decision allows us to see how philosophy uses science, derives a certain use value from it that it employs to produce its own surplus value of absolute truth. So, philosophy is a mix of metaphysics and science wherein metaphysics is taken to dominate and condition the aspects (empirical or ideal as is the case in mathematics) that science makes manifest. It requires that science do the work of manifesting certain empirical facts that it then mixes with and brands transcendentally to create an empirico-transcendental mixture. Various forms of philosophy – especially of the post-Kantian variety like phenomenology, but also logical positivism – make a claim to be acting transcendentally, to be providing the conditions and surety of knowledge, but then appeal to the empirical for support of their supposed transcendental claims.

Laruelle refuses this separation within science of the transcendental and the empirical. Instead of imposing the decisional structure upon science, Laruelle aims to disclose the identity of science. Before turning to see how he understands science, let us first look at how he is able to move from epistemology to non-epistemology. This requires a different sort of approach to science from the others available to standard philosophy of science which seek to ground science within certain epistemological conditions, as Kant and post-Kantian philosophy do in both the Continental and Anglo-American traditions. And it will even take a different stance than that of science studies (the most well-known example for readers of philosophy being the work of Bruno Latour). Instead Laruelle follows a kind of phenomenological example by going to the thing-itself (science) and looking not at its practices as the social sciences might categorize such practice, but at what phenomenologists call the transcendental structures of that phenomenon. Laruelle, however, does not look for instances of transcendence or transcendental structures that would have their genesis separate from immanent practice. While he claims that finding the "Identity-in-the-last-instance of scientific thought" is what will break the triple division of intellectual labor supervised by philosophy, he does so by bringing himself under the demands of science. He says that he will locate this Identity-in-the-last-instance with "a method of *immanent self-description*, science being capable of describing itself rigorously if it takes as its immanent guide its own radical or postural realism, meaning this very Identity, for its own understanding [*compréhension*]."[9]

We may now see how this approach differs in many ways from the standard epistemologies or even science studies. The second of these options is celebrated in many circles today as a nonreductionist approach to the sciences, available to those who still want to resist scientism. But this approach is not non-philosophical, precisely because it still subjects the practice of science to something outside of it, a kind of transcendence of human society rather than the radical immanence of the human scientist. This sort of quasi-philosophical decision is what Laruelle points to graphically when he highlights the Greek within certain disciplinary names like anthropo-logy (*anthropos* and *logos*). Science is still subject in science studies to the anthropological structures that are taken to be distinct from the human (beings) that practice science and, instead of attempting to create a unified theory of science and philosophy, thinkers like Latour still aim to police the boundaries and set up something like parliaments of thought. We might call this a reformist politics of thought.[10]

The *logos* inherent in anthropology, whether it is formal logic or a structural logic, is an instance of subsuming science, both in the general sense and in its particular instantiations, within what Laruelle calls a "hinter-world." I am translating here the French term *arrière-monde*, which is a neologism in French used to translate Nietzsche's use of the German term *Hinterwelt*.[11] The translation of this term into English has taken a few forms: the most common is Walter Kaufmann's rendering as "afterworld" in his translation of *Thus Spoke Zarathustra*. But Robert Pippin's use of "hinterworld" strikes me as more legible, despite being slightly Victorian-sounding. In Nietzsche the term refers to the projection of something beyond the earth, beyond the human. Christianity is hinterworldly, but so are the philosophers like Kant who perpetuate the notion that there is something behind the appearances.[12] The French *arrière-monde* also bears a relationship to the French word for "background" [*arrière-plan*] which becomes an important concept in phenomenology in which things always appear upon a background that recedes from perception even as it makes perception possible. Laruelle is indeed building off both of these notions so that philosophy is presented as always looking beyond radical immanence and hallucinating some transcendence beyond it. In so doing, philosophy creates a separation between the appearance of a thing and the thing-in-itself. And thus philosophy impoverishes the practice of science, setting it up for failure by claiming it only ever touches an appearance, only ever dreams, but never thinks.

Laruelle is very clear, in an essay from 1991, about what non-philosophy is not with regard to its understanding of science. First, it is not a positivism or a scientism. He says that both of these approaches to science in fact "are only familiar with the philosophical concept of science, this concept's kind of universality and domination, and not its radical transcendental concept."[13] Neither can it truly be described as a transcendental realism. While Laruelle clearly shows sympathy for this notion of a realism, he refuses the decision of the transcendent and a transcendental that is determined by the idea of the transcendent.[14] And finally it is not an appeal to science to come along and provide a bridge that one might jump on to get outside of philosophy or to bring about the end of philosophy. Rather, non-philosophy's understanding of science brings science to bear upon philosophy so as to make it more human, more habitable: "It is the destruction of its sufficiency alone, of its illusory authority, of its fetishism – the ultimate auto-philosophical fetishism that even grounds its 'deconstructions' – it is the real transformation of philosophy on the basis of the scientific posture."[15]

Non-Philosophy refuses the separation of the appearance of a thing from the thing-in-itself. It makes this refusal in a particular way, because the separation can be carried out heuristically within thought, but in-the-last-instance the object will be unified in-One. There is no separation in the Real. Laruelle tells us that this vision, which we have seen him call "vision-in-One," is not the creation of non-philosophy, but already exists in science. He writes in *Philosophies of Difference*, regarding his practice of providing a real or absolute critique of Difference (which may be extended to any philosophical proclamation that "all is X"):

> This is no longer and never has been a philosophical decision. Transcendental truth is absolutely autonomous and does not form a variable and indissociable mixture with appearance or illusion. This point of view for which thinking would no longer have to divide a mixture of truth and appearance that it would have first of all assumed given in order that it is able to move on to various reductions, various bracketings that are always relative to this given – the name of this point of view is science.[16]

We will now turn to his tracing of the immanent self-description of science in order to understand how it is that science unified with philosophy is able to act in this non-decisional way – which is to say, in this non-philosophical way.

On non-epistemology and the description of science

As Laruelle's work was becoming more recognized in the Anglophone world, the comment made by Gilles Deleuze and Félix Guattari was often quoted: "François Laruelle is engaged in one of the most interesting undertakings of contemporary philosophy. He invokes a One-All that he qualifies as 'non-philosophical' and, oddly, as 'scientific,' on which the 'philosophical decision' takes root. This One-All seems to be close to Spinoza."[17] Even in the midst of this positive appraisal, Deleuze and Guattari show serious misunderstandings of the non-philosophical project, most egregiously in the confusion of Laruelle's One (which is never linked to the All) with Spinoza's. The depth of this misunderstanding becomes fully present when they too pass judgment, writing: "François Laruelle proposes a comprehension of non-philosophy as the 'real (of) science,' beyond the object of knowledge…But we do not see why this real of science is not non-science as well."[18] Deleuze and Guattari are making a standard philosophical move here, attempting to speak for science rather than take its posture. Laruelle is not attempting to reform scientific practice. Instead he is concerned with philosophy in relation to science and how philosophy might be changed if it takes the posture of science toward itself. This is not non-science, because that would be to carry out a policing of science by philosophy. Instead, Laruelle calls this a non-epistemology, because it is concerned with changing the way philosophy casts science.

Logical positivism was cast as the boogeyman and antagonist for Continental philosophy throughout the twentieth century, largely because it was thought to reduce all phenomena to their logical foundation and to claim that phenomena would only be meaningful if they were empirically verifiable, essentially excluding art and other activities as meaningful human practices. But Badiou's own merging of philosophy and mathematics displays the duplicitous nature of philosophy far more starkly and clearly – for it would seem that he holds science in high esteem because of his claim that set-theoretical mathematics is the science of ontology or Being *qua* Being. Yet, while this would seem to impoverish philosophy or make it in some sense equal to other forms of thought, it his philosophy which also declares that all other forms of science are in fact not science: "physics provides no bulwark against spiritualist (which is to say obscurantist) speculation, and biology – *that wild empiricism disguised as science* – even less so. *Only* in mathematics can one unequivocally maintain that if thought can formulate a problem, it can and it will solve it."[19] Laruelle's response to such a claim is to refuse the split between science and the sciences, to refuse the split within science itself: "Every science, even 'empirical' ones or those called empirical by philosophy in order to degrade them, are also in reality 'transcendental'; they bear upon the real itself and, what is more, they know the real relates to science itself."[20]

It might be going too far to say that Badiou confuses such mathematics with the Real, but certainly he confuses his own ability to speak for the truth of a science (set-theoretical mathematics) that is itself mute with an ability to then decide upon what forms of thought are able to produce, or have already produced, truths. And in a certain sense, insofar as Being is often confused with the Real, Badiou acts under this philosophical confusion. As he writes, "The procedure is always the same: isolate some knowledge, abstract a theory, cut away from it what could be in it – the force (of) thought – and make it accept through coercion that it is under the law of philosophical decision."[21] Laruelle follows Gödel and claims instead that, "Science – even formal logic on the condition that it is included as already being an authentic science – is the best destruction of the confusion of the 'general logic' with the real within the mixture of a 'transcendental logic,' which is the heart of every Philosophical Decision. Science – even formal logic as science... – is an alogical knowledge (of the) Real, through its essence at least."[22] The tracing of this alogical knowledge (of the) Real is not the concern of epistemology, but requires a non-epistemology that places itself under the immanent practice of science.

In short, the identity of science breaks with every epistemology to the point that science's radical difference from philosophy leads Laruelle to posit an equivalence of epistemologies.[23] The division of labor imposed by philosophy is broken by the simple recognition that "science thinks."[24] Even radical forms of epistemology are broken when compared to the actually immanent practice of science: "Science imposes the distinction between a transcendent realism (which it destroys); a transcendental realism that is an object and thus ideal and semi-transcendent (which it partially destroys), only conserving transcendence in a simple or non-thetic form [sous une forme]; and a nothing-but-transcendental realism or "postural" realism where the real is immanent, even as an 'object'."[25] This is the summary of Laruelle's description of science: it is a posture toward the Real – not of Being and not of the Other – that does not claim to determine or condition the Real. It is in this sense that science is realist: it knows itself to be a real science or a science-(of the)-Real and it is not excluded from the Real.[26]

In this way science is an exemplary instance of the vision-in-One outlined in chapter 2. What this means is that science does not work through divisions in-the-last-instance (though divisions within thought may be heuristic), but instead thinks from a "non-thetic Identity (of) thought and (of) the Real."[27] Science is a reflection without a mirror, radically different from philosophy's speculative nature that always requires some form of redoubling. When science reflects or creates representations, it does so as a manifestation of the Real's invisibility: "the Manifest is invisible – it is the real; the Invisible is manifest – it is the science of the real."[28] What does this mean? That science never truly tries to uncover the ineffable. This might strike the reader as scarcely credible, since the spontaneous philosophy of science present in the media is one that constantly directs our attention to popular science. This type of science, the kind associated with public intellectuals like Richard Dawkins or Neil deGrasse Tyson, often makes claims that seem to be precisely claims regarding the Real. However, these claims are actually of the order of philosophy rather than science. They are removed from the practice of science and are at best meta-scientific statements, akin to meta-mathematical statements, in which the essentially meaningless representations (meaningless at least when treated outside that practice) produced by scientific practice are "translated." Or, more accurately, they are recast upon a new background into statements that are meaningful in a different regional form of knowing.

This helps us to understand what Laruelle means by science. For when Laruelle claims that non-philosophy is different from employing a science outside philosophy to bring judgment upon philosophy, to replace philosophy, to break and end philosophy, he means precisely that science does not make the really true pronouncements regarding Being or ethics or any of the other fields of philosophy. This is a popular vision of the end of philosophy, the gradual displacement and destruction of philosophy by other regional sciences that can answer more definitively the questions posed by philosophy. While this is often the stance of writers of popular science, as when Stephen Hawking declares philosophy to be dead, this is not the essence of science when it is practiced or – to use the non-philosophical vocabulary – when it is lived. Science is simply the production of thought. It does not tell us what Being *qua* Being is, it does not tell us the right way to live in the world, but it does disclose nucleic acids, it does make manifest wave functions, it does trace nitrogen cycles, and so on. A scientist may feel the need to philosophize, to bring these practices into a unitary vision of the world, but according to Laruelle this is not the essence or identity of science, and is a slippage into a spontaneous philosophical mode. For in its immediate practice, science really does nothing, it works without this unitary logic: in the immediate drive to science there is nothing promised and nothing truly gained unless it is found exterior to that practice. Science is blind and mute when it comes to anything beyond the Real, and its realism is what Laruelle calls *"irréfléchie,"* which in this context is best translated as "unreflected," but which normally is translated as "thoughtless" or "reckless." There is a certain sense in which the practice of science is as pointless as the lived (reality) of an individual life – pointless, that is, when brought under some transcendent or transcendental condition for its existence, when finitude is treated as tragic and couched within a hinter-world. But every human lives without this background in the radical immanence of their vector through the world. Science doesn't provide knowledge to use in the war of ideas or to trade in the marketplace of ideas, it just provides pointless knowledge free from exchange, even if the world attempts to alienate the practice and draw out some profit from it.

The aleatory finitude of science bears upon the way Laruelle understands ethics as concerned with victims rather than immortal heroes and we will turn to this in the next chapter. However, this understanding may cause some to wonder whether science truly operates in this non-decisional way. Do scientists not break apart objects in this or that science, or reduce objects to some other object in this or that science? Laruelle argues that this breaking apart of the object is ultimately organized by the logic of determination-in-the-last-instance. This understanding of science may create a local distinction between what Laruelle, following Althusser, calls the real object and the object of knowledge, but this distinction is never taken to be determinate of the Real. We will now unpack exactly how Laruelle understands this merely heuristic dualism to function according to the unilateral logic of the last-instance.

Real objects and objects of knowledge

Let us begin first by looking at the two definitions Laruelle gives to the real object and the object of knowledge, and then trace their specific relationship, which Laruelle thinks escapes philosophical decision. This will rely on the notion of determination-in-the-last-instance, which Laruelle claims is the way that science relates to the Real (rather than thinking under authoritarian philosophical concepts like Being), avoiding the need for some kind of dialectical relationship or any other relationship of mixed co-constitution.

Laruelle claims that "the *real object* in the narrow sense" is what "a science relates its forms of knowledge to."[29] He continues by unpacking this sense of the real object describing it as having a quadruple structure that is *a priori* to the "object of knowledge" and which, despite its seeming multiplicity, remains in-the-last-instance a single identity. His full definition of the real object is that it is a "non-thetic Identity effectively grounded upon a quadruple *a priori* postulation of reality, exteriority, stability, and unity." Furthermore, this real object is what constitutes the "*a priori* condition for the object of knowledge."[30]

This real object "finally grounds the *object of knowledge* as the articulation of empirical procedures (in the broad sense: every theorico-technico-experimental apparatus) as objective phenomenal data [*donnés*] and apriorical procedures of the real object (the insertion of this apparatus and its work within the real object, with knowledge in mind [*en vue*])."[31] In other texts, he writes this as "object-of-knowledge" to emphasize the unified character of the object and the knowledge of it. In either case, the intended meaning is that there is a separation between the real object and knowledge of it, such that the real object retains its autonomy even as the ability to create some representation of the real object is part of the autonomy of scientific thought. As Laruelle says, this object of knowledge is "an ultimate and transcendental condition" that must be fulfilled for scientific knowledge to be autonomous.[32] The autonomy of the real object is vitally important to the autonomy and identity or essence of science in distinction from philosophy's identity: "Science changes the order of its thought without claiming thereby to also change the order of the real: it is even a representation, but one that is also non-thetic (of the) Real."[33] The knowledge may be subject to change, but the real object and the Real that it is unilaterally related to are not. Laruelle goes on to explain this, writing that science must

represent the "real object" within an "object of knowledge" – the final product produced by the process – which has *the property of modifying itself without also claiming thereby, as is the case in philosophy, to modify the known real*. Knowledge [*connaissance*] is not an attribute or a determination of the known real, which is a cause that is absolutely anterior to its knowledge.[34]

Or, in other words, the new knowledge produced is dependent upon the object, and that knowledge is caused precisely by the object.

In both cases, the conception of the non-thetic is important for understanding what Laruelle is claiming, both with regard to the particular posture of science and to grasp the particular sense of "identity" he intends. A thetic statement is tautologous, like $A = A$, and as such fuses the idea of the posited and positing. This concept is derived from Fichte's philosophy, in which the principle of thetic identity is written as $I = I$. The existence of the posited I and the positing I are simultaneously *a priori* and as such, for Fichte, ground every other form of knowing.[35] For Laruelle this principle is generalized as the principle of radical immanence for all identities. It does not preclude multiplicity or difference, but rather multiplicity and difference in their radical immanence *qua* multiplicity and difference manifest identity in this way.

This notion of radical immanence leads directly into the important concept of determination-in-the-last-instance (which Laruelle takes from the philosophy of Marx and Engels) or unilateral duality (these two terms, as we have seen, are near-equivalents in non-philosophy), which Laruelle claims is descriptive of the practice of science.[36] With regard to the two objects produced within scientific forms of knowing, unilateral duality tells us that the object of knowledge is utterly dependent upon the real object, but that the real object does not rely upon the object of knowledge. Insofar as the real object may be affected by the object of knowledge, it is because such an object of knowledge was already virtually there as the radical immanence of the real object. This is in part what Laruelle means, then, when he says that:

> The distinction of two "objects" is a duality-without-synthesis, without a superior unity, because this distinction is not derived from a scission or a decision, but it does not lack a cause within Identity nor an *occasion* within experience....So, science is an activity that is intrinsically "dual" or crossed in a "dual way" by an irreversible cleavage that no longer results from a scission of some prior scission, a scission that would belong necessarily to it as the Dyad in the One.[37]

This duality-without-synthesis is expressive of the particular "realism" of the sciences or, more accurately, the posture toward the Real that science takes. For, in thinking according to this unilateral dualism of a real object and an object of knowledge, there is a recognition that the science produced by the practice of science is in some sense local and does not attempt to provide some unitary concept that would specify a prior unity, as philosophy does with the concept of Being, *logos*, Other, etc. Insofar as the terms "the Real" and "the One" are privileged in non-philosophy, they do not function in the legible form that other philosophical terms do, for science does not need to be concerned with the problem of Being, which necessarily implies a unity even if that unity is found within difference. The Real-One is a more abstract name that is necessarily more denuded of properties or attributes. This abstraction is what allows for the endless, fractal proliferation of scientific practices. Each object of knowledge may become a real object for a new science, such that the sciences are no longer related to one another in some hierarchy developed on some preexisting unity of the object, but are now related to one another along a flat field of relation, all equally foreclosed to, or unable to represent, the Real-One.

Homo sive natura: or, human science and human philosophy

In a certain sense, science promises nothing and this is how non-philosophy is a science (of philosophy). This probably seems a strange statement in the light of the dominance of techno-capital-ism and the ways in which science is ideologically overdetermined by capitalist demands for innovation and product creation. But science produces knowledge. In the practice of science one simply is in the midst of knowing something. There is often a drive to translate that knowledge into ordinary language and this carries with it its own pleasure without an end, but the actual act of knowing within scientific practice takes place separately from that translation practice. When one translates into ordinary language, this is a second operation, and while it may be a mode of knowing, it is dependent upon its own real object, which is the knowing found in the scientific practice. This may be difficult to completely grasp, since usually when one is taught science, it is translated into ordinary language. But this is often what leads to later misunder-standings, and as one advances in scientific studies one relies less and less upon ordinary language. One is able to know through the manifestation of the invisible present in the mathematics or in the list of symbols or through the diagrammatic models or whatever form of immanent representation is found in that particular science. This is ultimately what non-philosophy attempts to model and this is one reason why so much of non-philosophy is devoid of examples. For if non-philosophy does what it says and says what it does, then its very practice is the knowledge it produces.

This is one way of expressing the meaning of the concept of vision-in-One discussed in chapter 2, and it is this concept that Laruelle generalizes from scientific practice in his attempt at a unified theory of philosophy and science. Yet, as I have focused here on texts from the period Laruelle has called "Philosophy II," we see a certain kind of privileging of science over philosophy. Nowhere is his flirting with scientism more present than in his statement from the same period: "It is hurtful but necessary to understand this: there is more *real and really universal* thought in, let's say, Riemann and Einstein – but it is not only in them – than in Heidegger or in Hegel."[38] As, in Laruelle's view, scientism is a philosophical hallucination regarding science, he comes to criticize his own early stance in *Principles of Non-Philosophy* (part of the period called "Philosophy III"), claiming that during Philosophy II he had simply reversed the standard hierarchy in which philosophy dominated science, such that an image of science dominated philosophy.[39] It is important to see that, in the midst of this flirtation with scientism, there is a cause other than the simple ruse of power that he accuses philosophers of often employing. Laruelle is not attracted to science because it is the true arbiter of truth, but because he sees science as a more human practice than philosophy. The fractal nature of scientific knowledge helps us to understand this claim, for even when science attempts to think the human it will do so with a proliferation of approaches to the human that assumes a foreclosed radical immanence. We can affirm the representational nature of science, without the fantasy of a full representation. The knowledge produced by science is real, without having to capture or lock up the Real as such. Thus, despite the ways in which sciences may be used to reduce and murder human beings within the world, the human as known by science is very different from the perpetually weak human of philosophy that must always be determined by some second term (*Dasein*, autonomous individual, creature, Other, over-, etc.). There is an acceptance of the human-in-human, neither weak nor strong, but human.

Laruelle writes in *Théorie des identités* seriously, but with some humor: "*Homo sive scientia*. Let us translate it this way: 'man, therefore science (of man)', this is our new *cogito*."[40] Or, as he goes on to write, "*Homo sive scientia* is the formula that serves for us as a new hypothesis regarding the relation of science, philosophy, and man. It signifies that a god is necessary to make (something from) philosophy, but that only a man can make (something from) science, which does not mean that science exhausts man."[41] Science is only philosophy's other because philosophy projects science as its other, as the outside that secures the authority of philosophy. But science is closer to the practice of a *humane* form of thinking than philosophy is, precisely because of science's particular form of realism. By modeling the posture of science non-philosophy aims to foster a kind of humane form of philosophy that manifests as a unified theory of philosophy and science. The equivalence of the human and science is already suggestive of an ethics within thought itself. We now turn to an investigation of a human-ethics.

5

Ethics, or Universalizing the Stranger-Subject

Generic deracination

Alexander Galloway's *Laruelle: Against the Digital* provides a potent explanation of the difference between politics and ethics for Laruelle, as we saw in chapter 3. The political is often taken to be the name for the mechanism of decision, and in this way philosophy = politics (and we may read this equation both from right to left and from left to right). Thus, politics is about world-making in the sense of the French word for globalization (*mondialisation*) but also in the sense of the capturing and englobing of humans within the decisional parameters of that world. Galloway sums up the difference between politics and Laruelle's understanding of ethics, writing:

> In any case, the ethical is a question of the withdrawal of the law. What replaces the law is not so much a new super-law, a new law of laws, but the absence of all mundane commandments in favor of a single principle of unification. For this reason the ethical is best understood as a kind of virtualization, because it withholds decision in favor of a superposition of indistinction. And this is why, while there are many possible forms of political organization, there is only one kind of ethical organization – communism – a truth promulgated by Jesus just as much as by Marx.[1]

What does such indistinction or indivision (as Laruelle will say) mean with regard to how we live, though? What are the implications of such a division between politics and ethics? Does this division result in a political quietism?

To this last question, this chapter will reply with a forceful "no." As we will see, Laruelle's sense of ethics shares a great deal in common with militant practices, but it is not politically determined because, like these forms of militancy, non-philosophical ethics rejects the world, rejects the englobing function of the world. It rejects the world because the world is precisely a political world. The world is made by distinctions between friend/enemy, black/white, slave/free, even migrant/refugee – all sorts of scissions that are set by the world and perpetuate it. The Stranger-subject refers to a kind of subject that may have the end of the world as its object, without naming exactly what this end of the world might look like. Of course, this terms does not valorize some simple cataclysm, but rather refers to the overturning of the structures of the world such that the world as world would no longer be recognizable. It is akin to the way in which Frantz Fanon misquotes his former school teacher, Aimé Césaire, in an oblique but evocative way:

> This attitude, this behavior, this shackled life caught in the noose of shame and disaster, rebels, takes issue, challenges, howls, and as that's how it is, we ask him:
> "What can you do?"
> "Start."
> "Start what?"
> "The only thing in the world worth starting: the end of the world, of course."[2]

This is a certain kind of deracination, but it shares very little in common with the popular form of Anglo-pessimism with its hymns to Cthulhu and glee at the site of the impending destruction of humanity at the hands of an unrestrained techno-capitalism. It is more akin to the Afro-pessimism and critical theory of those like Frantz Fanon, Frank B. Wilderson III, Saidiya Hartman, Hortense Spillers, Jared Sexton, and others. Their pessimism, which is not derived purely from seriousness but has a kind of humor to its naming, is not derived from white fantasies and horror-fiction novels, but from the lived history of the world, the world as it is, its foundation formed by the deaths of millions of victims who are refused even the recognition of their victimhood by this same world.[3] Despite the fact that there is always a sense of things being unilaterally related to the One or the discussion of radical immanence (the etymology of "radical" being the Latin term *radicalis* meaning "of or having roots"), non-philosophy is not a project of rootedness but of deracination. Both non-philosophy and Afro-pessimism share an understanding of deracination in relation to the figure of the world (almost always capitalized in Laruelle's work). For Afro-pessimism, the Black subject is cast as an object by literally being cut off from natality and subjected to social death (explained in depth below). For non-philosophy, there may be a kind of "root-edness" in the One, but such a rootedness is beyond representation and beyond recognition. Philosophico-political rootedness takes place in the world, where one is recognized as belonging to this worldly family or this worldly tradition or this worldly history. This is a rootedness of relation and, insofar as the One or the radical immanence of the human is foreclosed to relation, there is no rooted-ness as such. The One is incommensurable with the world and so human (beings) are radically deracinated at the level of their lived identity. Therefore, Laruelle's own victimological pessimism has much more in common with this position than it does with those grim priests of a hostile capitalist future or with the liberal intellec-tuals paying lip service to the ideal image of a victim silenced by the same media that broadcast the image of the intellectual superim-posed on pictures of the dead. Laruelle sobers up those of us cap-tured by these narcotics of contemporary theory with the direct question, "What if this flood of ideal cadavers carried along by the black river of History hid from us the river bottom, its bed lined with very human victims?"[4]

Let's begin this chapter by laying out the stakes of Laruelle's ethical theory as bluntly as possible, by making it impossible to see this ethics as a political quietism or even a rejection of militancy, as its militancy proclaims a kind of messianity. Let's begin, then, by turning to a philosopher whose dedication to philosophical sufficiency discloses perfectly how such philosophico-political world-making accommodated anti-Semitism, if it was not directly grounded upon such a friend/enemy distinction and decision. Recently debate over the depth of Heidegger's anti-Semitism was reignited with the publication in German of what are being called the "Black Notebooks." Some of the most egregiously anti-Semitic passages were translated by Richard Polt for a paper he presented to the Heidegger Circle. Two of these passages will serve to bring out sharply the stakes of Laruelle's ethical theory, though my aim is not to interject anything into this debate about Heidegger, only to use these quotes to frame our discussion here.

First, Heidegger writes of the worldless character of the Jewish minority: "One of the most secret forms of the gigantic, and perhaps the oldest, is the tenacious skillfulness in calculating, hustling, and intermingling through which the worldlessness of Jewry is grounded."[5] Second, he goes on to write of the "world-historical task" of this worldless identity,: "The question of the role of world Jewry is not a racial question, but the metaphysical question about the kind of humanity that, without any restraints, can take over the uprooting of all beings from being as its world-historical 'task.' "[6] The worldlessness of European Jews is the locus of a metaphysical question regarding the identity of humanity for Heidegger, and in this very specific way it is interesting. Heidegger's anti-Semitism is, of course, despicable and ugly, even if at the same time we should not allow focus upon his prejudice and hate to comfort us as though the general structure of anti-Semitism was not found in a number of intellectuals today and accepted as part of various debates in the West that are not recognized as despicable and ugly (with regard to the figure of the Muslim or generalized anti-Blackness, for example). Let's say instead that Heidegger is wrong, but not for the reasons one might think. He is not wrong in marking an oppressed minority identity (European Jews in early twentieth-century Europe and Germany, in particular) as "worldless," but precisely in his negative valuation of that worldlessness of European Jews, manifested prior to the Holocaust. As Jared Sexton has recently remarked, there is a possibility for a "deracination of everything" evidenced by the natal alienation or the refusal of kinship that the middle passage and lingering social effects of slavery bestow on Black people marked by their Blackness (as Jews were marked by their Jewishness for Heidegger and other anti-Semites).[7] Following Sexton, we may say that Heidegger is right about a certain kind of people, a certain kind of subject, that can destroy the coherence of the world. Marx called this subject position "the proletariat," Frank B. Wilderson III calls it "slave." Theorizing that an identity with corollary subjects like Blackness or Jewishness could destroy the world, could carry out a generic deracination of "peoples" and "nations" and all such philosophical hallucinations of identity, is an ethical act that unifies in-the-last-instance as a universalization of the Stranger-subject. The end of the world as a self-sufficient and harassing world is what is at stake in ethics.

Stranger victims: from the theory of the stranger to the general theory of victims

Philosophers have their image of victims, not unlike how the media and their intellectuals have their ideal victims alongside their vision of acceptable violence. Laruelle's ethical theory is predicated on a complete rejection of this sort of theodicy, a kind of *victimadicy*, that underlies so much of philosophical ethics. This leads Laruelle to strong positions with regard to the way in which philosophers take up the Jewish Shoah as the unthinkable event that grounds the philosophically sufficient thinking of victims. Laruelle is asked a question in an extended conversation with the journalist and philosopher Philippe Petit about the move from victim to persecutor seen in the experience of European Jews who were first victim to anti-Semitic violence and murder in the concentration camps before then taking up the role of the executioner of Palestinians with the establishment of the State of Israel. I will quote his answer in full, since the sensitive nature of the topic requires that context not be left out, but the question ultimately bears on the stability of the identity of a victim, and we see that for Laruelle the lived (reality of the) victim exists completely outside of this justification of the "best of all possible victims," which may support a future violence in their name:

> Philippe Petit: This is very dangerous. For example, can we say that the former victims of the camps have become Israeli persecutors? Is that an untenable statement?

> François Laruelle: It is entirely tenable, but what kind of necessity does it have? Primo Levi's remark does not apply only to the camps. It is a philosophical and universal law that is inherited, like memory, from the preceding generation. I have even said that it was possibly planned by a perfected Western philosophy. Within the greatest disjunction, within the greatest difference, there will be some affinity between the Victim and executioner, the tortured and the torturer, etc. This is a universal scheme that allows us to understand, at least provisionally, certain relations of force or events within history. That this should be considered a particularly dangerous formula for Israel, I entirely believe, but because Judaism has a totally different reading of history from the one that we find in Greek philosophy. Judaism thinks history as a contretemps of the relation of the chosen people to God, their persecutor. This relationship of infinite transcendence does not end in a totalization of victims and persecutors, a totalization which is eminently Greek and which implies a kind of reciprocal approximation of the Victim or executioner. This proximity is a problem that the philosophers are unable not to put forward....It is philosophically legitimate and necessary to find some sufficient reason for violence – only philosophers locked away in their system can believe in the exceptions that they imagine and only they can believe in their logodicy.[8]

Laruelle here walks a tightrope. On the one hand he wants to indeed affirm that the Jewish people in Israel are tempted to, and may, fall into an easy reversibility of victim and persecutor. He recognizes that this reversibility is in some sense common, as we might see with the victim of a mugging then joining with the police to act as a persecutor of people systematically victimized by the State. Yet he also gives attention to the particularity of Jewish thought, identifying that within the radical aspect of Jewish thought there is always a rejection of the kind of "logodicy" that "Greek" (in the sense of European) philosophers cannot help but believe in.[9]

Because this is a fraught topic prone to misunderstanding, allow me to trace the structure of Laruelle's argument abstractly before bringing in the empirical element. Philosophy is marked by an ambiguous structure that brings everything back to relation. We have already traced the different forms this ambiguous structure may take in our survey of his theory of Philosophical Decision. When Laruelle talks about Jewish thought, he is specifically referencing the way Jewish thought has inserted itself into philosophy to resist philosophy's self-sufficiency. For Laruelle, this largely means Levinas and Derrida, as well as the discourse of psychoanalysis, which means it references the work of individuals like Lacan who were not themselves Jewish but were operating within a Jewish tradition of thought. The focus on alterity or otherness in their work arises out of Judaism without philosophy and so, when thought with regard to philosophy, acts as a resistance to it. However, insofar as Levinas and Derrida carry out a Judaic turn within philosophy, their act of resistance to philosophy ends up as susceptible to capture and colonization by philosophy. The other becomes relative, it is placed in a relation to Being, so that it becomes a part of the ambiguous structure of decision.

We may speak broadly of Jewish thought as understood outside its struggles with and resistance to European philosophy's attempts to colonize it or frame it. The particularity and power of such a distinct form of Jewish thought may be traced all the way back to the Book of Job (the first book collected in the scriptures of the Hebrew people), in which there is a sense of absolute or even unilateral otherness in the absolute monotheism of Yahweh. One may read this in Job as a transcendent and unilateral persecutor who does not relate to the unilateral victim. Job is the story of a man who is persecuted by the Adversary (the meaning of the Hebrew name "ha-Satan"), who was allowed to carry out this persecution by the only one who could authorize it: Yahweh. Job's friends try to convince him that he would not face such persecution unless it was just, and thus he must have done something to deserve it. There must be some reason, some act done in relation that would explain his punishment. Job, however, refuses this reasoning and demands that Yahweh manifests and explains the true reason. Eventually, Yahweh does appear to chastise Job's friends, but he offers no reason why Job suffers. There is simply no relation – Job remains a victim and God is simply God. One cannot think of Job's victimhood in relation to God, his persecutor, without falling into all sorts of paradoxes and ambiguities. The story resists such relational thinking – whereas in Greek philosophical thought there is always a relation. One cannot be a victim unless there is a relation of victim and persecutor that is recognized by some third aspect that stands outside of that relation while naming it as such. Israel manifests so much of the European project of settler-colonialism because Israel does not recognize the unilateral and immanent nature of the victim. The victimhood of the Palestinian is not recognized because Israel is cast as the memory of the Jewish victims of the Holocaust, whereas the Palestinian is not memorialized, the Palestinian does not exist in a relation, "Palestinian" is literally not formally recognized as a national identity by "the West" (Europe, the United States, Canada, and some others). Western media-friendly public intellectuals dishonor the murder of millions of European Jews as the final and ideal image of the victim, using this image to shut down any discussion of the nature of victimhood. That they are able to do this without ever engaging with the lived (reality) or tradition of European Jewishness, or even awareness of other forms of Jewishness that are not European – forms of Jewishness that also face exclusion and persecution in Israel – makes their attempts at victimology unethical to the core.

What we need, in order to deliver on the wager of non-philosophical ethics, are "stranger victims": victims who are foreign to the philosophical scene and impossible to capture philosophically. In this first section of the chapter we will trace Laruelle's work on the stranger or foreigner and its deepening through his theory of victimhood, before turning to an attempt to creatively bring non-philosophy into dialogue with some of the most radical voices in critical theory around the question of race – for it is in the image of the slave that we may find the stranger victim before which any kind of theodicy, logodicy, or victimadicy crumbles. The slave is by nature not recognized, incapable of being truly memorialized, and so forgotten without even ashes.

The stranger before self and Other

We are told as children not to talk to strangers. As citizens we are trained to fear foreigners. Even those in society who are pro-immigration couch their arguments within an overarching pro-assimilation paradigm that destroys or overcomes the foreignness of the foreigner. Laruelle's turn from politics to ethics marks a turn away from power to identity "in flesh and blood," a turn away from strength to fragility, from the same/difference circuit to what might actually be generic. Let the Stranger remain strange, let our thought become stranger yet, if it ever hopes to be ethical in itself, to practice an ethics immanent to thought itself, a unified theory of ethics and philosophy. We saw the importance of the Stranger in the preceding chapter, in which we explored the status of science as philosophy's Other and then, more precisely, as the stranger to philosophy that conditions the entire democracy (of) thought which non-philosophy aims to be. We have already seen, in the discussion there, how the stranger functions for Laruelle in his construction of a democracy (of) thought. Here we will trace the development of that concept with specific reference to how the stranger breaks the sufficient form of standard ethical theory, and then how Laruelle provides a unilateral character to ethical thinking with his linking of the stranger to the victim. This linking refuses the usual philosophical move of convertibility between victims and their persecutors.

Laruelle argues that standard philosophical ethics is structured and determined by metaphysics. For him, the essence of metaphysics is found in the *meta* which refers to a "distance or 'phenomenological' transcendence that allows it to transgress towards the whole of being [*étant*] in its double dimension."[10] This *meta* character is repeated in ethics "as prohibition or obligation," which are concepts that transcend the beings they are ethically saddled with. This distance marks a distinction, a division, between the beings and the form of transcendence taken to be ethical. In other words, standard philosophical ethics is not in itself ethical. Obligation and prohibition are not in themselves ethical, although they structure ethics, but require something other than those principles, i.e. beings, to inhabit or enact them. The beings subject to prohibition and obligation are always already unethical, for the distance marked by the transcendence of ethics means that there will always be a distance between those beings who carry out the ethical act and the transcendent ethical norms, regardless of whether that transcendence is simple, as in the "over" of *meta*, or a complication of philosophical decision, as in the Levinasian *epekeina* or beyond. In either case, what is at play is a form of decision and not a structure that seeks to find some way to be ethical and philosophical in a unified way. What is lacking is a unified theory of ethics and philosophy.

As should be clear by now, Laruelle's answer to the metaphysical–ethical *mélange* is to find some way to unilaterally locate the lived dimension of ethics. This is where the figure of the Stranger enters into non-philosophy and breaks the decision for sameness or difference, for self or other. The Stranger is the name for the most generic identity of human (beings). Laruelle understands identity to be something more lived than simply adding or subtracting a predicate or attribute to some abstraction or idea of the human. He writes, "Our principal hypothesis is that Identity is not only a property or an attribute, but that it exists 'in flesh and blood' independently of its use as an attribute."[11] Laruelle takes great care to think through and present how the non-philosophical understanding of identity is not subject to the usual philosophical decision that would direct our thinking of identity between the poles of difference and sameness. Within the field of ethics, this metaphysical framing comes to be inhabited by the figures of self and Other, even as self and Other are precisely structured by a distance philosophically located between them.

The Stranger does not exist in these coordinates. Laruelle crafts a fundamental theorem of his theory of strangers that may help us to situate how he understands the stranger to be foreign to the usual philosophical positional points of the subject. He writes: *"there is no alter Ego, nor is the Ego an Other, there is no specular game between Self and Other, because Self and Self alone may also be the Stranger – if there is one – and the Stranger is in-the-last-instance this Me [Moi] that I am."*[12] This might strike the reader as pushing back against philosophies of the Other, but in a particular way Laruelle is radicalizing such philosophies through the figure of the Stranger. He illustrates this through a reader of the popular phrase of Rimbaud usually translated as "I is another," though the French reads "Je est un autre" – or, literally, "I is an other." Such a distance, however minimal it may be in the construction of a philosophical subject, is marked by what Laruelle calls "ego-xeno-logic" that is marked by a reciprocal duality of self (ego) and other. What is lived by a human being as self and other is always still marked by a distance, by a necessary correlation of thought and Being – while the Stranger that I am marks my originary position in the world. To be a Stranger is to not be at home; to be a Stranger to oneself is not to be an Other to oneself, but to be without any stable reference point in the world, to be separated ultimately through one's radical immanence (to oneself) from the world. The duality of self and other is grounded unilaterally upon such an existent-Stranger, for it is this Stranger-being that we are which forms the ground for the projection of the thinking of self and other. This helps us to make sense of the theorem that follows the previous one, "*Self and Other 'are' not the Same, 'we are' identical-in-the-last-instance*. Identity and Strangeness [*Etrangèreté*] then cease to be confused – and their dyadic opposition belongs to their confusion and constitutes that confusion. It is in-the-last-instance-alone that they are identical rather than different or the same."[13]

Thinking under the victim as generic name

By basing his "human science" upon the Stranger instead of the philosophical *mélange* of self and other, Laruelle is able to shift the basis of ethics away from universalizable moral acts (Kant) or a kind of piety for the abstract Other (Derrida and – to a lesser extent in Laruelle's understanding – Levinas), or even from a kind of ethics of power that protects the weak from the strong (Nietzsche). Instead of such an ethics of power, always threatened with slipping into the worst kinds of oppressive violence or justification of that violence, or an ethics of abstract Otherness that within its own thinking is unable to think identity as such, Laruelle brings ethics *under* the condition of the victim. This might be surprising for those who have read *Intellectuals and Power: The Insurrection of the Victim*, in which Laruelle remarks, "To be honest, I am tired of 'after Auschwitz,' which has become a slogan."[14] Yet his weariness at the sloganeering that happens around Auschwitz is not the same weariness that inhabits certain promethean forms of philosophy that grow tired of caution signs before their attempts to make good on their promises. Laruelle shares very little with the forms of acceleration that want to unhinge human intelligence from ethical concerns, subjecting them to the demands of inhuman ideas. Instead his weariness grows from the way such sloganeering continues the vicious circle of victim and victimizer. This is clear as he continues to say:

> And "before Auschwitz," what happened, nothing, only accidents of history, just forerunners to the Shoah? Or was persecution at play? The before interests me as much as the after. I think persecution is completely forgotten by the duty of memory, those persecutions of religious heretics, dualists, and gnostics. Victims are not "suitors," like there are suitors for the truth [a reference to Plato]. This is the *substantia nigra* that flows through the veins of history. Still unimaginable crimes are for that matter readying themselves in its folds, still more invisible and more featureless, crimes according to the future.[15]

And so it is not some kind of anti-Semitism or universal abstraction that lies behind his weariness regarding the sloganeering around Auschwitz. The victimization of the Jewish people in the midst of the Shoah is real, and yet undeniably this victimization comes to be used as a victimadicy that turns the victims of the Shoah into the justification of a world where the genocide of another people is defended.

This fundamental point allows us to understand why in *Future Christ: A Lesson in Heresy* Laruelle focuses upon the forgotten victims of history, rather than those who have a popularly remembered history. For Laruelle, the name of these forgotten victims – the gnostics – remains a quasi-religious name in the same sense that the Jews take on a religious name. Laruelle marks this difference between the Jewish victims of the Shoah and the heretical gnostic victims of a long period of Christendom through a distinction between being "burned out" and being "burned up." As anti-Semitism gripped Europe, the Jews were repeatedly burned out of their homes, and in the Shoah that fire came to be a "technological fire" or an industrialization of this death. Yet, as Derrida and others have argued, there remain ash and cinders of the Jewish people that spark a memory. This is not the case for the murdered gnostics, who are forgotten – who, even as Laruelle references them, spark nothing within the readership in the way our remembrance of the murdered Jews sparks images of these victims, images that remain through their being circulated in the world. As Laruelle writes, "In one case our living memory of being dead remains in ashes, in traces that bind us to the dead in our unbinding them. In the other there is a radical consummation, without a trace 'to light' our memory. That without-remainder is the immanence of fire which 'remains' in itself, which 'immanes' as Man-in-Man."[16]

Laruelle is not arguing against remembrance here, though he does add an abstract theoretical argument to other more empirical arguments like that of Norman Finkelstein, who warns against the ways such remembrance may be turned against its own spirit.[17] Instead, he is moving toward a more generic understanding of the victim, an understanding of victimhood that might break such a circulation of victim and persecutor or victimizer. In such a generic understanding, there might be theoretical resources for resisting the insidious anti-Semitism of certain forms of remembrance of Jewish victims, as well as the way in which such remembrance makes new populations of human beings "killable."[18] It breaks the paradox produced by this remembrance of victimhood, which justifies victimizing: "The paradox that drives the holocaust – making the Other exist as Other by his total destruction but maintaining him in existence by consuming him – is thus resolved, *there is no holo-caust, no 'wholly burnt,' of heretics.*"[19] By virtue of being forgotten, gnostic heretics produce nothing. They are not exchanged, they do not circulate within ethical thought. And, as non-circulating, they give witness to a more generic identity of the human, not through being stripped of predicates abstractly, but through their predicates having no philosophical use-value: "The heretics reveal to us that man is in an ultimate way that being, the only one, who endures crime and is characterized by the possibility of being murdered rather than simply persecuted and taken hostage, exterminated as 'man' rather than as 'Jew'. Why ultimate? *Because man is without-consistency, he is on principle, in contrast to other beings, able to be murdered, he is even the Murdered as first term for heretical thought and for the struggle that it performs.*"[20] In other words, Jewish victims are murdered precisely because this particular predicate is taken to be heretical within a certain system, thus it is as a Stranger, as one who is abnormal or perverse *within a particular system of exchange* that the Jew is made a victim; "Jew" is a heretical name for what is more *generically* human than the system of predicates allows, "gnostic" is an even more heretical name for this generic identity because there are no gnostics left (having been killed over the course of hundreds of years through various inquisitions), and "victim" is perhaps the most generic identity of the human stranger.

Those who have not read Laruelle's work on the victim may hold an immediate suspicion that Laruelle is making a certain use of victims that erases them as victim. But Laruelle takes a very different posture with regard to the victim, and through that posture comes to be able to say things about the circuit of victim/crime that are perhaps more insightful and more compassionate than standard philosophical ethics. While, in *Éthique de l'étranger* (2000),

Laruelle argues that every crime is necessarily a crime against humanity, he summarizes this view succinctly in his very recent *General Theory of Victims* (2012, and 2015 in English translation), writing: "Crime is already an attempt to transcend a history once and for all, among other things a history of the 'mean' or the 'tool' object."[21] In other words, a criminal act has, in-the-last-instance, a human end driving it. Crime arises ultimately from the real separation of human beings from the world, from a transcendent or harassing history – it arises from an attempt to break alienation, even as it ends in violence and a form of failure for which there is no redemption. This is where the victim arrives without any sense of usefulness, without being something that thought comes along and dominates: "But the victim is not a tool to be damaged or capital to be destroyed; her essence is generic. And instead of appearing only to disappear or to survive, like a tool in the immanent circuit of being (of ontological pre-comprehension), she disappears radically in order to, perhaps, 'survive' and moreover to be 'revived' by superposition in Man-in-person."[22] Instead, Laruelle tells us, thought must come to think under the condition of the victim, which is the main argument of *Intellectuals and Power* and is found again in *General Theory of Victims* when he writes, "For us-the-Gnostics and us-the-generics, this is the role of the intellectual: to help victims in this uprising, to imitate and prolong this uprising in the human dimensions of thought."[23]

The victim is not to be pitied, but co-suffered with (the literal sense of *compassion*), this being the condition under which thinking of the essence of the human takes place.[24] And Laruelle is quite clear that victimhood is the cause-in-the-last-instance for insurrection and a kind of generic sense of resurrection which is not open to "heroes" or the victors of history.[25] So, thinking under the generic name of the victim, how does non-philosophy create a kind of thinking that is in its very act of thought ethical? Laruelle argues for the creation of a "determined intellectual" as opposed to the "dominant intellectual" who takes to the television or op-ed pages to play out various set pieces of sub-philosophy. The determined intellectual is determined by nothing other than the victim, refusing to justify that victim's suffering, but to think that victim unilaterally: "The determined intellectual lets himself be motivated by, but not determined by, history. He only finds occasions or contingencies that allow him, not to think the Victim, but to do 'victim thinking' [*penser victime*]. The great difference between the dominant intellectual and the determined intellectual lies here, thinking the victim or victim thinking."[26] As I explain in a translator's note, this locution shares many of the same difficulties found in translating Luce Irigaray's "parler femme." Laruelle's "penser victime" could be translated in a number of different ways, as could Irigaray's formulation, which has led her translators to leave "parler femme" untranslated. However, as this is not a phrase which recurs throughout Laruelle's work, I have chosen to translate it as "victim-thinking," though it could also have been translated "to think victim," meaning something close to thinking as a victim but without the sense of distance, and thus transcendence, implied in the "as."

So how does this conception of a Stranger that takes priority (or as Laruelle writes it in his attempt to avoid the implied sufficiency, takes the prior-to-priority) break the principle of sufficient ethics? Such a principle could be formulated as the ability to circumscribe any ethical problem within a metaphysically structured ethical system of thought that as a system operates at a distance from ethics as such. This returns to an undeniably provocative claim made throughout this book implicitly, but most explicitly in the introduction. Non-Philosophy makes no real promise, meaning if it promises anything it does so outside the circulation of wager and promise inherent to the history of philosophy, in which one philosophy succeeds another by virtue of offering better tools for interrupting or changing the world – keeping in mind the understanding of world as the background and hinterland upon which a human (being) is thought and thrown into that world. "The world" is the name in non-philosophy for the set of various forms of transcendences that become alienated from the immanent ground of their genesis. "The world" is the name for the complex apparatus of authorities and the various forms that decision takes as it – at best – obscures or – at worst – eviscerates the human-in-person. To bring attention to the Stranger, to the foreigner, is to bring attention to what threatens the world, to what escapes the world, to what moves through the world without worldly recognition. But how does this threat to the world by the Stranger manifest itself? It is simply through the strangeness of the stranger, the foreignness of the foreigner, and the victimhood of the victim as manifest within thought itself.

We see an example of the way such ethical thinking or victim-thinking manifests in non-philosophy when Laruelle considers the figure of the *sans-papiers* in France. The term refers to those immigrants who are classed as *étranger en situation irrégulaire*, akin to "illegal aliens" or "undocumented workers" in the American idiom, but literally strangers and foreigners, who are unable to work legally within France. The lived (reality) of being undocumented is far from easy and those who are subject to the State undoubtedly hope to be left alone by the State so that they may simply live their life. Laruelle claims they do not want recognition of the philosophical sort. The usual form of philosophizing the undocumented involves, "a wholly negative subtraction by the philosopher who, himself, can then return with all the positivity of the Good Samaritan."[27] Rather than seeking to take away the predicates of a human being so that what one is helping is precisely "universal man," Laruelle moves forward with his thinking of the undocumented as a name for generic humanity. Not a subtraction, but a generalization or broadening of human identity outside the coordinates of recognition by the world or State.

He thus reads the undocumented stranger as fundamentally a manifestation of the structure of the One. While the Human-in-Human is always already foreclosed as another name for the One, there is a projection of the subject in its thrown existence that plays out through the formal structure of One-in-One, (non-)One, and non(-One).[28] This structure is the formal way in which non-philosophy expresses the causality of the last-instance and from such an understanding goes on to carry out its pragmatic use of philosophy. In simple terms, this formalism is a sketch of philosophy made relative, a disempowered philosophy that is no longer sufficient, but still acts within the world. The One-in-One names the radical identity that is the last-instance where the various dualisms of philosophy are identical or superposed, rather than being the Same or forced to circulate in an economy of vicious circularity. The (non-)One is an effect of the One-in-One, but acts as a kind of clone of that One in the world. There is a negation within it, but it remains suspended. The non(-One) is the actuality of a relative transcendence that has its genesis in immanence itself and acts as the relative negation of the One within the world. We have seen that this general sketch is used throughout Laruelle's work to model various relationships and think their relative stability rather than their absolute identity. With regard to the Stranger or Foreigner and her status as undocumented, this may be sketched as Laruelle writes:

> The One being this time unifacial, there can be, according to the perspectives of the world, a thousand different images in which it

is incarnated as posture, but only one each time – even if this unifacial image is also, ambiguously, as we say elsewhere, the (non-)One (the one and only document of the Stranger) and the non(-One) (his thousand documents), through which we have the sole access possible to the One. The One itself is not an external access to the world, but something immanent that goes or under-goes or that transcends, without giving rise to a double transcendence. The One advances incognito before its image, or traverses it.[29]

The force-(of)-thought manifest here is powerful and it is important to understand that non-philosophy is directed here toward thought. What are documents to an immigrant? They are the means to work, they secure an identity grounded in a transcendent form of authority as manifest – often, if not nearly always, violently – through the State. Thus, when Laruelle claims that the (non-)One is the only document of the Stranger he speaks to the fierce power of the undocumented who lives *despite* the world, despite the State. This is a kind of fugitive-being, a refusal of transcendent authority as the ground of identity, and taking identity only from the One as the authorization of one's Stranger-existence. Laruelle marks an anxiety that unites the good liberals of Western societies with their conservative counterparts. For the undocumented is at the border and she "has visas in my name" (as M.I.A. declares in "Paper Planes"). There are a thousand papers, a thousand documents, that the undocumented may pull from the act of negating the world's power. These thousands of negations, thousands of documents that mark an identity within the world, are also tools that may be turned against those State forms of transcendence as the undocumented may mutate that negation into her own negation. This is a negation which reflects the absolutely foreclosed nature of the One, who does not even pass through its own image, but is clandestine (*clandestin* being another term for the undocumented in French) and incognito in the world.

"What does such an analysis do?", the politically minded theorist may ask, fancying himself an activist. Gloriously, it does nothing. To be more exact, it does nothing that can be recognized since such recognition is determined precisely by standard philosophical notions of decision and circulation. Such recognition is structured as a world, it englobes subjects with quasi-identities given from transcendent sources that harass the flesh-and-blood identities of those who, subjected, are cast into the world. The One does not grant us access to the world, though; it does not change or interrupt it. It refuses such recognition, even in the mirror, and is a generic deracination. In practicing this deracination within thinking itself, it offers a kind of end of the world. We will now turn to how such an ethics may be understood through a dialogue with a critical race theory that also seeks to understand such a deracination of the human as a form of good news.

Identity and the universal: non-philosophy and critical race theory

After the previous overview, I want to shift from explication to a creative reading of Laruelle in dialogue with other theorists, in order to show the way in which Laruelle's work and non-philosophy may generally enter into vibrant and vital debates ongoing in critical theory. I will focus here on critical race theory, though others have found the work useful in other forms of radical theory, such as queer theory and gender theory.[30]

Laruelle's seeming obsession with oneness and the frequent use of the term "universality" (though often critical) might suggest that Laruelle's ethical theory is at odds with popular identity politics and the sophisticated theoretical projects that emerge around questions of identity, such as queer or post-colonial theory. Yet, on the other hand, his frequent use of the term "identity" and focus on the individual as another name for the One, and the human individual, might suggest a natural alliance between non-philosophy and these theoretical projects that bear on political and ethical questions. Laruelle is no doubt haunted by his being formed in a French and European milieu, and this probably manifests in certain ways that may allow some nostalgic individuals to hold up non-philosophy as another instance of the drive toward an Enlightenment vision of universality, but this arises from a surface-level reading and is largely uninteresting. If Laruelle were simply another French or European philosopher who advocates for a universality that just happens to match the cultural values of Europe, then his non-philosophy would remain all-too-philosophical. And while there may be remnants of this in his thought, there is also a radical anti-racist core to non-philosophy. As he remarks in a conversation with Robin Mackay:

> If, within non-standard thought [another name for non-philosophy], the knowledge of human nature (to put it in traditional terms) remains entirely problematic, not at all becoming the object of some

dogmatic knowledge, this only goes to show that there is no absolutely determined knowledge of the human, of man; and in particular it aids the struggle against every dogmatic definition of human
nature – against racism, for example: if one has no absolutely certain
knowledge of human nature, it is far more difficult to develop a
racist thought.[31]

This anti-racism, rooted in a certain understanding of identity
and the universal, means that non-philosophy may contain tools
and analyses that could be brought together with critical race
theory and neighboring discourses to add yet another weapon to
the anti-racist, anti-colonial struggle to decolonize our theoretical
structures as well as the others. In order to make this argument, let
us begin with a seemingly difficult quotation, one from Laruelle's
book *Introduction to Non-Marxism* that might at first glance appear
to support the normal European sense of universalism that Marxism
carried forth into non-European struggles as well in the so-called
Third World:

> It is *also* necessary to read the tradition of Marx, Engels, Lenin, Mao,
> etc., as the symptom of a universalization in the process of a think-
> ing-according-to-the-Identity within which it may have, not the sin-
> gular, but the uni-versal; it is *also* necessary to stop criticizing uni(-)
> versality in the name of individual singularity, the authentically
> thought individual does not rise out of philosophical singularity and
> philosophical exception, but from Identity.[32]

Laruelle's argument here is subtle and requires attention. First, he
is rejecting certain rejections of universality, written here in such a
way as to emphasize its oneness and movement. In this case "uni"
of course refers to "oneness," while "versality" contains the French
vers or "toward" and *versalitié* may be read as "towardness." The
term may be read then as "moving toward the One."
    We then see a rejection of the singular as the determining term
with regard to this moving toward this universality or oneness.
Often the singular is taken to be an instance of pure individuality.
This is the popular image of thought critical race theorists labor
under, but it also describes well the position of the radical philosopher Gilles Deleuze who rejects transcendent political structures
on the basis of the radically singular nature of individuals as
instances of pure immanence.[33] For these reasons, one might be
tempted to read Laruelle's rejection of the singular here as a rejection of the identity politics of critical race theory. For those reading

it in this way, the universal should not be rejected on the basis of a singular identity like "non-European" or some more specific identity like "woman," "queer," "black," or so on. But, in a very precise sense, this rejection of the singular is a rejection of this European vision of the universal. For what Laruelle rejects here is "individual singularity." The individual singularity as found in Deleuze's pure immanence is an individual absolutely stripped of predicates in a way that looks a great deal like the claim of European universalism: that one should not be engaged with as a "black man" or some particular, but simply as a "human," denuded of qualities. There is something of this in Laruelle, but it is far less delusional and less artless than the usual liberal proclamation that one "does not see race," for someone making such a declaration often does not see race because they are white and their race, despite being largely a social construction, is never revealed as such.

Indeed, Laruelle does seek to strip away these predicates, but he does so in a way that is not about getting to some real essence of the human, but rather that posits a completely opaque identity of the human as lived. With regard to race this is important, because the identity of a (Black) man, for example, is created through creating a Black/white difference and so any attempt to break out of this system will require a destruction of the singularities produced by the dominant and colonizing term in this system: the whiteness which forces Blackness to circulate as Blackness. In fact, this whiteness is an example of the exception that the singular names for Laruelle. Bringing back to mind Laruelle's discussion of exception with regards to politics, the singular cannot express a democratic or communist form of thought precisely because it tries to step outside and circumscribe the One, it tries to create a differential system of politics rather than an ethical superposition of indistinction. Where do we see – or rather, not quite see, as the case may be with this opaque identity – the human? We see it in the lived identity of the victim of this decisional politics. In the case of the world structured by whiteness and casting a (Black) outside to define and undergird that world (quite literally since the wealth of the Western world is largely built off the slave labor of Black human beings) the victim takes the name of the (Black) slave.[34] Note that (Black) is written in parentheses, a grapheme that I will return to and which relates fundamentally to the way, within the white world of philosophy, the (Black) functions both as a blind spot and as the structural negation of the human as philosophically overdetermined.

Universalism in the standard sense forms a philosophical amphibology with the singular. The singular slips into the role of the universal, and the universal into the role of the singular. When the singular slips into the role of the universal, it is a matter of stripping away all predicates without ending the world that produces those predicates, and when the universal slips into the role of the singular it is an example of the way universalism has played out historically, with Europe proclaiming itself universal and refusing to recognize others as human. These others are then able to be murdered in the service of setting up the universal. This "able to be murdered" is of course not recognized within this singular universalism since the (Black) slave is not recognized as human within this structure. This provides a strange and productive resonance with Laruelle's pronouncements that the Human-in-person (which is a human outside of the circulation of recognition) is not born and does not die.[35]

In many ways, nothing here says anything different from the standard schema of philosophical anthropology. To be a human is to be recognized and to recognize: that is, to be human is to form a world. In this terse proclamation, there are nevertheless deep resonances with Hegel's anthropology, along with Marx's, Heidegger's, and Sartre's. But we also find it in Fanon, albeit in a different mode – one that is closer to non-philosophy despite Fanon's use of the standard philosophical coordinates of self and other. However, in his mutation of philosophical universality he shows the white sufficiency at play in the philosophical construction of the world. As he writes, "The black man is *comparaison.*[...] Whenever he is in the presence of someone else, there is always the question of worth and merit."[36] This is powerfully illustrated by Fanon's phenomenology of the only way in which he is given recognition: as a black object, not a human, englobed in a white world. Owing to the power and clarity of this famous passage, it is worth quoting at length:

> "Dirty nigger!" or simply "Look! A Negro!"
>
> I came into this world anxious to uncover the meaning of things, my soul desirous to be at the origin of the world, and here I am an object among other objects....
>
> "Look a Negro! Mama, a Negro!" "Ssh! You'll make him angry. Don't pay attention to him, monsieur, he doesn't realize you're just as civilized as we are..."
>
> My body was returned to me spread-eagled, disjointed, worn out, looking dismal on this white winter's day. The Negro is an animal;

the Negro is bad, the Negro is wicked, the Negro is ugly; look, a
Negro; the Negro is trembling, the Negro is trembling because he's
cold, the small boy is trembling because he's afraid of the Negro, the
Negro is trembling with cold, the kind that chills the bones, the
lovely little boy is trembling because he thinks the Negro is trembling with rage, the little white boy throwing himself into his moth-
er's arms: "Mama, the Negro's going to eat me."

The white man is all around me; up above the sky is tearing at
its navel; the earth crunches under my feet and sings white, white.
All this whiteness burns me to a cinder.[37]

Frank B. Wilderson III expands upon Fanon's analysis to argue
that the (Black) as the enslaved and colonized does not enter into
the world as a human being, is not recognized and is not given the
power to recognize. Yet, the (Black) slave is also treated as the
excluded term that grounds all circulation. In a way, the (Black)
slave is akin to the Real in the sense Laruelle intends, since it is
outside of the circulation of the structure of the world, though with
the caveat that this character is something that remains precisely
in defiance of the world's death-dealing. And so everything unilaterally flows from the identity of the Real and there is nothing more
unilaterally real in this way than the (Black) slave. Thus, the Slave,
like the Real, is unrecognized or recognized as "nothing" – for
slavery is constitutive of the world, both in terms of the grammars
that allow us to construct discourses on the world and in terms of
the means of subsistence for the world. Primitive accumulation is
slavery.

But, in this way, as Wilderson and the early work of Orlando
Patterson argue, the Marxist grammar of suffering, of exploitation
and alienation, is insufficient for an understanding of the Slave.
Work, or forced labor, Patterson argues, is not a constitutive element
of slavery. The subjective dispossession of the Slave is more complete, the negation of the (Black) goes deeper. Wilderson writes:

Once the "solid" plank of "work" is removed from slavery, then the
conceptually coherent notion of "claims against the state" – the
proposition that the state and civil society are elastic enough to even
contemplate the possibility of an emancipatory project for the (black)
position – disintegrates into thin air. The imaginary of the state and
civil society is parasitic on the Middle Passage. Put another way, *No
slave, no world*. And, in addition, as Patterson argues, *no slave is in
the world*.[38]

Wilderson goes on to say:

as a grammar of suffering, the Slave is not a laborer but an anti-Human, a position against which Humanity establishes, maintains, and renews its coherence, its corporeal integrity; if the Slave is [...] generally dishonored, perpetually open to gratuitous violence, and void of kinship structure, that is, having no relations that need be recognized, a being outside of relationality, then our analysis cannot be approached through the rubric of gains or reversal in struggles with the state and civil society, not unless and until the interlocutor first explains how the Slave is of the world.[39]

Now, this requires moving outside of philosophy and engaging with empirical realities like the refusal to even discuss reparations or the way in which police officers are, in the last instance, allowed to murder unarmed black men. "No angel," John Eligon writes of Michael Brown in the *New York Times*.[40] In order to not be killable, the black man has to present as an angel. Writing as an intellectual fully embedded in the anti-black world and spontaneously reproducing its philosophy – in spite of his own subject position – Eligon could have simply written: "Michael Brown was no human."[41]

Philosophy's structure is the structure of the white supremacist world as explored by Fanon. Laruelle's non-philosophy is – lest we forget – a science of philosophy and a form of thought that is generalized, thereby allowing for a certain use of philosophy. This is important precisely because the hallucinatory world – the thought-world not the earth – that we live in as subjects is structured by that philosophy. The thought-world may be the capital-world, again structured with the same self-sufficient faith as philosophy, but as a world it is formed of strata, and so we may also include the race-world or, more directly, the anti-black-world. This repeats the structure of Philosophical Decision and philosophical duality: from the perspective of the white, to be human is to be white all the way down – whiteness is even taken to be the stripping-away of color or specificity in our everyday speech. Yet this transcendent whiteness is rooted in a transcendental difference – that is, the white human is only known to be white in relation to the (Black) slave. This Black/white world now challenges the transcendent character of the white human by showing that the very empirical basis of that world (its primitive accumulation) is built upon some second thing: the (non)labor of the (Black) slave. Suddenly, there is an X and Y within the anthropological world, and European philosophers must perform the usual transcendental-empirical back-flips to erase this difference, while attempting to exploit its founding move at the same time, forming once again an amphibology.

Fanon's and Wilderson's casting of the (Black) as object and the (Black) as slave operates as the negation of the philosophical human. We may write this subject position as (Black) to indicate that the identity is not given by the world, that this suspended identity is precisely closer to the Human-in-Human than the white human of philosophy. The universalism of European philosophy is an ersatz-universalism. The assumed "ordinary human" is not the same as the one cast by non-philosophy – indeed the only thing usually subtracted from this image are minority predicates like Blackness and the category of woman. To be ordinary is to be bleached, to pass as without the conditions of color. This universalism comes under critique by Laruelle as well and he opens up to a possibility of something beyond it – a grammar that takes up the immanent impulse or power within appeals to the universal, but that is built upon a truly worldless (Black) human.

Laruelle writes:

> The supposed "universality" of philosophy gives place to the worst misunderstandings. It is not its universality that is dubious, it is its restrained character of "abstract" generality (metaphysics as "abstraction" of its objects), thus of partially empirical "generality" which appears too strict or too limited when it is measured by what the vision-in-One tolerates. Philosophical universality, as we know, is double or divided: at once *generality* and *totality*.[42]

Philosophical universalism is the name for the unilateral duality of the universal and the particular, or the universal and the singular. If we are to regain something of the uni(-)versal, then we must think beyond its capacities and move to the generic: "This is why non-philosophy announces itself from the outset as a universalization, *of the 'non-Euclidean' type* if you will, of the philosophical generality/totality."[43] We enter into this unilateral duality of the universal and particular and attempt to generalize this relation – generalization being the meaning of "non-Euclidean." What would it mean to generalize the unilateral duality of the universal and the particular? Well, it would require we at least negate the white. And to negate the white we must, as Fanon's analysis suggests – and translated into the technical language of non-philosophy – think under the condition of the (Black) victim. As we will shortly come to see, Laruelle's victims are never passive or worthy of pity and contempt, they are the cornerstone of humanity and in their "no" is their insurrection and resurrection. As Fanon writes with reference to the same Fichte who is so important for Laruelle:

The I posits itself by opposing, said Fichte. Yes and no.

We said in our introduction that man was an *affirmation*. We shall never stop repeating it.

Yes to life. Yes to love. Yes to generosity.

But man is also a *negation*. No to man's contempt. No to the indignity of man. To the exploitation of man. To the massacre of what is most human in man: freedom.[44]

This element in Laruelle, the general theory of the victim, when thought with the analysis of Fanon's and Wilderson's recognition of the non-recognition offered to blacks in the white world, helps us to avoid the objectification of the (Black) again and begins to reveal how non-philosophy may become more what it aims to be. It does so, however, through the further universalization of objectification, turning the white world's decisional globalization into material for human liberation. This requires objectifying in a certain sense the white/Black dyad cast by that political decision. But the purpose is always to break that world, to end the world so there may be space to be the humans we already know we are prior to worldly harassment.

Conclusion: the good news of deracination

Ethics is still differentiated from the way in which the Human-in-person lives her immanence. Philosophical ethics remains a matter of acting in the world and, insofar as non-philosophy fosters some kind of unified theory between philosophy and ethics, it is still a matter of disempowering and recasting those materials. When we turn to Laruelle's discussion of what he calls "philo-fiction," we will see the way in which that ethics may be united more directly with positive projects by returning again to critical race theory, specifically the debate and mutual building of theory between Afro-pessimism and Black optimism as developed by Fred Moten, particularly in relation to aesthetic creations as a form of resistance. We consider this work in order to help ground Laruelle's vision of the philo-fiction of insurrection that comes from the victim, and that arises out of suffering.

What we have seen is that Laruelle's use of the universal stretches the capacity of the concept past its breaking point. To make it function non-philosophically he has to graphically break it as he writes "uni(-)versality," to indicate the true sense of the concept ("moving toward the One"). He continues to deploy the term, but the concept of "the generic" comes to gradually replace it and functions with a greater capacity for his purposes. A generic ethics is then about indivision or indistinction, as Galloway says: "If the political is a question of points, of introducing a hard distinction into a hitherto smooth field, the ethical reverses the logic: not point but curve, not distinction but indistinction."[45]

Yet, as we have seen, such an ethics of indivision takes place by situating itself under a condition, a figure produced by the division of victims and their persecutors. In taking up this division as material, such an ethics becomes also a pragmatic in the world. Thus, because ethics is a matter of universalizing the Stranger-subject or – it amounts to the same thing – thinking the true generic identity of the human, it refuses recognition as a goal. Recognition is the purview of the world. What we see in Laruelle is something shared with Wilderson and Sexton. To show the power in being incognito, or "incognegro" as the title of Wilderson's memoir has it, or being kinless as Sexton advocates, is what Laruelle's ethics does and this is presented as good news. But how could being kinless be good news? Because it is a breaking of the (political) world, the end of the world, since the world is all about distinctions for the purpose of exclusion and domination. Even as insurrection is always a kind of running, it looks for a stick, for weapons in that world it may turn against it, recalling again George Jackson's famous line taken up by Deleuze and Guattari. Insurrection is a movement out of the world, a movement toward indistinction. Generic deracination is one way of saying that the human only exists as a multitude of Strangers.[46] Such a generic deracination is the only way to break the vicious circle of victim/persecutor. Furthermore, recognition of this deracination, as a kind of immanence of the future, is a way of saying that humans are always separate from the world, that the world does not truly determine humanity. We will see how this looks a bit more clearly in the next chapter.

6

Fabulation, or Non-Philosophy as Philo-Fiction

Art is the world without the world

Laruelle has used many names to describe his project. The term "non-philosophy" clearly has more prevalence than others, but he has always deployed other terms, to refer either to aspects of his thought – like "science of philosophy" or "non-epistemology" – or to the project in the general sense – as he has most recently with "non-standard philosophy." But there is another term he has deployed alongside of these that appears to be both general, like "non-standard philosophy," and particular, like "non-epistemology." This term, "philo-fiction" and its variants (photo-fiction, christo-fiction, art-fiction, amongst others), is derived in part from his work in the standard philosophical domain of aesthetics (which I am framing here as "fabulation" because of my focus on fiction), and yet also refers to what non-philosophy creates when it enters into the various domains of philosophy with its logic of the "non." When Laruelle enters into these domains, he does so without regard for an authenticity that would be granted by following the rules of discourse, even those of the art-World.

Instead, the purpose of fiction is a kind of counter-creation to that of the world. The act of creating fiction or "fabulating" is the goal of a non-philosophy – something is made by non-philosophy with the materials of philosophy and the world it creates. While non-philosophy also describes that world, as we saw in Laruelle's theory of Philosophical Decision, such a description is given in order to relativize and disempower what self-presents as sufficient and absolute. Stepping outside of the terms that Laruelle might himself use – but nonetheless consistent with the practice he engages with in his books – we might say that philo-fiction operates in a way similar to science fiction, though the kind grounded in visions of social justice and moving from the experience of the victim. We might indeed call this, along with Walidah Imarisha and adrienne maree brown, "visionary fiction." As Imarisha writes in her introduction to an anthology of works of speculative or visionary fiction, "Whenever we try to envision a world without war, without violence, without prisons, without capitalism, we are engaging in speculative fiction. All organizing is science fiction."[1] That is, in thinking how the world might be otherwise, how it might be stripped bare of its structures of authority (war, violence, prisons, capitalism), we engage in a practice of drawing from what appears in that world but under the logic of the without, of the otherwise: "Art is the world without the world, the entire world but without its over-determining concept."[2] Importantly, Laruelle is not arguing for the continuation of the world or even a better world. It is on this point that Laruelle may differ from a certain optimism found within even the most grim speculative fiction. After the creation of a fiction, whether it be philo-fiction or any other form, the radical immanence of the One still remains foreclosed. The radical (lived) human remains unrepresentable. But, as we will see, how that radical (lived) human lives in the world, how the radical (lived) human is *performed*, does matter. For while the coordinates of the world are not everything, while there remains something of the Human-in-Human always already foreclosed to the world, the existence of the human is performed in the world. Survival is important and should be relatively valued, even though survival always takes place by definition within the limits set by the world and through means derived from the world even if in-the-last-instance these means remain human. There is, for Laruelle, a way of valorizing fiction: as a force of insurrection that disempowers the world and operates without concern for its parameters.

This chapter is separated into two parts to attend to the particular material engaged with – again, that is fabulation – and then to see the way in which non-philosophy's practice is a philo-fiction generally. Our discussion of Laruelle's aesthetics will not focus on the particular object of photography, which has been the focus of two of his most explicitly aesthetic texts (*The Concept of Non-Philosophy* [2011 in a bilingual edition] and *Photo-Fiction, A Non-Standard*

Aesthetics, 2012), but rather focus on the general shape of his work on aesthetics as fabulation before looking at the way philo-fiction may play out as the performance of the subject.[3] In attempting to craft a philo-fiction Laruelle is attempting to create a unified aesthetic and philosophical practice, both aestheticizing philosophy and philosophizing aesthetics. Because of the centrality of ethics to Laruelle's work, we return to his conception of this performance via problems posed by the specific critical race theory seen in the last chapter, as this allows the stakes and aims of philo-fiction to be seen more clearly. While art is never simply distinguished from ethics or politics, the way in which ethics and politics manifest in art is often covered over by philosophy by either making the art serve a didactic role or reducing art to a tool for philosophy's own use in playing the didactic role. As John Ó Maoilearca's work persuasively argues, Laruelle's conception of non-philosophy assumes that the regional forms of knowing (like visual art, fabulation, and aesthetics in this case) already think.[4] We will explore then the way in which Laruelle's victimology drives his thinking regarding art. Keeping in mind that in this victimology – or, perhaps more accurately, "victim-fiction" and victim-thinking – the victim is not understood as weak and in need of saving, but as the very power of insurrection, as fiction-making or fabulating. Thus, his own conception of art as a form of thought is that art may be directed by the victim and join in her insurrection too, as crafting a form of life within the world.

The art of thought

There is a difference between art and philosophies of art. This might seem like a simple truism, but such a distinction is often elided between what philosophy says about something and that thing-in-itself. While philosophers (and perhaps theorists more generally) often claim to make something understandable, they often do so by disempowering the abstraction inherent in the object they are philosophizing. Perhaps this is nowhere clearer than in philosophical reflection upon works of art. While the multiplicity of different forms and styles of art makes general statements inherently likely to occlude various important nuances, nevertheless, when one stands before a piece of art, there is something abstract about the experience which remains even as one attempts to produce something discursive about that piece of art. Even classical or figural painting is abstract in this way. Perhaps this is what leads Laruelle to claim that artists are more sensitive than philosophers to the abstract nature of non-philosophy: "There is an abstraction to non-philosophy, but that abstraction is sometimes much more difficult for the 'trained' (or 'formatted' – meaning that they've been wiped to prepare them for philosophy) philosophers than it is for [psycho-]analysts or artists. Often artists are more sensitive to non-philosophy than philosophers themselves are."[5]

The abstraction of art and the abstraction of non-philosophy are found not in looking for the underlying idea of art, but in the abstraction of its practice. Laruelle provides a succinct description of his understanding of how non-philosophy may produce a non-standard aesthetics, writing: "I propose considering every art form in terms of principles of sufficiency and no longer in terms of descriptive or theoretical or foundational historical perspectives. To do this, one must construct non-aesthetic scenarios, scenes, characters, or postures that are both conceptual and artistic and based on the formal model of a matrix. We will not start from a question, we will not ask *what is art, what is the essence of a photo?*"[6] One of non-philosophy's hoped-for outcomes is to distinguish itself from philosophy's domination of those objects philosophy hopes to develop knowledge of. Non-Philosophy disempowers that domination by attempting to create a minimal gap between what philosophy says about something and how it does that. Badiou, as I have repeatedly claimed, is perhaps the most explicit proponent of the need to recognize philosophy's ability to come along and speak the truth for domains of knowledge that mutely produce those truths.[7] In distinction to his contemporary, Laruelle instead hopes to perform these domains, but to do so in a philosophical way. When non-philosophy engages with art, then, it cannot simply be through writing a gallery catalogue, but must find a way to turn itself into a kind of artistic practice by using artistic materials.[8] In this way, any aesthetics within non-philosophy must perform the art of thought rather than produce a thought about art: "Let us suppose that 'aesthetics,' to retain its name as such, is now of a superior power of art to thought, thought itself striving to be an art 'in-the-last-instance,' so an art of thought rather than a thought about art."[9]

This calling upon forms so as to go under them as conditions of philosophical work is the impetus behind Laruelle's philo-fiction. This means the various materials will necessarily modify some of the ways in which non-philosophy manifests in each instance. With regard to his recent work on quantum physics, this has meant attempting to think of non-philosophy as akin to the style of science-fiction: "Philo-fiction is scientifically based and is not science-fiction that is philosophically based, it is 'broadening' of the term science-fiction in every sense of the word through its transfer to the terrain of philosophy so as to raise it to something besides literature alone."[10] Undoubtedly, Laruelle is taking a great risk here by the standards of what counts as respectable work in philosophy. For running throughout non-philosophy is a kind of aesthetic vision as he attempts to bring together various forms of thinking, but without endeavoring to provide the usual philosophical arguments regarding the conditions for scientific truth or judgment regarding the beauty of art. His engagement with a determinate science, quantum physics, risks being seen as "merely" aesthetic, especially when he makes claims such as this:

> If it is necessary to justify this kind of attempt, we prefer to say that it is a matter of generically knowing, with an eye towards our human under-coming, the gnosis that constitutes the first forms of knowing that we are without knowing it. Philosophy alone does not suffice for all of this and even is opposed to it. Another form of knowledge is necessary, at once scientific and of some philosophical kind, one without reflection but through superposition of the quantum and philosophy. Without this no one can understand more clearly this formula: philo-fiction, indeed even theo-fiction, is a science-fiction with possibly its classical technology augmented with that of philosophy, but the sense of which is human or the vector that is "messianic."[11]

After all, normally when we think of people bringing together various "messianic" ideas with ideas derived from the science of quantum physics, we think of controversial figures (sometimes simply described as "charlatans") like Deepak Chopra. The crucial difference, however, is that Laruelle's non-philosophy does not make claims about the "true nature" of the world, and does not enter into debates regarding the ways quantum physics supports materialism or some form of vitalism or some other already constructed philosophical position.

In terms of non-philosophy's framing of the science of quantum physics, anything that science tells us about the universe is necessarily partial and open to being revised with new findings and when new models are developed. Human existence (what Laruelle refers to in his later work and is seen in the quote above as "under-coming") speaks to a form of knowledge from which even scientific knowledge comes. We will examine in the next chapter what Laruelle means by the term "messianic" and its relation to his understanding of science. But we may begin to understand if we take him to mean that this human knowledge is already a kind of messianic act. For scientific knowledge about the fundamental building blocks of the physical universe speaks to the human under-coming into that universe, rather than being thrown (existing) into the world. Again, to point out a difference between the universe and the world is to point to a difference between a form of existence that is not sufficient (universe) and a hallucinated totality that in reality refers to the set of actual but not necessary forms of authority (the world). Thus the proliferation of various kinds of fictions within the universe can be seen as a proliferation of various kinds of knowledge: not producing knowledge separate from those practices, but understanding those practices as themselves forms of knowledge – "To think 'aesthetics' in the form of scenarios, quantically conjugating a variety of arts and philosophies, would enrich and liberate possible productive forces and would justify the existence of art not as thought, as was talked about with postmodernists, but [as] a veritable art-thought, entirely specific and worthy of being called 'contemporary'."[12]

Laruelle's engagement with the arts is much like his engagement with the other domains we have examined, and perhaps is closest to his engagement with science, since science for Laruelle takes a fundamentally immanent stance within the Real in much the same way the artist does before being forced into a philosophically reflexive position regarding his/her work. When one thinks from a kind of naive and spontaneous realism of the photograph, it simply becomes a tool for the self-sufficiency of that spontaneous philosophy.[13] In those instances, photography or any other kind of art "is a way of taking ontological care of being in its entirety in order to be surprised by being in its entirety, for example to be surprised that there are victims as if victims were 'being'."[14] However, in the immediate experience of a photograph that captures something of suffering, the world fades away and instead the human may become outraged or "indignant." Laruelle is making reference to the Spanish people's anti-austerity movement, the *indignados*, when he writes: "The photo is the way in which the world astonishes itself whereas it should be that in which man becomes indignant. Photo-fiction would rather be a way to take pity on the human rather than astonishing the world, the poor world that does not quit making war with itself via interposed photographs."[15] So there is here a human cause behind the art of thought. It would not be correct to claim that art is then subordinated to some purpose other than art, since the human herself lacks any purpose or end, but rather art raises up humans in a kind of "weak resurrection" by bringing attention to the human, instead of encompassing the human within the world.

Let us now put this vision of aesthetics as fabulation in dialogue with a problem raised in our investigation of Laruelle's work on ethics. Namely, how are we to distinguish the human as separated from the world, while still understanding the real effects the world's enframing has on the human as a particular subject?

Fiction is a matter of insurrection

In a certain sense, the world is already a fiction. Think of all the regional forms of knowing that philosophy deploys: ontology, epistemology, anthropology, and even the ways in which the Philosophical Decision may be traced through discourses around biology, cosmology, and so on. The Greek *logos* carried by the suffix in each of these terms is familiar to all of us. These discourses may be seen as crafting stories about the objects they claim to elucidate and reveal, whether they be Being, knowledge, the human, life, or the cosmos itself. With regard to anthropology or the fiction told of the human, (Western) philosophy has played its part in the fabulation of what it means to be human. We have seen in the chapter on ethics the argument that Black intellectuals like Fanon and Wilderson have made regarding the way this fabulation operates through a series of constitutive exclusions. Even when philosophy is unable to see itself as a tool, confusing its ability to fabulate and the fictions it crafts with the Real itself, philosophy still operates as a tool. It joins and sometimes drives what Alexander G. Weheliye calls "racializing assemblages" in construing "race not as a biological or cultural classification, but as a set of sociopolitical processes that discipline humanity into full humans, not-quite-humans, and non-humans."[16] In his own fabulation of certain fictions, Laruelle joins major thinkers in Black studies like Fred Moten, Hortense Spillers, and Sylvia Wynter in attempting to "disrupt the governing conception of humanity as synonymous with western Man" (despite his own subjective position as a white European French man).[17] Here we will again elucidate Laruelle's position through contrasting it with work carried out in Black studies. Not because Laruelle, as a white European man, has the better position, but precisely because those in Black studies are clearer about the stakes behind various subject-fictions. They also allow us to locate a dualism that runs throughout non-philosophy, between the Real (the Human-in-Human which is not a subject) and the world (where various subject-fictions operate as the force-[of]-thought within theory).

Laruelle's non-philosophy offers resources for thinking through a debate within critical race theory today, between the position of Wilderson's Afro-pessimism and that of Fred Moten's "Black optimism."[18] Of course, and this bears repeating, this is not about offering *the* solution to the debate. It would be, as has been stated, a rather (white) philosophical move to think that a white American male explicating the work of a white French male could come along and enter into a difficult debate amongst black theorists and simply proclaim that a philosopher living in Paris has already solved this problem of the social death and social life of Black people in the anti-black racist world. It is, rather, to show the ways in which non-philosophy may be yet another tool, either as framework or as offering particular concepts, for such debates, if those involved wish to take it up. The form of the political world I sketched in chapter 5 is largely faithful to Wilderson's own and it is an analysis of the world that I think is correct. In Laruelle's terms, the world is not everything, and Wilderson would probably agree even though he directs his attentions toward a diagnosis of the world. His diagnosis shows that the discourse of the world takes place philosophically through the discourse of Being and thus the differential between black and white that structures the anti-black world is a philosophical discourse about Being that ultimately denies Black (slaves) their being, such that ontology cannot account for blackness. Fanon makes this claim, writing: "Ontology does not allow us to understand the being of the black man, since it ignores lived experience [*vécu*]. For not only must the black man be black; he must be black in relation to the white man.... The black man has no ontological resistance in the eyes of the white man."[19] We see here a resonance again with Laruelle as ontology (or philosophy more generally) is found wanting in terms of being useful to understanding the (Black) human, because it does not take into account the *vécu* or the way in which such a subject position is lived.

Moten – whose project is marked by a distinction from Wilderson's, but overall they share much – is concerned with thinking through what he calls a "paraontological" analysis of blackness in this world as a site of resistance, and as the way in which oppressed people manage to live "in the break" or in the midst of violence and the denial of their humanity within the (white) world. This performs the reversal of valuation that we see in non-philosophy with regard to authoritarian philosophy that seeks to interpret or change the world, as we gleaned to be inherent in Heidegger's anti-Semitism and its explication through his philosophical terminology. In non-philosophical terms, we could say that the Black and white in this sense are subjects and so determined or in some form of relation or lack of relation to the world, but the lived (reality of) blackness is beyond such ontological concerns. This matches well with Moten's double injunction concerning blackness: "On the one hand, blackness and ontology are unavailable for one another; on the other hand, blackness must free itself from ontological expectation, must refuse subjection to ontology's sanction against the very idea of black subjectivity."[20] While Moten has not yet published a full exploration and analysis of this "paraontological" distinction, he is clear about the demand that has conditioned the conception of the idea when he writes: "The paraontological distinction between blackness and blacks allows us no longer to be enthralled by the notion that blackness is a property that belongs to blacks (thereby placing certain formulations regarding non/relationality and non/communicability on a different footing and under a certain pressure) but also because ultimately it allows us to detach blackness from the question of (the meaning of) being."[21] There is something lived and performed outside of the parameters of Being, outside of the parameters of the world, that no philosophical grammar has attended to. That something is blackness and, as Wilderson has argued, it looks like death to the world: "Because, I contend, in allowing the notion of freedom to attain the ethical purity of its ontological status, one would have to lose one's Human coordinates and become Black. Which is to say one would have to die."[22] As Jared Sexton has argued, those seen within the world as the walking dead have a life in the world that manifests as social death.[23] This notion of social death as the story of blackness is a philo-fiction, it is the fabulation of a new conception of lived (realities of) humans that challenges the story of the world.

Laruelle allows us to make clear that the social death forced upon certain subjects takes place within the world: it is the purview of subjects that emerge from the Human-in-Human foreclosed to worldly representation or recognition. The paraontological distinction between blackness and Black people is an instance of philofiction, but in the same way as the non-philosophical distinction between the Real and the world more generally is also a philofiction crafted by thinking from the radical immanence of the Real-One or Human-in-Human. Wilderson's distinction of these worldly subject positions into Human (white), Savage (indigenous), and Slave (Black) speaks to the structure of the world as such. Wilderson's remark that freedom for the Slave ("the end of the world," since the world is constructed on the basis of a decision between free and slave, master and slave) comes with hyperbolic demands also speaks to the radical immanence of the One that underlies and is foreclosed to these subject positions: "For the Black, freedom is an ontological, rather than experiential, question.... the riders that one could place on Black freedom would be hyperbolic – though no less true – and ultimately untenable: freedom from the world, freedom from Humanity [another term for white subjectivity in Wilderson], freedom from everyone (including one's Black self)."[24] Why freedom from this Black self? Precisely because the self is the subject formed by the world. It is the fiction one lives, and if one lives it according to the standard rules of narrative then one lives the world with all its attendant harassments – and, in the case of the slave subject, as socially dead. That the fact of this freedom is possible – even though hyperbolic and untenable, at least within the frame of the world – speaks to the fact that one's lived immanence underlies any fiction, any creation of the subject, and moreover that this possibility is not provided for on the basis of any universal subject, but on the basis of a radical immanence of a (lived) identity.

So the principles of non-philosophy would allow us to affirm both the position of Wilderson's Afro-pessimism, which claims that within the parameters of ontology the subject position of the Black is cast as nothing, and that of Moten's Black optimism, which claims that there is a paraontological distinction between the subject position and the immanence of blackness that disrupts the world as such. Laruelle's theory allows us to be clear on why both positions are tenable in the way that Moten and Sexton have tried to think them together – for the position of a subject may be produced by the world, but there is a potential underlying that encompassed subject that may disrupt the world through which the subject is ontologically determined. To expand upon this and the ethical drive behind philo-fiction, let us move away somewhat from the technical language of Wilderson, Moten, and Laruelle.

When one engages in critical theory around the question of race, it is not uncommon for well-meaning individuals to ask whether it is truly anti-racist to recognize and name another person as raced in any way whatsoever. Race is, after all, a fiction, or what Laruelle would call a hallucination of the (lived) human. So is it right to engage with that fiction, when it has driven some of the most sadistic violence imaginable against other human beings? Would it not be better, such a well-meaning individual will ask, to drop this fictional account and treat all human beings simply as human beings? Does not such treatment arise out of a refusal to recognize racial difference or distinction? It may even seem as if such a question is grounded upon strong non-philosophical commitments to the generic nature of the (lived) human. The reality, as can be derived already from the preceding two chapters, is very different. Laruelle's theory is interesting precisely because of its strangeness to standard liberal conceptions of politics, ethics, and aesthetics. Such liberal accounts, even when they are radical liberal accounts, are largely dependent upon a philosophy of recognition and representation played out between two terms that occludes a third term which determines that relationship. This is another way of saying, of course, that such a philosophy manifests the structure of Philosophical Decision, but it surfaces in a different way why there might be something of Philosophical Decision to resist and struggle against. The occluded third term of Philosophical Decision may come to oppress or control in nefarious ways the other two terms, and it is naturalized or normalized in such a way as to be beyond criticism.

How does this abstract structure relate to the question of insisting on a certain set of names as privileged fictional names for the Human-in-Human that lies beyond naming? With regard to the way the fiction of race manifests in the world, the two terms could be many things, but if Wilderson and others are correct that there is something fundamental to the construction of race that is rooted in the systematic dishonoring and subjugation of Black people by white people, then it would not simply be correct to say these two terms are "white" and "nonwhite." It is more rigorous to name them as white and Black, for the way in which race is constructed ultimately depends upon these two extreme poles. While in the past such a relationship was dependent upon a recognition of "not black," as the white human secured his humanity in not being a slave (that is, in not being nothing), this has changed in an age of "color-blind racism" or "racism without racists."[25] Now the demand is that the Black and white poles be recognized simply as two people, and that they enter into mutual recognition based upon some basic commonality. This is often what lies behind the refusal to take into account very different material conditions for a white subject and a Black subject. While segregation of communities continues, this is thought to arise "naturally," ignoring the ways in which Blacks and whites have very different access to business and housing loans or health care or education, or any number of other institutions that correspond to quality-of-life indicators. The demand is that one strip away various determinations of one's subject position so that recognition takes place simply between two people, instead of between a victim and her oppressor or one complicit with making her a victim. What is left unthought, occluded from vision altogether, is that there is an implicit whitening of what it means to be human here. There is a third term – what we might name as the anti-black world since it englobes the other two – that determines the relationship of the two. One does not see the world, for the world is the name for that framework through which you see everything else and you do so seemingly spontaneously. To be a recognizable person, entering into a relationship of good faith with another person, is to enter into certain conditions of the world. In simple terms, when the demand is to "treat people like people" this means ignoring the ways in which the world determines who gets seen as a person and who is not extended that privilege. It ignores that the demand is to see the person in the way one sees a white subject. Others have discussed at length Laruelle's valorization of cosmic blackness and they have done so with skill.[26] They tell us that Laruelle valorizes and names the blackness of the universe because it is more generic than light, it is less than light – as a visual metaphor within philosophy, which has social consequences, it is valued less than light and thus it is named and celebrated by non-philosophy. From the universe to the breaks in the social world, it is blackness that names the radically lived and unrepresentable.[27]

The subject position of the black is created by the world, and one names that blackness precisely because of the way in which the world has attempted to construct that subject as socially dead. Of course, from a non-philosophical perspective too, humans should all be treated as equal. But until the world that constitutes their inequality is ended, then one names these subjects either as Black, or victim, or (as we will see) Christ, because the (socially) dead may rise and in so doing disrupt the very world that brought about their death. This is how Laruelle understands victims. Not as weak and in need of saving, but as a fiction – as a subject – that is produced in a relative way by the world but that manifests a radical imma-nence that breaks from the dialectics of the world:

> By its intrinsically in-person real, the victim is the counter-witness to nihilism, the same way that before it was the counter-example to creation *ex nihilo*. The victim carries with it resurrection, or rather the prior-to-the-first insurrection, against the dialectic of being and nothingness, which has no real or lived sense. The victim is a power of "awakening" or "reprise" in the order of the lived experiences opposed to the simple dialectical or differential repetition of sur-vival. Survival reinforces transcendence, an act that exceeds death or persecution and prolongs the world, whereas insurrection, which is the root of resurrection, weakens or debases this transcendence of a world to the state of lived experience.[28]

The rising of the dead outside of the dialectic of being or nothing-ness is a way of speaking within the world of what is "beyond" the world, or otherwise. In the next chapter, we will see how non-philosophy submits religious materials (taken to be a kind of fiction as well) to such victim-thinking.

7

Religion, or a Rigorous Heresy

Beyond philosophy's orthodoxy

The scene is dramatic. Likely, after decades of film versions of the story of Christ, every Western reader can bring to mind those films' *mise en scène*. The color palate takes on a certain orientalist hue, some mix of sun and sand, while a steely old Hollywood tone and look are given to our white actors of European descent. And we see a version of Jesus as white Western man – that burdened absolute image of the human provided for in philosophy's ersatz-universalism – speaking with gravitas and graveness amid the orientalist background, emotionally but directly demanding of Peter "But what about you?" "Who do you say I am?" he asks, with Peter's response – a triumph of sorts for the audience – "You are the Christ" (Mark 8:29). It is strange that in the next moment the actions of this declared Christ are described in this way: "Jesus warned them not to tell anyone about him" (Mark 8:30). But, as this text contradicts itself in its performance, the original disciples did, and this Hollywood-esque domestication is what resulted. Perhaps it is owing to the Hollywood *mise en scène* we have adopted that the drama of this scene can be safely foreign, with its strange mix of orientalist images and (however bronzed they are for the scenes) white actors speaking with refined gravitas. This safe foreignness covers over the demands being made; the distance created by the *mise en scène* makes it seem that the question being posed by the one declared to be Christ is posed in the past and so does not bear on the present or the future.

What is true is passed over in this exchange, the true strangeness of it. Today Christianity is but one choice amongst many acceptable religions to believe in, one option amongst various plans, as you might find when comparing different mobile phone contracts or brands of cereal. But, according to Søren Kierkegaard – writing at perhaps his most pious in *Practice in Christianity* – if one is to believe in Christ, one must be contemporary with the strangeness of Christ: "as long as there is a believer, this person, in order to have become that, must have been and as a believer must be just as contemporary with Christ's presence as his contemporaries were."[1] He goes on to write: "This contemporaneity is the condition of faith, and, more sharply defined, it is faith."[2] Perhaps though, contrary to Kierkegaard, making this question contemporary will have nothing to do with Christianity, not even the Christianity purified of Christendom that Kierkegaard hoped for. This may be because, as Kierkegaard and Nietzsche argued in their own ways and others after them have argued in theirs, the Christ of Christianity has nothing to do with the real Christ. If these heretics are correct, then the wager is that one can do a Christology outside of Christianity and its institutions. Doing so would reveal Christ as a contemporary in a way that Christian theology obscures and may be productive of a different kind of philosophy of religion from the kind we have seen in the Continental tradition.

This is the wager that is explored in this chapter. I have elsewhere written at length on non-philosophy's relation to religion and the possibility of a non-theology, and, as usual, I do not repeat that analysis here.[3] Instead, for the sake of introducing students to the way in which Laruelle's engagement profoundly affects the style of non-philosophy, I focus here on his engagement with the figure of Christ (in theology, this focus on and investigation of the figure of Christ is called "Christology"). First I do so by teasing out two other Christologies in contemporary French philosophy as they engage with orthodox Christian material: the Christology of Michel Henry and then the Christology of Alain Badiou. Together with Laruelle's, I have chosen to call these "secular Christologies" because, even with certain caveats around the work of Michel Henry, all three speak without any churchly authority and speak about Christ in a specifically philosophical manner. I have chosen to contrast Laruelle with two of his contemporaries in part because of their shared reference point to Christianity and, in the case of Laruelle, because of an eradicated tradition that was defined, destroyed, and disfigured in memory by Christianity (heretical

Gnostics). But I also contrast Laruelle with these two philosophers because their engagement with religion is more familiar and takes on a more radical nature than that of other French contemporaries since they connect the various religious materials (Christology in this case) to a philosophical form often thought to be antagonistic to engagement with religion: philosophical materialism.[4] What does materialist philosophy, assumed to move philosophy to this world, have to do with Christ? The goal of the first major part of this chapter will be to see how these philosophers writing in the secular age have made Christ contemporary for their philosophy, and specifically how Laruelle does so in a different way that is not beholden to orthodox forms of religion – Christianity in this case – but moves through its heretical materials. I will attend to the questions: How does this engagement with the problem of Christ reveal how philosophy engages with religion generally, and how does non-philosophy engage differently? Does this engagement modify anything about the thought of the three figures discussed in this chapter? Does it do any philosophical work or is it just the work of thinkers returning to piety in their twilight years?

In a certain sense this speaking of the one claimed to be the Son of God, God incarnate, is a reiteration of Deleuze's question regarding the moderns: "Why is philosophy so compromised with God?...Is it a dishonest compromise or something a little purer?"[5] Our reiteration might be phrased something like "Why is philosophy still concerned with Christ? Is it simply piety, a bit of playfulness, or something a little more interesting, more productive?" Perhaps this isn't quite the way Kierkegaard would like us to pose this question or to be concerned with Christ's contemporaneity, seeing as he railed against the idea of the interesting in *Fear and Trembling* and *The Point of View of My Work as an Author*, but what I refer to as interesting is precisely what is worth giving our attention to, what we should allow to capture our attention within thought – what challenges the smooth functioning of the philosophical machine.[6] For the problem of Christ is ultimately a problem of the identity of humanness, a recurring – if not *the* recurring – question of non-philosophy that drives it from its very core, as we have seen play out in the preceding chapters: not what it means "to be" human, not what it means to be a particular man or a woman, but what at our most generic and in our most radically lived (experience) our humanness consists of. To ask "Who do you say that I am?" and to hear back the answer "the Christ" cracks open the real drama of each life.

Orthodoxy and heresy in French secular Christologies

Christ, the firstborn Son of the Father

Michel Henry's work is a limit case in how far one can go philosophically with religious materials. Without falling into the trap of thinking that philosophy and theology can be easily separated out into their pure forms, there does seem to be some difference between religious organizations of thought and philosophical ones. The philosopher may come up against the religious material, but it is far from clear at what point the work of the philosopher is completely determined by their religious belief and experience and when their understanding of these religious modalities is being shaped by their philosophical work. Michel Henry's work is a limit case because the line between philosophy and theology is even more razor thin and tarries closer to heresy, in the light of orthodox theology, than is the case in the work of other Catholic phenomenologists. In fact, there is something of a tug-o'-war over Henry's work, between those like Jean-Yves Lacoste who see in Henry's late Christian works a sign of the philosopher's "resolute commitment to Christianity" and those like Michelle Rebidoux who see in this "Christian turn" an attempt to solve the philosophical problem of solipsism that threatens Henry's phenomenology of radical immanence.[7] Of course, none of the secondary work on Henry would go so far as to present such a stark choice. It is not the case that in Henry we find an either/or between theology and philosophy, but the tension in what is emphasized by his readers points to a real tension in Henry's work between theological determination and the auto-mutation of philosophy with religious materials that we see in each of our three philosophers.[8]

Henry's engagement with Christology over the course of three books takes a decidedly phenomenological approach. His phenomenology is radical as it attempts to create a thought that is immanent to the material it is investigating, which requires that Henry take the words of Christ as if they were true. This is of course largely self-grounding, but in terms of investigating a phenomenon in its "for-itself" modality it is potentially more fecund than reductionist or relational accounts of religious phenomena. This would seem to suggest that the organon for evaluating Christology will be Christ himself, and this would seem to be in accord with such

a radically immanent method. However, there is always a tempta-
tion to let the *logos* come to define Christ (rather than holding them
both in what Laruelle calls "superposition") – a *logos* determined
not by Christ but by those who speak about him. Henry gives the
game away from the start in *I Am the Truth: Toward a Philosophy of
Christianity* by making his Christology a philosophy of Christianity.
He writes:

> I do not intend to ask whether Christianity is "true" or "false," or to
> establish, for example, the former hypothesis. Rather, what will be
> in question here is *what Christianity considers as truth* – what kind of
> truth it offers to people, what it endeavors to communicate to them
> not as a theoretical or indifferent truth but as the essential truth that
> by some mysterious affinity is suitable for them, to the point that it
> alone is capable of assuring them salvation.[9]

The question begged here – of what Henry means by Christianity
– is quickly answered by him when he writes:

> What we find expressed in a set of texts designated by the title *New
> Testament* is what we mean by Christianity – and rightly so, it would
> seem. Where else would we seek the "content" of Christianity, so as
> to reflect on what it considers truth to be, if not in the corpus con-
> stituted by the Gospels, the Acts of the Apostles, their Epistles (by
> Paul, James, Peter, John, and Jude), and last of all in the Revelation
> attributed to the same John? Were not the dogmas defining Christi-
> anity elaborated on the basis of this corpus? Does not the knowledge
> of Christianity – and thus all reflection on its possible "truth" – come
> by way of these texts? Only a meticulous analysis of them can lead,
> it would seem, to understanding of what Christianity is at its essen-
> tial core.[10]

But this decision on Henry's part to make the New Testament the
material revealing of the essential core of Christianity is not nearly
as obvious as he makes out. Why not a material analysis of
the communities who take the name "Christian?" Is Henry blind
to the problem of supercessionism raised by limiting the analysis
of Christianity (and so, for him, of Christ) to the New Testament,
excising the Christian experience of its Jewish origin completely?

A decision will always excise something, leaving a thinker open
to some rebuke, and while the issue of supercessionism is very real
considering how it has undergirded anti-Semitism throughout the
centuries, something else is at work in this decision by Henry. It is

the real separation of the radical immanence of some phenomenon from the world in the philosophical sense of the field of projected transcendental signifiers. He puts this starkly, writing: *"the truth of Christianity differs in essence from the truth of the world....Living is not possible in the world.* Living is possible only outside the world, where another Truth reigns, another way of revealing."[11] For Henry, the world is synonymous with the scientistic reduction of everything to what can be measured, thus the truth of the world always reveals itself through some relation, never getting to the ipseity or radical immanence of the thing itself. This is ultimately the meaning of his anti-modernism and seeming hatred of the natural sciences on display whenever he speaks of the Galilean failure of Western thought.[12] This is not some kind of "natural" Roman Catholic distrust of the secular and modern analogous to Pope Emeritus Benedict XVI's constant warnings about science unmoored from Christianity, as some commentators may want to suggest, but there is something perhaps troubling about such an easy dovetailing of an institutionalized theology of fear alongside a real philosophical commitment. What does such closeness reveal about Henry's Christology?

To answer that question, we need to first look more closely at what Henry's Christology is. While this plays itself out in increasingly complex levels of nuance over the course of three texts, moving from the way Life, the Body, and Speech are manifest purely in Christ, the structure of this Christology is given in a relatively simple way in *I Am the Truth*. What Henry sees in Christian Christology is a response to the problem of pure manifestation as opposed to the reductionist or relational philosophies that cover over the thing-in-itself. In *I Am the Truth* this is related specifically to the way Life is manifested as such – not life as studied in the natural sciences, which according to Henry only truly studies living beings and not Life itself – whereas a philosophy of Christ must look to life as manifestation, as Life is in and of itself. This is then a problem of how Life engenders itself within the living and on the basis of itself, so without any reference to a relationality that would erase the Ipseity (or individual identity) of identity. The self-grounding relationship of God the Father and Christ the Son provides Henry with a model of this non-relational but not solipsistic Ipseity. He writes:

What was clearly established was this: absolute Life experiences itself in an actualized Ipseity, a Self that is itself actualized and, as such, singular. It is in this way that the self-engendering of the Father implies within it the engendering of the Son and is one with this engendering. Or rather: the engendering of the Son consists in the Father's self-engendering and is one with it. No Life without a Living. Not one Living without Life....*Life engenders itself like the Living that Life itself is within its self-engendering.* And this is why that Living is the Unique and the First – "That man," as John says (1:33).[13]

In other words, what Christology does for Henry is allow for a thinking of Life grounded in nothing but itself, not in the world, nor in living beings, but Life as pure actuality. Thus, Christ comes to be but the Firstborn Son of the Father, where each of us is a Son:

> I myself am this singular Self engendered in the self-engendering of absolute Life, and only that. *Life self-engenders itself as me.* If, along with Meister Eckhart – and with Christianity – we call Life God, we might say: "God engenders himself as me." The generation of this singular Self that I myself am – the living transcendental Me, in the self-generation of absolute Life: this is my transcendental birth, the one that makes me a *true man* [my emphasis], the transcendental Christian man.[14]

All of this is in itself interesting, especially reading Henry's later works as attempts to deal with problems raised by his early philosophy. But, without accounting for the generation of Christianity as such, Henry leaves his philosophy open to a theological determination that suppresses the power of his thought. Instead of addressing this issue of *religion* as such, rather than assuming Christianity as the bearer of truth, Henry ends up grounding a new dualism between *Christianity* and the world in a cultural monism that he critiques as in the world itself, "To reduce man to a part of the material universe, similarly subject to the physical and mathematical approach of modern Galilean science, it is necessary to have previously reduced any form of knowledge to such an approach: *to presuppose that there exists no mode of knowing other than Galilean science, that is to say, modern physics.*"[15] But Henry has done the same in his immanent approach to Christianity, as can be seen in the quote above where Christianity reveals *true man* – not the human as a multiplicity, but the human as truly invisible in the sense that everything that matters to our transcendental Self is invisible, like pain and love. Only Christianity reveals that, says Henry, ignoring the plethora of religious traditions outside of Christianity that deal with the invisible and the occulted as well, perhaps in ways that institutionalized Christianity does not.[16]

But ultimately it is institutional Christianity that haunts Henry's phenomenology. Interestingly, nowhere to my knowledge does he consider the role of the Church as such. What is institutional for Henry is the scripture that records the words of Christ and that the Christian community engages with in its development of dogma. It is spoken by Henry in a way that assumes them, without paying much attention ultimately to their political or social reality. So, what we are given in Henry's passing over of the institutions of Christianity in silence is simply the idea that there is an ethic developed and that it is distinctly Christian. He writes, "The Christian ethic aims to allow people to overcome the forgetting of their condition as Son in order to rediscover (thanks to it) the absolute Life into which they were born."[17] So Christianity ended up doing what the Marxist demands but is unable to do except in a Galilean way – it changed the world. These sorts of claims about the efficacy of one religious tradition over others, about how medicine or care of the vulnerable develops, are always highly speculative and ultimately idealist. Is charity a fundamentally Christian notion or a fundamentally human one? For Henry, this question is unintelligible, for the answer is that to be truly human is to be truly a Son of God. But this means for him not to be a Christ, but to be a Christian. And this suturing of Christ to Christianity is not only not necessary within the bounds of Henry's own philosophy, but also not necessary within the bounds of reason and experience. The evidence for that will be seen not just in Laruelle, but in the traditions that Laruelle draws upon – like certain Gnostic sects – and those he didn't – as with the Christologies and Imamologies found in various strands of Islam.[18] But is it not fear of the barbarism of this age, the barbarism that Pope Emeritus Benedict XVI also spoke about from his gilded throne, that drives Henry into the arms of not Christ, but Christianity. The Christ spoken about by Henry is ultimately a manifestation not of Christ himself, but of the *culture of* Christ – not Christ crucified, but a world transformed into a Christian-world after Christ's resurrection. Christ stands as a ready-made example for Henry's own philosophical concerns and is derived from his own personal faith commitments without placing them under critical scrutiny.

Christ, consubstantial with the Father

Slavoj Žižek has pointed out that there seems to be a fifth truth condition of religion that should be added to Badiou's identification of four other ones (art, science, politics, and love). This is because of the role of religion in Badiou's engagement with St. Paul.[19] Žižek's point is that Badiou's theory of fidelity to an event determines the relationship to philosophy of the other four conditions as a kind of metacondition. It is not a demand that Badiou engage more directly with religious material, instead it is a demand that Badiou recognize how his own subtractive method already presupposes a certain Christian notion of faithfulness. While Badiou has not yet added religion to his list of truth conditions, he has engaged with Christological material directly in a way that shows his subjective method at work and often declares a certain fascination with Christianity that he does not have with Judaism or Islam (just to name the main varieties of monotheism). Even though he claims, in *Saint Paul: The Foundation of Universalism*, that "For me, truth be told, Paul is not an apostle or a saint. I care nothing for the Good News he declares, or the cult dedicated to him," we find him in his *Theory of the Subject* and *Logics of Worlds* discussing Christ in a way that illuminates a different approach to the relationship of Christ and philosophy than the one we have seen with Henry.[20] However, it is still in his *Saint Paul* that we find a clearer exposition of his subtractive method than the one in *Theory of the Subject*, and a less complex one than in *Logics of Worlds*, so before turning to his Christology we will remain there in order to understand his early engagement with Christ before he turned to Paul.

Badiou's evaluation of Christianity is in line with his generally polemical stance as can be seen when he writes:

> Let us be perfectly clear: so far as we are concerned, what we are dealing with here is precisely a fable. And singularly so in the case of Paul, who for crucial reasons reduces Christianity to a single statement: Jesus is resurrected. Yet this is precisely a fabulous element [*point fabuleux*], since all the rest, birth, teachings, death, *might* after all be upheld. A 'fable' is that part of a narrative that, so far as we are concerned, fails to touch on any Real, unless it be by virtue of that invisible and indirectly accessible residue sticking to every obvious imaginary.[21]

Badiou is quite clear that his only reason for engaging with such a religious fable and the apostle who preached it is to "organize" his "own speculative discourses," as Hegel, Nietzsche, Freud, and others have done before him.[22] Indeed, for Badiou, there can be no compromise with the fabulous element in the way we have seen Henry fully embrace and think from that element (being, of course, Christ's life, death, *and* resurrection). For Badiou, "it is a question of restoring the universal to its pure secularity, here and now."[23] Thus Paul can only be of use to Badiou if he is separated from the fable. Badiou is explicit that this will be his method, he will subtract Paul from the very fable that Paul rightly could be called the inventor of and examine him only formally as a "subject devoid of all identity and suspended to an event whose only 'proof' lies precisely in its having been declared by a subject."[24] In other words, for Badiou, the figure of Paul, and really any religious figure, will only be of interest for his philosophy as an *example* of some element of his philosophy, in this case the coupled theories of the event and the subject. The example is only useful as a point of reference if it reveals the formal structure of fidelity to the event, this fidelity being one mode that subject creation takes in Badiou.[25]

The subtractive element of Badiou's philosophy is where the power of his thought would seem to lie and it is in many ways the most radical contemporary version of universalist subtraction touched upon in chapter 5. It is what could be most productive for those who want to do something with Badiou's work, and so the most powerful outside of the particular instantiation of philosophy through the Badiou-subject. The process of subtracting allows for the philosopher to take what is most powerful within some particular phenomenon, religion in this case, and remove it from the structures surrounding it that would sediment and ultimately disempower that element. Subtraction is then not a negation, or if it is it is a positive instance of negation, which opens up thought to new forms of coherence and construction. Thus Christ may come to challenge the current understanding of the human, mired as we are in the drive not toward a fulfilled life but, in many ways, what Badiou thinks of as "mere survival." Whether that is the mere survival forced upon the majority of people in the world today or it is the mere survival of the denizens of the First World, living without any sense of what Badiou calls "the Idea." The message of Christ, which spoke against the power of this world, opens up to a vision of the human who, to paraphrase Aristotle, lived as if immortal.

One might expect Badiou's subtractive engagement with Christianity to produce a vision of Christ subtracted from orthodox theology. However, turning to his own remarks on Christology in *Theory of the Subject*, one is confronted with something strange:

Badiou seemingly endorses the strict Christological orthodoxy established by the Council of Nicea, which he calls "the first of the great politico-ideological conferences in history."[26] The only thing that is seemingly subtracted from Christian theology is the notion that any of this is true and not simply a fable, albeit for Badiou it is a helpful fable for delimiting what he sees as an authentic Maoism against a right-wing Statism and an ultra-left fanaticism. For Badiou reads the consubstantial being of God the Father with God the Son as a dialectical arrangement, expressing the fundamentally decentered and split identity of the absolute. If the Arians (who were condemned at the Council of Nicea) had been triumphant over what became Christian orthodoxy, it would be but an example of "right-wing opportunism" whereby the "revolution is dissolved within the state."[27]

Badiou doesn't go into great detail on why he associates this particular Christian heresy with that particular Marxist deviation, but it seems to have something to do with the overly hierarchical and thus ordered and secure anchoring of identity that comes out of Arianism. Regarding the ultra-left deviation, this is lined up with Gnostic Docetism (a heresy that declares the body of the historical Christ was an avatar and so Christ did not die), which is fanatical in prohibiting Christ "from truly dying on the Cross, from having a sexed and precarious being."[28] Badiou's true target here is not, of course, actual Gnostics (as if there were any left), but rather the ultra-left theory of Guy Lardreau and Christian Jambet, which played out in practice through their leading roles in the ultra-left organization Le Gauche Prolétarienne (The Proletarian Left). What Lardreau and Jambet (with whom Laruelle engaged in his early political works) were concerned with, as were other ultra-leftists in Europe at that time, was the complete overturning of the current order of things. They called such a complete overturning a Cultural Revolution, rather than an Ideological Revolution. Badiou puts his fear this way:

> Gnostic radicality maintains an ironclad divergence between the original purity of the divine Father and the blemishes of sex, the world, and death. If God comes to *haunt* the world in order to indicate the true way, he cannot establish himself therein in his essence. Obsessed by the pure and the original and violently inclined toward Manichaeism, this ultra-leftist heresy blocks the fecundity of the message just as much as the rational and peaceful hierarchical ordering proposed by the Arians.[29]

In other words, what Badiou is concerned with is finding a way to articulate a message that is seemingly unable to be articulated. The message of consubstantiality is one of a dialectical operation between what is and what is to come.

It might seem that relegating Christianity to a fable is enough to disempower the claims of its worldly authorities, but in actuality it is revealing of something deeply conservative within Badiou's thought. Badiou's philosophy vacillates between the extreme of supporting absolute revolution and ultimately finding no way to express this desire or even the actuality of such a revolution outside of the terms already given. As he writes in his *Logics of Worlds*, "As we've already said, the Christian paradox (which for us is one of the possible names for the paradox of truths) is that eternity must be encountered in time."[30] The question remains: does modeling one's revolutionary philosophy upon orthodox Christology really confront us with eternity in time or does it merely provide a divine cover over the world. In other words, in religious terms, does Badiou's philosophy not remain all-too-worldly?

Badiou notes in *Theory of the Subject* that the imaginary and theology provide an advantage that is found in working out such paradoxes in fabulous and affective language, but he recognizes that these fables have a dark side. He writes: "To enjoy them [the advantages of the imaginary and of theology] to the fullest, the heretics must be burned. Which is, it must be admitted, quite real."[31] Badiou's subtractive method, with regards to his Christology, fails precisely because it treats religion and theology as mere fable and does not treat their "quite real" aspects, like the burning of heretics, in the same way. It is not just eternity that must be encountered within time – tales of eternity and the material structures that organize and safeguard them must also be encountered within the lived. It is to this that we turn with the Gnostic Christology found in Laruelle.

Christ, victim-in-person

At this stage, I want to return for a moment to Kierkegaard's *Practice in Christianity*. For there is a difference marked in Laruelle's heretical account of Christ that strikes me as fundamental if we are to see what differentiates his account from both Badiou's and Henry's. For both Badiou and Henry, there is a certain privileging of the institutions of Christianity that we have seen in the previous sections, a certain being beholden to orthodoxy. In Laruelle's account this is rejected and it is this *radical* separation of Christ from Christianity that moves us closer to the generic truth revealed in Christ. Consider, then, Kierkegaard's words again:

> So look at him once again, him the abased one! What effect does this sight produce? Should it not be able to move you in some way to want to suffer in a way akin to his suffering, to want to witness for the truth with the danger that just because of that you will have to suffer? If possible, forget for a moment everything you know of him; tear yourself away from the perhaps apathetic habitual way in which you know about him; approach it as if it were the first time you heard the story of his abasement. Or if you think you are not able to do that, well, then, let us help ourselves in another way, let us use the help of a child, a child who is not warped by having learned by rote a simple school assignment about Jesus Christ's suffering and death, a child who for the first time hears the story – let us see what the effect will be, if only we tell it fairly well.[32]

To forget everything that one knows about Christ, to forget what has been learned by rote in Kierkegaard's day, and what has been learned through the play of light and magic on the screens of movie theaters, televisions, and whatever other screens we watch today, to forget that and to see this as just the story of a human being – however innocent, however loving, however much others claimed he was God against his own demands not to tell anyone about him – means we simply watch, with childlike horror, a human being murdered. Nevertheless, he is not particularly brutally murdered nor is it a particularly unjust injustice, despite what Kierkegaard tells us his hypothetical child would think.

Such an injustice is enough. This is where Laruelle begins his engagement with Christology, separating out Christianity from Christ. He writes, "What an error in ever having said the 'essence of Christianity'...Man is without essence and he removes the essence of Christianity more so than Christ removed the sins of the World."[33] Unlike both Badiou and Henry, Laruelle is more explicit in his account of the identity of Christianity and his heretical stance toward it. We will first examine that heretical nature before turning to look with more depth at the secular Christology he develops. Christianity, for Laruelle, is not simply a fable as it is for Badiou, nor is it the bearer of a culture safeguarding Truth and Life as it is for Henry. Instead, Christianity, or as he calls it here "the-Christianity [*le-Christianisme*]" – or what we might translate more idiomatically as "Christianity-with-a-capital-C" – is "that mixture that we know, in its infinite tensions between faith, dogma, temporal and spiritual authority, which yet hopes to confess an ecumenical faith from a common origin – a unitary aggregate validated by common sense, history, and finally theology and philosophy brought together."[34] In other words, Christianity is just another material created by human beings that can be worked with, that can be used to burn the flesh of other human beings, that can be a source of creative resistance to the world, and that can be repeated without the institutions of Christianity.

But in this way Christianity and Christ are separated. Christianity becomes just another material through which the "messianity" of Christ is manifest. It is important to emphasize this Docetic aspect of Laruelle's Christology, its unorthodox direction, precisely because, amongst the few things written on Laruelle and theology, there has been an attempt to neutralize Laruelle's challenge and bring his non-philosophy under a Christian *mandatum* – or formal recognition of full communion between a teacher and the Christian Church – that he never signed.

This attempt is made by Gabriel Alkon and Boris Gunjevic in their article "Theology and Non-Philosophy," found in the collection of Laruelle's essays they edited entitled *The Non-Philosophy Project*. Their essay is thin on citations, but this aspect of their essay is forgivable considering Laruelle's own practice of theory as living thought and his emphasis not on the history of philosophy but on the construction of theory. So, even though there are issues with their essay on the level of scholarship, I do not think that this is really where any criticism should operate if it wants to get to the heart of the matter. Rather, any critique of this kind of writing has to take place in the science of theology – what I've termed elsewhere as "non-theology." From such a perspective, aiming to identify and disempower the self-sufficiency of theology, what Alkon and Gunjevic miss in their advocacy of the centrality of Christianity is precisely the way this would inscribe a principle of sufficient (Christian) theology in the place of the principle of sufficient philosophy. The authors at one point write: "But why...does Laruelle focus on the figure of Christ? Why does Laruelle invoke *this* name? The answer cannot be, as Laruelle sometimes suggests, that he is simply making non-religious use of given religious and theological material."[35] Why couldn't the answer be the one Laruelle gives? Well, Alkon and Gunjevic tell us the reason is that Laruelle connects his most recent work very strongly to the figure of Christ, which is true, but that does not mean there is any necessity there either! What we see the editors doing here is something akin to when Pope Emeritus Benedict XVI said in his infamous "Regensburg Address" that there was a certain providence in Christianity, originally a Jewish religious movement, merging with Greek philosophy and European culture. It turns something completely contingent, ultimately insufficient, into something necessary, and absolutely sufficient unto itself. What the authors are claiming is that Christianity has no need of non-philosophy, but non-philosophy secretly needs Christianity. This is perhaps Christianity's oldest trick, at least as it plays out in philosophy, for Christianity is necessary because, like the capitalism which it provided fecund with ground to grow out of, it can always overcode anything that comes before it.

At one point the editors try to argue that Christian theology already has put forward some of the central ideas of non-philosophy, like Laruelle's theory of the "given-without-givenness" of things since the pure transcendence of God is immanent in creation as a gift (more true of Jewish and Islamic monotheism). And here they point toward, though do not develop, a more interesting theme concerning the role of transcendence and immanence in non-philosophy. For Laruelle, transcendence isn't rejected, but instead is made relative to its genesis in radical immanence. Which means, of course, that transcendence is no longer transcendence as its boosters would like to present it: it is no longer absolute or redoubled. But Alkon and Gunjevic try to move us toward the notion that transcendence, theologically understood, isn't really like this. Instead, they write:

> Transcendence is internal to the structure of things that exist in mutual determining relation to each other, a relation that is *positive* and not just differential or dialectical; and so transcendence cannot, even in-the-last-instance, be foreclosed from any form of worldly knowledge. Transcendence *as such* is foreclosed: that which gives the world as a whole is as unknowable for theology as it is for non-philosophy; the doctrine of creation insists that the world is given without a philosophically recoverable givenness.[36]

What else is this but a "weaponized apophaticism?" That is, transcendence here is said to be positive – meaning we ought to be able to engage with it, to see it – but it is positive in such a way that its positivity cannot be confronted like the positivity of all other things: it is both positive and above engagement, thereby making any rebellion against transcendence, against the underlying structure of the world, impossible. For what you would be rebelling against is simply an appearance, while the truth underlying the appearance always slips away. It is an unsaying, but this time it is the unsaying of creatures – the denial of their dignity – always in the name of the creator.

The authors are deploying old theological tricks, analogous to the philosophical ones Laruelle rejects, that require the humiliation of human beings in the face of transcendence. And why? For Laruelle the point of emphasizing Christ over God the Father is that Christ is human, Christ is in-person, whereas God the Father, for Laruelle, has the same structure as Hell and the world, through their hallucinated transcendence and absolute sufficiency.[37] Non-Philosophy is a gnosis and as such it is a radical rejection of this world, not in the name of Michel Henry's transcendence-in-immanence, as the editors suggest, but in the Name-of-the-Human. What Alkon and Gunjevic want to do by insisting that Laruelle has a faith in the Christian version of Christ is to make non-philosophy submit, not to the Name-of-Man, but to the Christian tradition, all the while realizing that what fascinates Laruelle about Christ is that he refused to submit to tradition as such – for it isn't Jesus Christ of Christianity, but the Christ of victimized gnosis. Christ in this sense is much more akin to the heresy (to Christianity) of Docetism, as already mentioned. In this way, one could develop a non-theology out of Laruelle without any of the primacy that Alkon and Gunjevic think belong to the Christian version of Christ. One could look to Shi'a Islam and the Hidden Imam, or to Hinduism and its avatars, or any number of religious materials that are not Christianity. But in each case it wouldn't be enough simply to inscribe non-philosophy into those systems, as if it were the occasion of their thought, but, just as Laruelle does with Christianity, those systems have to be inscribed as occasions of human thought and practice. "Could Laruelle have articulated his non-religious faith without the direction provided by his personal belief [sic] in – his inclination towards, his attention to, his imagination of – Jesus Christ?," Alkon and Gunjevic ask us.[38] The only answer that rigorously holds to the principles of non-philosophy is, "No, because *Laruelle* did not. But that doesn't make it sufficient, it only makes it an occasion and other non-philosophers may do what Laruelle did not."

As in Kierkegaard, Laruelle's Christ is an abased one. A victim-in-person, which is the way that Laruelle signifies in writing a concept in actuality, or "flesh and blood" as he likes to say. What is present in Christ, not just the historical Christ of Christianity, but the plural Christs that appear throughout history, whether it be a Gnostic manifestation of Christ formerly hidden or the divine martyrdom of Imam Ali, is the disempowering of the vicious circle that is the dialectic of victim and oppressor – the refusal to let the identity of the human be determined by the death-dealing that comes from oppressors and the victors of history. The victim-in-person that are these Christs reveals a certain radical identity of humanity, a unilateral identity, in which the oppressor is denied their role and made ultimately relative in their autonomy to the radical autonomy of the victim, which is where this abasement becomes insurrectionary. Laruelle writes, "Radical humanity, non-ontological, is *proven* when men are murdered and persecuted. The performation of their being-murdered and burned is in the manifestation and only persecution reveals as such the victim's irreducible non-consistency, only that non-consistency determined death as that of a human subject rather than of a 'beast.'"[39] "Beast" here refers to the notion that the human is just some brute living thing, a concept that is overturned in the rebellion of victims against their oppressors that is both endless in the sense of eternal and end-less in the sense of having no true *telos*. From this point of view, Laruelle claims:

> *onto-biological death is already defeated by Man-in-Man* [i.e. the human manifest in nothing but the human, without relation to some *logos*]. The prosecution of the world against the heretical Christ reveals the already-defeated-death and therefore New Life from which we thus understand the irreducibility to the world. Not that the historical Christ's sacrifice had been the necessary condition for that victory. Human death can only be in-the-last-identity the effect of the hallucination brought about by the world of Man-in-person, with the constitutive repression of the subject.[40]

In other words, it is human beings who kill human beings; the reasons for doing so are ultimately hallucinations, projections that cover over the radical immanence and common name of the victims with their oppressors. This is a fact that brings judgment upon the heads of the oppressors and speaks to a radical freedom of the victims. And it is this victimological reading of Christology that avoids Laruelle's Docetism turning into some defense of new age cults or an inability to evaluate when someone is suffering from Jerusalem Syndrome.

Ultimately, Laruelle's engagement with Christology combines the most interesting elements of both Henry's and Badiou's. For here we see the combination of Henry's radical immanence of the human with the subtractive method of Badiou.[41] Both are ultimately taken farther in Laruelle than in either Henry or Badiou, precisely because Laruelle's drive to separate out Christ from Christianity allows him to avoid the mistake of tying his engagement to the idealism necessary for holding to but an aspect of the Christian tradition. This idealism is present in Badiou, when he turns away from the real burning of heretics, and is present in Henry when he considers Christ only as the triumphant Christ of orthodox, institutional scriptures. Laruelle's Christ is ultimately contingent, but for that reason all the more revealing of the true abasement and power of Christ.

Theory of the Future Christ

So, why is philosophy concerned with Christ? Is it just piety, as it may seem with Henry; a bit of playfulness, as it may seem with Badiou; or is it something a bit more interesting, a bit more theoretically interesting, as I want to suggest it is with Laruelle? What even counts as "interesting," since this word's normal function in this field is to politely acknowledge another intellectual's work: "Oh, that sounds interesting," we politely say and move on. I hold "interesting" in this case to refer to something that disrupts philosophy's normal mode of functioning, that breaks philosophy's drive to be respectable in this world. Engaging with the material of religion – both the intellectual traditions that constitute religion and their practices – will simply be another instance of philosophy's drive toward domination, toward self-sufficiency, rather than the mutation of philosophy for a mode of thought that isn't worldly, made for humans and other creatures, instead of being made for the hallucinations we create.

There has been an assumption made throughout our remarks – an assumption shared with Kierkegaard, who has framed this chapter, but also with the other great nineteenth-century philosopher, Nietzsche. This assumption holds that Christ was an event in the world, but an event that has been obscured. For these two great anti-Christian thinkers, the radicality and contemporary nature of Christ are obscured by Christendom (Kierkegaard) or already betrayed by the so-called slave morality of St. Paul (Nietzsche). For any true secular philosophical engagement with Christ, one must go a step beyond the nineteenth century, where so much Continental philosophy of religion has remained, ripping apart the identity of Christianity into a true Christianity, one that lies at the core of the message of Christ: a worldly Christianity. From here, philosophy of religion has fallen prey to a trap of its own creation. Unable to bring together the ideal with the actual or concrete, it has either had to reject the edifice of Christianity altogether, at best merely tolerating it as in Marx's philosophy, or found itself strangely defending the Christian legacy as able to go beyond itself into the European version of the secular. All of this is ultimately blind to the invention of Christianity and the subsequent invention of religion and the secular as categories dependent upon Christianity as institutionalized in Europe and its colonial projects.[42]

This is the trap that Badiou and Henry fall into with regard to their relatively orthodox Christologies. Both thinkers have a vision of the world that follows this same split between the ideal and the actual that is only reconciled in appeals to paradox, but paradox does not think an unsplit object even if it brings attention to the difficulty inherent in such a thought. For Badiou, it is Christianity's paradox of eternity encountered in time that is taken as a model for the faithful subject, and for Henry it is the paradox of attempting to think a radical immanence separate from the world that ends up creating a Christian world. The secular engagement with Christology that we find in philosophy will continue as long as philosophy cares about the ultimate questions of human being and the salvation of humanity. But if we are to think Christ in a way that is truly radical, we must think Christ separate from eternity and from the Christian world. As Laruelle says, "Through their divinity religions think of themselves auto-foundationally, refusing to be born or being born from an ageless process."[43] This must be reversed. Rather than ripping the object apart in order to think it, the philosopher of religion who wants to truly encounter Christ (that is, the generic human), the philosopher must then begin to think of Christianity as having an identity. So a more interesting engagement with Christ and with Christianity cannot simply play this old philosophical game, but must engage in a rigorous critique and mutation of this material. Engaging with Christ in the light of Christianity must be like going to a respectable midnight mass on Christmas Eve, surrounded by the droves of respectable families, but, during the sharing of the peace, you realize that you must now shake hands not just with these respectable types but also with the homeless who have come in for warmth. That sickly sweet smell of a dirty human body, a human body in pain, ravaged by a climate and an economy. Dirty. You have to touch him. But in the liturgical practice of "sharing of the peace," in the touching of this man, you cannot think that this moment is the truth of an ideal Christianity and the other historical form of Christianity that is more respectable and more worldly is some mere appearance. This split object is Christianity, fraught as it is with contradictions – not paradoxes – but the homeless person is Christ radically separated from even this split object.

Those in the Continental tradition doing a kind of philosophy of religion are concerned with Christ, and the reasons are not so obscure. Christ names something human, a hope beyond this world, a human and divine protest against the way things are. It is not simply piety, though there is some of that, nor is it simply playfulness: the murder of a human subject in the world is a real thing. But if this concern is to be interesting and productive, then we must separate out the confrontation with Christ that Kierkegaard speaks of from the Churches that bear his name. For the actuality of these Churches is that this protest has gone cold, it has died the death of overfamiliarity. For the original message of those who followed the historical Christ was that a peasant was put to death by the State and that this murdered peasant was resurrected and is God. It is as if we are looking into the eyes not of a bronzed white actor but a black death row inmate. It is as if Troy Davis, put to death by the State of Georgia in September of 2011, were looking at us and asked, "Who do you say that I am?," and we answered back "You are the Christ." Philosophy has shown that it can think Christology, despite the protests of Kierkegaard, but can philosophy think the ordinary human victim as Christ and still remain philosophy, or must it be transformed into something a bit more human and, following Laruelle's *homo sive scientia* equivocation, a bit more *scientific*? It is this question we will now attend to as we move deeper into Laruelle's Christology.

At the basis of Laruelle's description of the Future Christ (or Christ-subject – the two terms are equivalent) is the idea that the radical immanence of Man-in-Man is cloned as a subject with different materials which give that subject its particular, intentional modality as differentiated from its presentation as a transcendental illusion or Christ-world:

> Now who is this "we" who suspend their faith and refuse to give into faith? It is certainly not planetary or worldly philosophers, those who do not wonder what to make of the World-in-person. It is the

"we" of the Future Christ, the Christ-subject who we are without
having by hope or obedience identified in ourselves as such, identifying that we are already in every way as Man-in-Man, subjects
merged with their non-Christian performance. The theory of the
Future Christ is the immanent practice of its theory; our only faith
is practical and additionally a pragmatic of the old Christianity.[44]

One of the aspects of non-philosophy that is often maligned but
misunderstood is Laruelle's distaste for so-called examples, the
idea being that words like "Christ-world," "Man-in-Man," "Christ-
subject," or the like are just jargon for already-understood ideas
that these jargonistic terms can be reduced to. But Man-in-Man and
the Christ-subject are not representations, they are theoretical practices. To understand them, one has to *understand them*. Reducing
things to other things is not the full practice of thought, but practicing thought is more closely related to religious practices or scientific practices than philosophers often realize. For example, the
practice of a religious faith is never simply a matter of assenting to
some belief = X, but that belief = X is always inscribed in a number
of religious practices like prayer, confession, reading, writing,
giving alms to the poor, and so on. With regard to the theoretical
practice of non-Christianity, it is a matter of bringing assistance to
the world, of saving the world even though one's identity is radically separate from the world, by way of knowing or modeling the
world theoretically. As Laruelle himself puts it regarding his theory
of non-Christianity and the Christ-subject, "*thinking it is already to
practice it.*"[45]

    That said, without reducing these ideas to some already prede-
termined meaning, what exactly do they model? They model precisely what elements are at work in what can be done with religion,
specifically Christianity. What can be done with Christianity? Well,
quite simply, it can be turned into a material that will be generically
useful to humanity in dispelling the transcendental illusion that
human beings are something other than a radically lived humanity.
In a less twisted manner, we can say Christianity can be used, when
one no longer ascribes as a Christian but instead as oneself a Christ-
subject, to assist in showing that human beings are not reducible
to something else, that human beings have a radical identity prior
to subsumption of any transcendental term. "Man-in-Man" names
that aspect of one's humanity that is always foreclosed, or unable
to be understood relationally, to the world. "The Christ-subject"
("Future Christ") names the way that this Man-in-Man is cloned as

a subject using religious material. And "the Christ-world" is a kind of figure of the Anti-Christ, always already caught up in the identity of Christ given by the various churches, where Christ is taken as transcendent and sufficient. Laruelle summarizes his entire theory of the Future Christ in one of my favorite quotes from that work, which captures how non-philosophy is able to mutate and make use of religion as well as the immanent reason for the theory of the Future Christ in general. There he writes:

> With the cloning of every man as *subject*, humans, despite or because of their in-sufficiency, take up existing under the form of an *organon*, precisely the Future Christ, the authentic relationship to the World and to history in totality rather than in the manner of their phenomena. The old Christ had been conceived in transcendence and the World (in sin?), he was without doubt an organon but still on the model of mediation or instrument (for a reaction or rebirth). Christianity cannot overcome its failing of identity and faith by a profusion of churches and orders, of dogmas and authorities, saints and priests, actions and ritual operations. The Future Christ rather signifies that each man is a Christ-organon, that is to say, of course, the Messiah, but simple and unique once each time. This is minimal Christianity. We the Without-religion, the Without-church, the heretics of the future, we are, each-and-everyone, a Christ or Messiah. ... By its practice, this is only a half-programme, only unilateral, of a constitution of the Christ-subject giving aid to the World and against it.[46]

Gnostic hatred of the world

Philosophers love the world too much. Husserl wants to reaffirm the life-world, Heidegger obsesses with being-in-the-World, even Deleuze laments that we no longer believe in this world, while Badiou teases out the very logic of how worlds are formed. In some sense this explains why French philosophy is always so compromised with Christianity. Yet there are some who hate the world. Perhaps the most extreme case – and for that extremity all the more interesting – is in the early work of Jambet and Lardreau. Although not well known in the Anglophone world, their co-authored work *L'Ange* is an attempt to think the radical break with the world, with the way things are, so as to think a revolution that would be one, that would be an actual revolution.[47] Their attempt to think such a radical break proceeds through an investigation of the structural similarity between the early Gnostic-Christian ascetic communities which attempted to overturn culture: not just ideology (merely replacing one master for another), but an overturning of the very culture of masters and slaves. This theory rose out of the many cultural revolutions taking place in the late 1960s and 1970s. Of these cultural revolutions, the most notable was, of course, in China, but perhaps the most catastrophic was the one that took place in Cambodia. The second co-authored work by Jambet and Lardreau is the mark of failure that follows their revolutionary angel, for after declaring their fascination with and theoretical suturing to the Khmer Rouge they then witnessed the brutality that characterized the regime in Cambodia. This manifested as an attempt to make peace with "the World" in their *Le Monde*.[48] While it is unfair to lump their work in with that of the *nouveau philosophes*, as it was and sometimes still is, there is a similar trajectory that moves from this desire for a complete overturning of things, for an apocalypse and a making of all things new, to a settling with and into the world, with the way things are structured.

This movement from fervor to failure, from revolution to death, is a story that seems to me common to the religious mystics, fanatics, heretics, and even established figures we often look to with fascination, and who cause us to think that there may be a form of living as if immortal, withdrawn and indifferent to the world as such. But the comfort of the world so often turns us away from the undecidable moment of either madness or holiness manifest there. The work of Laruelle attends to and tries to generalize what happens in this holy foolishness. For the religious materials of mysticism, messianism, and gnosis don't just have an allure for him, but are a material that actually helps him to practice theory, to think through problems in his project that he has named "non-philosophy," and more recently "non-standard philosophy." Specifically, it allows him to avoid the fall – that Jambet and Lardreau experienced – from the angel to the world. And this is not something that comes late in Laruelle's career, as, since its earliest instantiation, Laruelle has declared that non-philosophy is a mysticism, even as it consistently declares itself a science.[49] And it is precisely because both are effects of the Human-in-Human that have forms which protect this lived (reality of the) human. Laruelle turns to gnosticism (or simply "gnosis" since it is not a tradition in the sense that Christianity is) because it performs a thinking of the human. The figure of the Christ, or Future Christ, is the figure of such a human salvation and such a generic humanity.

The strange appellation "Future Christ" used by Laruelle may bring up many questions for readers and it certainly wouldn't seem to touch on a project that, at first, was known for its radical valorization of science and the attempt to think the relationship between philosophy and science anew. Yet the relationship between the particular subject formation discussed in *Future Christ* and the various attempts to bring together theory and practice are all part of the same fundamental project. For underlying non-philosophical practice is the axiom of relative autonomy for all things, a kind of equality at the level of causality and effect, since both the human and science or religion are relative to or caused by the Real. This notion of relative autonomy allows the non-philosopher a kind of flat ontology, without ascribing any form of sufficiency to this ontology or to ontology in general, since it too is just an effect of the Real. The world is not just a human construct and the inhuman elements of science and religion (tannins in wine or the history of the Eucharist) do have their own actual powers, but to confuse this flat ontology with a being itself (as all ontologies tend toward) is an act of auto-inclusion or co-determination of the Real it describes.

Laruelle has been making explicit references to gnosticism since at least his 1981 book *Le Principe de minorité*, in which we first see his twin interests in religion and science emerge, but in *Future Christ* Laruelle makes this nascent connection between non-philosophy and gnosis most explicit. There he writes, "Gnosis, above all Mandaean Gnosis, along with Christianity, is one of the greatest thinkings about Life, and it wants to radically distinguish itself from the thought of Being without always reaching precisely there for the reasons of philosophy."[50] Gnosis, as a largely forgotten and murdered religious and philosophical practice, is to be valued for its irreductive thinking – a thinking that aimed (though ultimately failed, according to Laruelle) to think the radical identity of things separate and withdrawn from any kind of totalizing sufficiency. In other words, the popular image of the Gnostics (whom Laruelle entreats us to remember no longer exist because they were all murdered and turned into victims) as anti-body covers over the truth of their real object of critique. For what we take to be the Gnostics' hatred of the material is actually hatred of the world, of this-World, of the notion that life radically had to submit to or enclose itself within the identity of the world and therein lose itself.

The world is such an important concept for non-philosophy, albeit in a negative mode, that it is considered to be an element of both the vocabulary of non-philosophy and the syntax, as we have already seen. To review, in Laruelle's "Glossary Raisonné" to *Future Christ*, he gives us this definition of "world" as vocabulary: "Other name for philosophy under its two forms. Philosophy is world-shaped, the World is thought-world."[51] In the form of syntax, "world" is deployed by Laruelle to further "world-shape" other forms of material taken by philosophy as something it can dominate: "A composition by addition of the suffix '-world' to the term in question (God-world, Christ-world, etc.) indicates a sense of sufficiency."[52] And, of course, sufficiency is the "pretension of philosophy to co-determine the Real or Man who is foreclosed for it."[53] The resistance to this sufficiency is not some childish act of rebellion against philosophical adults who know better – rather, the struggle, rebellion, or revolt against the world arises out of the fact of its failure: "The divine creation – the World – is a failure, this knowledge is one thing gnosis was assured of."[54]

So the messiah, the future Christ, is not of this world and there is a radical separation of human-in-person and the world: this is the central gnostic impulse of non-philosophy. But non-philosophy moves past the traditional and disappeared practice of gnosis insofar as it does not aim for a total destruction of this world. The world, as an image of sufficiency, remains material, and, indeed, Laruelle says:

> If it is necessary to start again completely differently from that failed knowledge that is philosophy, we do not simply reject it on religious grounds like the ancient gnosis rejected the World as evil and illusion. *It is our only material*, and the science that the Moderns have acquired meanwhile gives us a means of knowing, that is to say of modeling, that complex object, failed knowledge, and a means of making use of it on the basis of Man-in-person who is not modern or ancient. We are the new Gnostics who think that there is a salvation even from evil. Philosophy, form of the World, is our prison but the prison has the form of a hallucination and a transcendental illusion, not the form of flesh – it is itself knowable.[55]

So Laruelle's struggle against the world is always a struggle not only against the bad demiurge, but against the bad theoretician, "the Philosopher or the Theologian, who have created a failed knowledge."[56] And thus salvation is always a matter of saving gnosis, of a theoretical practice that allows human beings to craft something completely different from the failure of divine creation, the world that begins in a kind of hatred of the world.

Some may ask why this hatred of the world is desirable. Even in popular secular discourse, there is a general feeling that gnostic theory is to be avoided and is a bit too extreme, too fanatical. For Laruelle this gnostic element still does important philosophical work. It manifests the radical separation of the human from the world just discussed. Before moving on, I want to take a few more minutes to make sure that this is understood properly along with the same lines as Laruelle understands the gnostics specifically. It is not that this separation is a claim about humanity's separation from the physical elements of lives, the conditions for existence, the creatures that populate the earth, the trees, the air, and whatever else, but "the world" names also the way we try to take these all together as a sufficient All or Whole. The identity of the human struggles against those structures, it struggles against those structures that try to pass themselves off as what truly determines one's identity, one's place in this world. And it is with the maligned gnostics that we see this most radically, according to Laruelle, because they not only thought and theorized this separation, but manifest it in their being murdered.

As I've argued consistently over the past few chapters, Laruelle attempts to think a more radical identity of the human than did attempts at universal humanity we find in the Enlightenment tradition of a largely Greek philosophical origin, as well as one more radical than the Other in the French Jewish thinkers Laruelle has been heavily influenced by. This task remains that of discovering "generic man," that common name we continue to return to which does not make the European mistake of elevating a particular image as the universal, or the mistake of thinking there is no common name or figure. For Laruelle this genericness is seen in part in the contingency, finitude, and struggle of victims, their manifestation as humans who are oppressed but reassert themselves against the structure that aims to determine and alienate them in their oppression. This struggle between a world that sees nothing of special significance in the aspects that make it up – and the creatural life that is right to rebel – is more generically the burned-up flesh and blood of heretics rather than the singular instance of the burnt-out memory of the Shoah.[57] Laruelle takes great pains not to denigrate the disaster and violence that befell a people, but he refuses, rightly I think, to allow for this singular instance to stand as the only instance of radical evil, to stand as the measure of the crime against humanity. As we already saw in chapter 5, for Laruelle, what differentiates these two murders is that the murder of the Jews is a singular horror captured in memory and the murder of gnostics is forgotten. No one is called to account for the crimes against the gnostics, no one re-members them, so they only remain insofar as the crime itself "immanes" in their flesh and blood – they only persist in the fact that these were human beings for whom no one has built a cathedral of memory, no one has reinscribed the crime into a cultural economy. They suffer unilaterally in this way, forever victims never bringing revenge or emerging as victors before the law.

But Laruelle sees that this hatred of the world can lead to a mere simple reversal. He even writes, "What is more hopeless than a Principle of Sufficient Rebellion?"[58] In other words, Laruelle isn't blind to the way that rebellion can become sufficient, can burn up everything, overcode everything and erase the human. Rebellion, while it is privileged insofar as it reveals something about the identity of the human, must not be taken to determine the human. The human determines rebellion. He tempers the hatred of the world, then, not in the name of the world, but in the Name-of-Man. He discusses this in the opening of *Struggle and Utopia at the End Times of Philosophy* (2004, and 2012 in English translation), in which he writes: "Non-philosophy is an attempt at a reply to perhaps the most determining if not unique question of science fiction and gnosis: *should we save humanity?* and *What do we mean by humanity?* Towards this end, non-philosophy raises the generic name of man to the level of a proper noun and places it under the sign of the Name-of-Man."[59] It is under this Name-of-Man that Laruelle deepens his understanding of the way rebellion can burn itself out and become a problem for understanding generic man if you aim simply to burn up the whole world. He distinguishes his notion of rebellion from such a self-destructive one writing that he:

> [calls] back into question the axiom that it is right to revolt, refusing that there is some sufficient reason in rebellion, that would be to deny rebellion, distinguish rebellion from every reflex of auto or self-defense, of vengeance or hatred, posit an *a priori* defense of man which would not be a self-defense or auto-rebellion. The problem of rebellion is one of risking the introduction of resentment and reaction into the struggle against "mastery" and so returning to the war, to the project of waging war against war.... We must think a mastery that is not merely a reaction but an occasion, a human (non-)action that is pure force of action-without-reaction."[60]

Indifference to the world and assistance to the human

So how does Laruelle develop this "action-without-reaction?" By turning to the mystical tradition. If a philosophical engagement with religious material is going to be interesting, then it has to do some productive theoretical work for what is being produced. Laruelle has tried to bring about just such a superposition of mysticism and philosophy since his early work, but most notably in his major work *Principles of Non-Philosophy*. In standard philosophical terms, this is a book about epistemology and metaphysics, explicitly trying to create a "unified theory of philosophy and science," but there he finds it necessary to bring in the mystical in order to make such a theory function. He writes:

> We distinguish mystique and the mystical [*la mystique et le mystique*]. Mystique is an experience of the soul's identity with transcendence. It therefore entails transcendence *within* a certain immanence, a mix of the two; it does not separate the soul from transcendence through a real mode but rather ties it to transcendence; finally it makes immanence a property or attribute of the relation of the soul and of God rather than a subject-essence as such. On the other hand, we call the mystical a real and actual essence, an already-performed-without-performation as we will call it, an absolutely autonomous instance rather than an attribute, property, event or relation. This essence therefore no longer involves transcendence, rather it excludes it absolutely. The "reduction" of the soul is confused with this essence; it is not immanence to transcendence, to a subject or a substance, to the Soul or God, but (to) itself.[61]

This is a reference to the fourteenth-century Christian mystical theologian Meister Eckhart – something common in French philosophy – even though it could just as easily be a reference to the ninth-century Muslim mystic Mansur al-Hallaj – but it is to Eckhart that Laruelle turns more explicitly in his later investigation of mysticism: *Mystique non-philosophique à l'usage des contemporarins* (2007, and forthcoming in an English translation as *Non-Philosophical Mysticism for Today*). There, when discussing the format of the book, he makes one of the few direct references to Christian religious figures, writing that the book conjugates (a term used in reference to both its biological and grammatical senses) heretical thought with "Christian and Neo-Platonic mysticism through Eckhart and

Russian Hesychasm, the general sense of which we invert, giving primacy to the Real as Man-in-Man rather than to God or the Deity."[62]

Laruelle is marked by many of the usual elements of Eckhart's influence on some of France's radical thinkers. Most notably, of course, is the influence you find in thinkers like Henry where the kind of radical immanence found in Eckhart is taken as inspiration for a fuller philosophical account of how ipseity manifests itself. Henry often quotes Sermon 6 in which (in Henry's specific formulation of the German) Eckhart declared, "God engenders himself as myself." And it is this kind of working-out of identity that Laruelle picks up as well. What is arguably distinctive about Laruelle's engagement with Eckhart is the focus on and subsequent recasting of the kind of detachment that follows and under-determines this kind of mystical sense of identity. Eckhart's remarks on detachment are well known even outside of the narrow discipline of mystical theology and are, if not completely enigmatic, at the very least extremely challenging. He writes, explicitly against St. Paul, "But I extol detachment above any love."[63] Indeed, "only pure detachment surpasses all things, for all virtues have regard to creatures, but detachment is free of all creatures."[64] In other words, as Bernard McGinn explains, "What becomes clear is that detachment is not just another virtue, such as love and humility, but is the form, or perhaps better, the ground of all virtues."[65] There is in Eckhart's kind of transcendental detachment something of the gnostic hatred for the world, but is this the most interesting and edifying way we can read this passage? Doesn't this detachment exactly give us the answer for how to bring about a rebellion that would be an action-without-reaction?

Laruelle's reading indeed suggests something that is to my mind more interesting. For Laruelle reads Eckhart's real target not as the singular and significant creatures-in-person or creatures-in-creatures (creating our own formulation using Laruelle's grapheme or formal way of signifying identity or radical immanence), but rather as the way that concern for the apparatus or machinery of creatures – i.e. the world – tries to overdetermine identity, whereby such rebellion woven into the fabric of the world and driven to blind rage at the harassment of the world can only but desire to burn it all down, to find a form of peace in the immanence of flame. Laruelle takes this detachment even further when he writes "the detachment of the subject is carried out without any relation not just to "creatures," but neither in relation to Being or God, rather it is carried out by a unilateralization of their correlation which is the World."[66]

But such detachment still requires a supplement for Laruelle – a supplement that is grounded (Laruelle would use the term "underdetermined") upon this detachment and flows out of it, but that is precisely an action. This action is the construction of names, a giving of assistance to the world, using theory to free up the world from itself and its assumed sufficiency – but a theory that is modeling its object in a way that unifies the object and the theory, creating a superposition between the two: not a synthesis, but a genuine identity separate from the dialectical process or the *logos*. For that, Laruelle takes his inspiration from the Hesychasts, a group within the Eastern Orthodox Church who practice both silence and the repetitive saying of the name "Jesus." Their detachment is manifested in this silence and in the simple utterance of the name "Jesus!" What interests Laruelle about this tradition is that it was a form of Christian mysticism delivered from philosophical over-determination while using, in some sense, many of the same techniques of Neo-Platonic philosophy that was and is so pervasive in the theological scene of Christianity. The practice of it varies, but it essentially is an attempt to practice in *prayer* a similar kind of detachment to that championed by Eckhart through an attempt to think "no thing," to withdraw even from God in order to reach union with God:

> Certain mystics have understood that the cry, the brief succinct and repeated jaculation [i.e. the utterance doesn't go outward] ("Jesus!") was the epekeniaphoric [not metaphoric] speech and that it should delight conceptual theological discourse in an ecstasy of non-sense. If another step is necessary to make theological discourse invalid, it cannot consist in a supplementary transcendence of speech, but rather in the radical impoverishing of the Logos, something like the empty axiomatic cry, the symbolized and formalized cry no longer adding itself to the cry in order to form a Logos. "God," World," "Man," "Christ," these are such as p, q, r, or x, y, z, the cries of a transcendental formalism.[67]

In other words, what Laruelle sees in the Hesychasts is an empty but immanently productive practice that can be used by philosophers in order to free themselves from the thought-world of philosophy, that can be a kind of way of disempowering the world while yet remaining in it – a way to be free and in that freedom assist the world as it, in its creatural forming, moves away from itself as sufficient and absolute. This is illustrative of the link that Laruelle locates between heresy and mysticism. He writes,

> We know why mysticism has always stood alongside heresy – it is paradoxically speculative and simple, claiming to overcome the order of philosophy and onto-theo-logy, even fulfilling them, using their conditions in order to address reputedly "simple" souls. The "vulgar" predication of "subtleties" risks dogmatic error and "catholic" unintelligibility. *The conjugation of speculation and the "poor in spirit," the effacing of the hierarchy between the simple and learned*, the collusion of humility and transcendence through *epekeina*, the setting of the *meta* between parentheses, well there we see an intolerable short-circuit, a "heresy" meaning something that cannot take on a catholic meaning even after explication as the burning-stake makes its argument with burning brilliance.[68]

In other words, we are all threatened a bit with being burned at the stake. None of us are particularly safe from the world, but we have a desire for something other than the world anyway. That is, we want good news. But can such a theoretical engagement really be translated into practice, into social and political action-without-reaction? Well, when Laruelle writes, *"The desire for God is the eternal form of Hell, the Bad News concealed [dissimulée] within the supposed Good News,"*[69] he is making a real claim about our experience in the world, for God (not Christ, but the Father) in this formulation and our desire for God is the form of the Big Other, our Golems that we create and turn upon us – it is a desire that leads to violence, but, more so, that leads us to commit violence.

Even if Laruelle does not have the desire for God-the-Father, he does have a certain desire for the *a-priori* defense of the Human, of the Victim-in-person, in a way that is very different from a banal and ultimately harassing form of humanism. He has a desire for salvation, even for fulfilling the function of this refractory world, which is a machine for the making of Gods or at least creatures. It is a machine then, and so something that can be worked and produce. And this machine includes our religious theories, our religious experiences, *our mysticism*. We can create theories that free us, that disempower our violence-producing narratives. He writes: "Mystic-fiction is nothing other than a *spiritual exercise without spiritual things but with immanent rules*, with imperatives performed in-the-last-Humaneity."[70] Mystic-fiction and Christo-fiction are forms of struggle in thought, which, while not sufficient or absolute or all-determining, are not nothing – and may be a great deal more

as is evidenced by the way he brings together this Christology with his understanding of science.

From the Future Christ to generic messianity

Laruelle's interests in material outside philosophy, whether it is science, religion, or something else, has always had a dual nature in that it was never "just science" or "just religion," but the two somehow always arise in his thinking together. So it is unsurprising that Laruelle develops his theory of the Christ-subject, moving from the Future Christ to a generic messianity in his 2010 work *Philosophie non-standard*. Here Laruelle aims to "achieve" non-philosophy by bringing together philosophy material with the material of quantum physics, banging them together in a virtual particle collider, and it is the figure of Christ that comes to speak to the subject that science requires if science is going to be put to the work of assistance spoken about in *Future Christ* and discussed above. There he writes:

> It is of course strange to speak of messianity as concerning the human cause of the science of philosophy, even though the notion of "determination-in-the-last-instance" should have set down the path of this completely apparent paradox....Here Christ is the simple historico-concrete model of genericity under the form of the superposition of the One and the Multiple, a mediation which "saves," as generic, human subjects.[71]

And, yes, it is indeed strange to speak of messianity in this way! Messianity translates the French neologism "messianité," and indicates an activity, rather than the usual messianism, which would refer to a constellation of ideas. Of course, Laruelle is not saying that these ideas are not active, but he is directing our attention by focusing on the active element here. This is not the place to examine the concept of determination-in-the-last-instance in detail, but what Laruelle is indicating by creating a kind of equivalence between messianity and the human cause of science is that messianity is the real cause of science. That science, whether it be the science of physics or the science of Christ (theology or Christology, more precisely), arises out of a certain messianic act. But what does Laruelle think this act consists in? Simply, it is a kind of embodiment, not of a worldly identity, but a generic identity between the

irreducibility of one's individual identity and the individual multiplicity of humankind.

This is what the "superposition of the One and the Multiple"
refers to. Superposition is an incredibly interesting phenomenon,
one that the scientist and phenomenologist Peter Steeves thinks can
help unify biological and cosmological theories in line with the
work of Lee Smolin, in a way that is not altogether different from
Laruelle's own advocacy of a proliferation of unified theories.[72]
When two wave-particles are in superposition with one another
they can be expressed by a non-philosophical re-expression of
mathematical idempotence as "$1 + 1 = 1$," referring to the fact that
when these two waves are superposed with one another they don't
produce a synthesis but instead their individual identities remain
while a new third identity is produced that nevertheless remains
those two waves at the same time. When two particles are in superposition, when one particle spins the other particle also spins in an
opposite and equal way, meaning that the spin is always balanced
between the two. This is what Laruelle is calling the generic identity expressed by the historical Christ. There is some relationship,
a kind of media-without-mediation – which is to say, without
synthesis – between the One and the Multiple that is developed in
this non-philosophical unified theory of philosophy and quantum
mechanics.

In Laruelle's recent work, the generic functions as a matrix
within which thought develops; a generic matrix provides certain
determinations for thought (the matrix itself is determined not by
a meta-matrix, but by its in-One character). Laruelle's formulation
of this generic, which characterizes this matrix, is derived from
philosophical materials. The importance of the generic for non-
philosophy has only recently come to the forefront and comes, to
my mind, to replace the idea of "minimal" that is more operative
in *Future Christ*. Laruelle tells us in *Introduction aux sciences génériques*
(2008) and *Philosophie non-standard* that he derives the generic from
the line Feuerbach–Marx–Badiou. What's important in each of
these philosophical constructions is the connection between humanity and science, a connection – or, more accurately, "idempotence"
– that is thought more radically (that is, more immanental) in Laruelle. The importance of the generic in Feuerbach is largely lost to
us in the Anglophone world since *Gattungswesen* is usually translated in English as "species-being." However, the French translation captures this as *être générique*, literally "generic being." Now
this formulation of the generic is taken up by Marx and it is Marx,

Laruelle claims, who truly initiates the generic science-thought that thinks scientifically from the universality of the human. He takes this up in his thinking of Christ writing:

> The messianic force of thought is not a metaphorization of Christ, rather it is generic secularization [*laïcisation*], and less still does it give a Christian interpretation of science in general. Though it is through a certain reference to the mediation of Christ as unity of God and man consonant with the unity of the Undivided and the Divided that the generic is called messianic according to this material or this symptom that integrally belongs to philosophy, and so an immanent messianity as superposition is affirmed of Man-in-person. But the messianic is not simply religious, it is a complex cause, also partly scientific, and more profoundly constituted as *ensemblage*, a generic alliance or unilateral complimentarity.[73]

So the generic element of messianity is central to our understanding of what Laruelle aims to do through his mutual complication of religious and scientific material within a relationship of unilateral complementarity, referring to the fact that all of this always is ultimately for the service of assistance to the world, but more importantly to the human beings that all of us are. Ultimately, non-philosophy is concerned with liberation, which is why it considers religion and engages with religious material. This isn't a possible liberation, but a kind of virtual liberation that is always present within the radical immanence of the human. When one is able to actualize this, these human beings are not merely a sign of possibility (what we may call saintliness from a non-philosophical perspective), which Laruelle suggests is too easily reinscribed within the world, but is "in flesh and blood" or Man-in-person, the future itself. Laruelle often refers to the future under an adjectival form as "the futural" and he defines it in this way: "The futural is an excess which, as generic, contains [a number of attributes] but pushed through a certain indetermination within immanence, it is discontinuous and continuous, unilateral, predictable within the limits of certain givens as conditions of the least reference, but ultimately unpredictable."[74] By using this adjectival form, "the futural," Laruelle disempowers certain philosophical systems that confuse the future with a kind of substance or power that gets separated in idealist philosophical forms from human pragmatics. One is futural, but one is not the future, and so when a human being is a messiah, as any human being can be, they express this characteristic of being "ultimately unpredictable."

Consider again Badiou's theory of events which produce subjects. The subject is formed in relation to their response to a particular truth-event in some field (though only four are really allowed: love, art, science, or politics). That response is predictable, while the event is not. Under Laruelle's theory of radical immanence, the subject is always a kind of superposed clone with a body that is itself something like Badiou's truth-event. Meaning, where Badiou posits a split between event and subject turned into an inconsistent unity, ultimately by some transcendent and determined action (fidelity or infidelity), Laruelle rejects that split and instead says that the One-Real of the body is unilaterally related to the truth and the subject produced. In other words, to turn away from the difficulty of this language, the existence of the messiah, which any person may be, is the truth. Within science and religion, we see that the practices form, but are not a saintliness, but rather expressive of a wild liberty that has no equivalent of exchange. Take traditional theological proclamations about the Being of God being in God's action, of God's freedom being in God's necessity, and apply them instead to human beings. This human being is the messiah of non-philosophy which needs no mediators, but is herself salvation: "Human beings have a problem that only they can solve: what to do with the World? Salvation or rebellion? Exploitation or therapeutic? Consumption or consummation?"[75] All of this concerns the antagonism between two kinds of futures and it is to this difference we now turn.

Conclusion: The Future of Non-Philosophy

The future, you ain't seen nothing yet

Where is all of this going? From the start I said that I would not challenge the charge that non-philosophy was fruitless. I said then that I am not looking for the sentence to be overturned on appeal. The authority of the court is simply not recognized. Of course, such a decision has consequences. Foremost of these consequences is that the refusal to recognize the set social norms of philosophy does not release the non-philosopher from the vicious circle of recognition. The non-philosopher will be recognized in a certain way by the philosopher who excludes the non-philosopher. Moreover, the philosophical world will keep spinning with or without her. In this ceaseless spinning, philosophy reproduces itself endlessly. It creates a future where there will be philosophy, where it will be. This is true even of nihilist philosophies and the implication of anti-natalism they carry. Even those philosophies exhibit a localized pro-natalism concerning the reproduction of philosophy itself. In this way, despite the challenge nihilism presents to philosophical society, nihilists are still within the frame of good manners. Philosophy loves the future because philosophy loves its children, even those that some may see as usurping philosophy in the future. After all, what parent does not want their child to inherit a better world?

Does non-philosophy have a future? Will there be non-philosophy in the future? Will it reproduce? Or, like an animal in captivity, is it fruitless and without a future?

I've already claimed that non-philosophy is fruitless. The true question is: does the future require that it be produced? Is it necessary that the future is the reproduction of the past? Laruelle's conception of the future has at least two senses, which we will consider as a way of concluding this survey of his thought. In the first sense, non-philosophy aims to be a hedge of protection from the worst of all possible futures in which the future is taken to be a form of the harassing powers of the world. In the second sense, the future is taken to be a mode of the lived that may disempower the future as harassing authority. To summarize this view, we may say that non-philosophy is already future, without any hope that there will be a future for non-philosophy. Non-Philosophy's future is always now, though one should not confuse the now with the present. As Laruelle sardonically states, "Either peace is an ultimatum or it is only the expectation of a war and perhaps a war of expectation."[1] If the future is to be anything, it will have to be now, not merely an expectation.

Laruelle claims that his project assumes something like the worst of all possible worlds. Laruelle is clearly interested in navigating the Scylla and Charybdis of the technophilia of everyday capitalism and the technophobia of Heideggerian authenticity when he writes:

> we should be under no illusions about the possibility of stopping this version of cloning. I don't understand how people can get so morally bothered by cloning since we know that everything that is technically possible eventually ends up happening. Cloning will happen – it happens under forms that are imaginary, mediatized, and delirious-sectarian, but it will also end up happening in forms that are more moderate, more therapeutic.[2]

To navigate these twin dangers requires a certain disinterest in technology as a sufficient form of thinking, along with the ability to recognize the human qualities of technology in-the-last-instance. Technology has to be subject to a kind of thinking, rather than taking "human thought" as a form of what we might call "sufficient technology," even while technology says something about the radically immanent posture of the (lived) human within the world. Technology will undoubtedly be used by the powerful against the weak; the very production of technology is already a form of violence against those who are required to build the gadgets that fill up our lives and our landfills. As we already saw, Laruelle grimly states, "Still unimaginable crimes are for that matter readying themselves in its folds, still more invisible and more featureless, crimes according to the future."[3] How can one respond to these crimes according to the future with a call to the same future that conditions these crimes?

In one sense of the future, contrary to Laruelle's, suffering is simply the price paid to get from what is to what will be. And what will be becomes simply the new what is. For Laruelle, we have to instead assume a kind of thinking from the generic human present in subject positions that manifest the generic identity of the human within the frame of the world. This victim-thinking gives attention to suffering without reifying it.[4] This form of thinking responds to suffering without treating suffering as something to redeem and thereby forget. Victim-thinking is developed in direct antagonism to theodicy as developed classically by Leibniz which states that the actual world is the best of all possible worlds. Laruelle's principle of victim-thinking instead begins from the logic of the "worst necessary." He writes, "The prudence of non-philosophy follows from the logic of the 'worst necessary' – this is not the principle of the "best possible" but the principle of the worst ('you ain't seen nothing yet')."[5]

We get a sense of what this logic of the worst necessary means when Laruelle writes, "I believe that this method – that of the worst – is the only method that still remains available for us if we are to hope for a salvation and not identify ourselves with the unfathomable psychology of dictators and tyrants."[6] To understand this claim as something beyond simply anti-fanaticism, the reader must notice that hope is the driving concept in this claim. Hope for salvation is an ambiguous concept, one that produces tyrants and dictators – not simply because they try to save the world (though there is that), but precisely because they think the world is something to save, because their hope is overdetermined by a kind of drive toward the best possible that can be brought about in the future instead of now. Even when one makes the decision to force someone else's survival, one is doing the worst necessary. Pretending that this is for the greater good, for the production of the best possible, this is the thinking of one who commits a crime against humanity.[7] But the point of the logic of the worst necessary is not to give up on struggle or to assume simple managerial politics such as one finds in mainstream liberalism. Laruelle claims instead that, "We have not yet explored all the possibilities of thought, and so all the possibilities of struggle. I form this hypothesis of the worst, but under human conditions, so as not to sink into the worst of the worst."[8] The worst necessary, then, and not the worst possible. To turn again to the question of technology, it is a question of being honest about the possibilities of the future opened up by technological progress. There will be something about this progress that is necessarily the worst. The only way to push against that is to face it, to refuse to see it as a necessary sacrifice for the best possible. It will always remain, and the complicity of philosophy in this future should not be forgotten if one hopes to explore the real possibilities of a human thought beyond grim necessity.

Why is this important? Because it leads to a different conception of the future as well – one that is no longer presented as a quasi-divinity, albeit a divinity that takes on a decidedly secular character while remaining just as blood-thirsty as any other god demanding sacrifice. Instead, we may perhaps think of a future that is immanent insofar as this futurity is lived, rather than framed and determining of that lived (reality).

The future, a mode of the subject

For Laruelle it is clear that in his work the future refers to a mode of being or existing for the subject. He places the adjective "future" alongside of other subject positions privileged in non-philosophy as first names for the human: "'Future,' always being an adjective, gives us in itself a first name to designate man as liable to being-cloned. As much as the Self, the Subject, the Other, the Stranger, etc., the Future must acquire the primacy and dignity of a first name intended for the human. This ultimatum? Man-Messiah exists..."[9] Elsewhere he states this more clearly, "The subject is not an existant *in* the future but an existant subject from the mode of the future and exhausts itself in it."[10] The future is not a background within which the subject operates, but a mode that the subject lives.

Some might find this problematic as it appears to psychologize time. Before we can state why this may be a potentially powerful way to conceive of the future, we need to address the question of where Laruelle fits between realist conceptions of time and psychological conceptions. Let us consider a quote from Laruelle that at first glance is opaque, but which, after we unpack it, will help us understand Laruelle's broader conception of time:

> only the time of the subject is constituted from a double source, worldly time and One-time which clones the subject-time. Cloned

time, neither pure past nor transcendence "in-memory," is the Future as ecstasy non-ecstatic (of) self. Returned to its principles heresy extracts the past, the present and the future in every historico-worldly eschatology. Heretical time, a human identity of time, thus avoids this solvent splitting and that philosophical necessity of being that which could only be called too justly a "recollection" or a retreat from time.[11]

From the first line we see that Laruelle posits something like the real/psychological split common in philosophical discussion of the nature of time. However, he locates this split as the double source of time for the subject – that is, the human as lived within the parameters of the world.

Instead of simply separating these two instances of time into a simple distinction between real and psychological, worldly time may be taken to refer to both the spontaneous philosophy of time which takes it as simple progress from past to present to future and the spontaneous psychological explanations of the experience of time. This form of philosophical mixture is contrasted with what Laruelle calls "One-time." In a very strict sense, One-time might be understood as referring to what one means when one thinks of "real time" distinct from psychological time. The difference is that, for Laruelle, for such a time to be One or Real in the non-philo-sophical sense, that time must be unrepresentable and already manifest. Turning from his religious example of messianism here and instead thinking of the scientist may help us to understand this claim. The future may be experienced now by the scientist-subject through scientific models of that future. This is what scientists do when they investigate the nature of time, even though they are unable to experience the purity of that model or extricate them-selves from their lived experience of the passage of time. The expe-rience of the scientist in this way witnesses to what Laruelle is calling here heretical time or a "human identity of time." For the scientist is able to conceive of time as radically distinct from human experience, time as radically given without time being subject to the structures of givenness. And, simultaneously, the scientist is able to experience time in the everyday way that one experiences time even if the scientist's model tells her that time is ultimately in some sense "illusory." Insofar as the scientist is a subject position, then she is the site of manifestation of a time that is not split, that witnesses to her a kind of relative transcendence of time and the radical immanence of that time which does not retreat from the human.

In a certain sense this is a more phenomenological description of the future than a scientific model of the future. Laruelle even refers to his description of the nature of the future as "non-phenomenological" in *Philosophie non-standard*.[12] However, within Laruelle's non-phenomenological description of the future is an inherent understanding that the future may be a name for a real time beyond any spontaneous philosophy of time. Following the logic of unilateral duality, the past, present, and future exist as effects of the One-time. From the perspective of One-time, there is no break between the future and the past and present. Instead, there is simply a flowing thickness of a futural now. Insofar as these three aspects of time can be located at the level of the subject (which is distinct from the One-time), then they are present as modalities of that lived subject. Laruelle writes:

> The past re-turns [*re-vient*], the present be-comes [*de-vient*], but the virtual future under-comes [*sous-vient*]. Introducing the indeterminate future into the cause of thought is how we are delivered from the harassment of the past and the present. The nature of the futural [*futuralité*] is not one of an empty future but a void of living determinations, a flowing thickness, a future ceaselessly renewed as a non-cumulative and non-ecstatic wave that under-comes in the subject.[13]

No future and the non-future

Undoubtedly, again, the above is more phenomenological in presentation than physical in its description of time. While Laruelle's turn to a determinate science, quantum physics, in the period of Philosophy V takes seriously the findings of the hard physical sciences, he is not attempting to provide a popular philosophy of quantum physics. Quantum physics does not necessarily need philosophy to come along to correct it or speak for it. What Laruelle's current "non-standard philosophy" aims to do is think alongside of quantum physics, to let this science underdetermine his own more philosophical work, and to unleash a new kind of activity in the work. We saw in chapters 2 and 6 how this conjugation of philosophy and quantum physics aims to create a philo-fiction. The question that remains is: What future does non-philosophy have? What does it want to produce?

Production is not reproduction. Non-Philosophy is interesting because it identifies cracks and finds ways to produce within them.

Such production does not require a goal or aim to be meaningful. It need not produce fruit. The elements of fugitivity found in non-philosophy's practice find an analogue in the non-human world as well, for it is in the interstitial spaces of sidewalk cracks in Mid-western American towns that the remnants of prairie ecosystems may find space to live after the majority of the environment has been colonized by elements of European ecosystems. Is this inter-stitial existence fruitful? What kind of answer could there be to this question inasmuch as fruitful normally means the reproduction of something that a corporation can come along, pluck, sell, and eat. No, the existence of non-philosophy has no future. It is the expres-sion of the radical immanence of human (existence) and such exist-ence has no purpose, has no future other than what has been hallucinated as the determination of lived (reality).

But non-philosophy's fruitlessness may have something useful about it, at least when the sense of usefulness is radically changed under the conditions of the radical immanence of the One. Non-philosophy models a way of thinking that is open to the construc-tion of a radically different world and a radically different philosophy from those that structure our world. One might call this a positive nihilism, or again bring to mind Fanon's misquotation of Césaire that the only thing in the world worth starting is "the end of the world."[14] If there is to be anything meaningful – or even meaningless – in a humane way about this claim, it must mean something other than a naive empirical end of the world. It is the end of a certain vision, a certain theodicy regarding the future of this world. To live in the light of the end of this world is to live in the non-future as the modality of a certain kind of heretical subject. Important theorists like Fanon too often lapse into a kind of philo-sophical heroism regarding these subject positions, but this linger-ing aspect of (European) philosophical sufficiency (likely another of colonialism's lingering effects) can be undone, and non-philos-ophy offers resources for that.

In the face of the constant harassment that comes from media-friendly images of the future, dystopian visions, and even every-day demands to constantly be worried about one's own future, non-philosophy joins with other forms of thought that demand a future to the measure of the human. A humane future is no future at all, but rather a kind of proliferation of the whyless now.[15] In this way, there is no future for non-philosophy because non-philosophy seeks to make meaning in a way that is strange to the norms of the philosophy-world. It is the very fruitlessness, the whylessness, that others accuse Laruelle of that is the good news of non-philosophy in the face of the failure of the world. Derived from the most entrenched forms of colonialist and theodical philosophy, non-philosophy operates at the level of philosophy itself, an austere, abstract, anti-colonial, anti-theodical theory that emerges and is authorized only from the radical immanence of the (lived) human. This is a strange thought. It may even be the strangest thought to emerge from French philosophy to date.

Notes

Introduction: What Is to Be Done with Philosophy?

1 Plato, *Letter VII*, 337d.
2 There is a common misunderstanding that non-philosophy is an "end of philosophy" project. To cite just two examples, the foremost proponent of object-oriented philosophy, Graham Harman, and his most virulent critic, Peter Wolfendale, both make this mistake regarding Laruelle. See Graham Harman, "Review of François Laruelle's *Philosophies of Difference: A Critical Introduction to Non-Philosophy*" in *Notre Dame Philosophical Reviews*, http://ndpr.nd.edu/news/25437-philosophies-of-difference-a-critical-introduction-to-non-philosophy, June 21, 2013, and Peter Wolfendale, *Object-Oriented Philosophy: The Noumenon's New Clothes* (Falmouth: Urbanomic, 2014), p. 228 n. 286. Laruelle has consistently rejected the discourse around the "end of philosophy" as a way that philosophy continues itself under new forms, but he has done so most forcefully in SU. For a further critique of Harman's reading of Laruelle see Anthony Paul Smith, "Editorial Introduction: Laruelle Does Not Exist" in *Angelaki: Journal of the Theoretical Humanities* 19.2 (2014): pp. 1–11. There I expand upon this critique of Harman's view of philosophy as "illuminator" and defend Laruelle's sense of blackness as the essence of identity. I will revisit this in chapter 5, where I show the ways in which non-philosophy may come into dialogue with critical theory especially on the question of identity and race.

3   As this text aims to introduce readers to Laruelle's own writings, I have sometimes adopted his own stylistic choice of capitalizing certain important terms, which he appears to have inherited from his studies in German philosophy. While I do not follow Laruelle's style completely, preferring to try to perform non-philosophy in an English idiom, the hope is that the occasional use of his style will allow the reader to turn to Laruelle's original work without the shock that some experience. While some have expressed a certain exasperation at this stylistic choice by Laruelle, I tend to see it as akin to certain forms of literature that eschew the idiomatic rules of writing in favor of a particular expression. That said, some have likened Laruelle's writing to a Frenchman who has overdosed on German philosophy, and it is true that there is a kind of internalization of Kantian, Husserlian, and Heideggerian writing tics, as if he was thinking German through French. This may be true, but at the same time there is also the clear intention in many of his texts to parrot or even parody the standard philosophical writing he is engaged with as a material practice.

4   See Anthony Paul Smith, *A Non-Philosophical Theory of Nature: Ecologies of Thought* (New York and London: Palgrave Macmillan, 2013), pp. 73–81, and *François Laruelle's Principles of Non-Philosophy: A Critical Introduction and Guide* (Edinburgh: Edinburgh University Press, 2016), pp. 11–21.

5   Ray Brassier, *Nihil Unbound: Enlightenment and Extinction* (Basingstoke: Palgrave, 2007), pp. 132–3, 252 n. 19.

6   Ibid., p. 118. It's interesting to note that this characteristically acerbic remark follows the earlier statement, "our aim is not to denigrate Laruelle's achievement, which strikes us as nothing short of extraordinary, but on the contrary to dislodge a rebarbative carapace which, far from warding off misinterpretation, seems to have succeeded only in barring appreciation of his thought's significance" (ibid.). This attempt to save Laruelle from himself resulted in further misinterpretations of Laruelle's work by those attracted to Brassier's project of deflationary rationalism-*cum*-nihilism – a project that, aside from being self-avowedly philosophical in forms antithetical to Laruelle's non-philosophy, includes an anti-humanism that borders on a misanthropic drive toward human extermination. Any confusion with that project would require massive excisions – likely performed sadistically without anesthesia – from

Laruelle's actual project of "human defense." Regardless of these misinterpretations made by Brassier's readers and the distaste I have for his project, the skill shown in his recasting of Laruelle is undeniably clever – and remarkably so. Despite that skill, Brassier's work has shifted a great deal in focus since the publication of *Nihil Unbound*, at least based upon Brassier's most recent published work, and so does not include any further engagement with Laruelle. At the time of *Nihil Unbound*, he found Laruelle's work to be useful for a particular purpose: "The nub of this philosophical re-interpretation will be that Laruelle has not achieved a non-philosophical suspension of philosophy but rather uncovered a non-dialectical logic of philosophical negation: viz., 'uni-lateralization'" (ibid., p. 120).

7 François Laruelle, "What Is Non-Philosophy?," trans. Taylor Adkins, in *From Decision to Heresy: Experiments in Non-Standard Thought*, ed. Robin Mackay (Falmouth: Urbanomic, 2012), p. 210.

8 SU, p. 3.

9 The claim that Laruelle's non-philosophy is a fruitless enterprise was made by Brassier. While I have a certain positive valuation of this claim – namely, that non-philosophy is fruitless from the perspective of producing more philosophy – it is worth noting here that the comment was made prior to any other real engagement with Laruelle in English. Readers will have to make their own decision as to whether or not Brassier's claims regarding the general fruitlessness of non-philosophy remain true in the light of his own impressive project in *Nihil Unbound* and a number of other recent texts taking up the method of non-philosophy in less nihilistic forms – namely, through pragmatic engagements with environmental theory, film, animal studies, feminism and gender theory, media studies, and others. See Smith, *Ecologies of Thought*; John Ó Maoilearca, *Philosophy and the Moving Image: Refractions of Reality* (Basingstoke: Palgrave Macmillan, 2010), ch. 8, and *All Thoughts Are Equal: Laruelle and Nonhuman Philosophy* (Minneapolis: University of Minnesota Press, 2015); Alexander R. Galloway, *Laruelle: Against the Digital* (Minneapolis: University of Minnesota Press, 2014); Katerina Kolozova, *Cut of the Real: Subjectivity in Poststructuralist Philosophy* (New York: Columbia University Press, 2014); and Ian James, *The New French Philosophy* (Cambridge: Polity, 2012), ch. 7, which also promises a forthcoming book that engages with Laruelle in a central way

to examine questions of technique and the experimental nature of contemporary philosophy.

10   I have done this to some extent in Smith, *François Laruelle's Principles of Non-Philosophy*, especially in ch. 6.

11   This may bring to mind the words of Aimé Césaire in *Discourse on Colonialism* (trans. Joan Pinkham, New York: Monthly Review Press, 2000), when he writes: "at the very moment it most often mouths the word, the West has never been further from being able to live a true humanism – a humanism made to the measure of the World" (p. 73). However, despite the terminological differences, Laruelle is in fundamental agreement with Césaire's point since Césaire is arguing for an expanded, potentially infinite understanding of the human based upon the many different ways the human manifests. "The world" names, in a certain sense, the set of those differences, which Laruelle would object to as a concept that may obscure the human, but this is not in any way a major distinction between principles.

12   All translations from the Bible are from the New Revised Standard Version.

1   Theory of the Philosophical Decision

1   PNS, pp. 7–14.

2   DNP, p. 116 (translation slightly modified).

3   Alain Badiou, "Interview with Ben Woodard" in *The Speculative Turn: Continental Materialism and Realism*, ed. Levi Bryant, Nick Srnicek, and Graham Harman (Melbourne: re:press, 2011), p. 20.

4   DNP, p. 117 (translation slightly modified).

5   Laruelle is, of course, not the first to make such a claim. The work of Max Horkheimer and Theodor W. Adorno and those working in their tradition of critical theory also offers a reading of philosophy as mythological. Undeniably, there remain important differences in their theories and Laruelle affirms the idea of science in ways that Horkheimer and Adorno do not in the main thrust of their work. See Smith, *François Laruelle's Principles of Non-Philosophy*, pp. 94–100, for a longer discussion of their similarities and differences.

6   PD, p. 204. Cf. Ray Brassier, "Laruelle and the Reality of Abstraction" in *Laruelle and Non-Philosophy*, ed. John Ó Maoilearca and Anthony Paul Smith (Edinburgh: Edinburgh

University Press, 2012), pp. 100–21 for a subtle meditation on finitude in Laruelle's work.

7 PD, p. 210 (translation slightly modified).
8 PD, p. 16. Cf. Rocco Gangle, *François Laruelle's Philosophies of Difference: A Critical Introduction and Guide* (Edinburgh: Edinburgh University Press, 2013), pp. 153–4, and Galloway, pp. 192–3.
9 PD, pp. 204, 210.
10 John Ó Maoilearca illustrates this by looking to the example of the choice between various psychotherapies. The assumption of the metapsychologies behind these different psychotherapies "implies that *only one should work* – their own. Their claims to truth are mutually exclusive.... *And yet they still do both* [behaviorism and Freudian psychoanalysis] *work*" (John Ó Maoilearca, *Post-Continental Philosophy: An Outline* [London and New York: Routledge, 2006], p. 148).
11 The phrase "the lived (reality) of the human" does not quite express the idea in strictly non-philosophical terms. Laruelle would prefer we create neither the hallucination of distance by modifying the "lived" with reality nor a relation of this dyad of "life" and "reality" with the human, a relation marked by the preposition "of." He would simply have us write "the contingency of the lived human," something that French grammar allows for with less awkwardness than English. Perhaps we could write it as "the human contingency of the lived (reality of the) human."
12 PD, p. 211.
13 Brassier, *Nihil Unbound*, pp. 122–4. Cf. Smith, *Ecologies of Thought*, pp. 65–72, for an earlier attempt to trace this formal structure, with specific reference to Brassier's reading and Meillassoux's criticism of non-philosophy. It strikes me that Brassier overemphasizes the repetition of immanence in his reconstruction. With regard to the internal structures of Philosophical Decision, Laruelle writes that it is "a structure combining a Dyad and an immanent *and* transcendent unity in the Dyad. This is the concrete structure of the categories of 'mixture', 'amphibology', and of 'antinomy', of 'auto-position' which we use here and there, but always understood on the model of Philosophical Decision" (PNP, p. 244). The point is not that immanence features twice, but that one of the posited terms features twice. The character of this "something" will depend upon the particular shape of that philosophy. Thus Laruelle recognizes a major and minor tradition within

transcendental philosophy, where Henry's focus upon radical immanence is said to push the limits of the structure of philosophy itself without recourse to the same kind of transcendence one finds in Kant or Hegel.

14 See François Laruelle, "The Transcendental Method" trans. Christopher Eby, in *From Decision to Heresy: Experiments in Non-Standard Thought*, ed. Robin Mackay (Falmouth: Urbanomic, 2012), p. 143.

15 Ibid., p. 137.

16 PNP, pp. 199–200.

17 See Immanuel Kant, *Critique of Pure Reason*, trans. and ed. Paul Guyer and Allen W. Wood (Cambridge: Cambridge University Press, 1998), A70/B95.

18 PNP, pp. 234–6.

19 PNP, p. 234.

20 PNP, p. 234.

21 See PNP, pp. 234–6.

22 See Jacques Lacan, *The Seminar of Jacques Lacan, Book XVII: The Other Side of Psychoanalysis*, trans. Russell Grigg (New York: W. W. Norton & Company, 2007). As Lacan inherits and arguably deepens Freud's psychoanalytic analysis of the subject, he is engaged with at length in *Principles of Non-Philosophy* in chapter 3, which attempts to perform a unified theory of the ego and the subject rather than repeat the antagonism between philosophy and psychoanalysis.

23 Michel Foucault, *The Order of Things: An Archeology of the Human Sciences* (London: Routledge, 2002), p. 172.

24 PNP, p. 235.

25 PNP, p. 236.

26 PNP, p. 236.

27 Brassier, *Nihil Unbound*, p. 133.

28 PNP, p. 4.

29 PNP, p. 232.

30 See François Laruelle and Jacques Derrida, "Controversy Over the Possibility of a Science of Philosophy" in *The Non-Philosophy Project: Essays by François Laruelle*, trans. Ray Brassier and Robin Mackay, ed. Gabriel Alkon and Boris Gunjevic (New York: Telos Press Publishing, 2012), p. 80. I will discuss this in more detail in chapter 3.

31 Arguably, Brassier would have been better served by another brilliant but neglected French philosopher, Guy Lardreau. Lardreau presents a remarkably similar theory of the last instance

(without the hyphens, indicating that it is purely philosophical in its lineage from Marxism and more explicitly materialist in the standard philosophical sense) without the aspects of Laruelle's non-philosophy that Brassier goes to great pains to distance his own project from. See Guy Lardreau, *Vive le matérialisme!* (Paris: Verdier, 2001), for the most explicit and polemical development of his understanding of the last instance, and Lardreau, *La véracité: essai d'une philosophie négative* (Paris: Verdier, 1993), for the fullest and most Kantian development of his own negative philosophy. But Brassier is clearly commiserative with those who find themselves annoyed by Laruelle's style and bold claims regarding the essence of philosophy, while at the same time finding value in this work. Notably he finds value in the machinery of non-philosophy, its method and the concepts that flow out of it. And, despite his criticisms, Brassier's reconstruction of Laruelle's theory of the philosophical decision remains, and likely will remain, one of the clearest and most rigorous readings of the concept. In this chapter on philosophical decision, I have attempted to respond to some of Brassier's criticisms, which are strong and required serious consideration in ways that the previous critiques simply do not warrant.

32 See Galloway, pp. 25–48. Galloway's reconstruction of Laruelle's depiction of the standard model is invaluable for the way that he is able to faithfully present Laruelle's work without being overburdened with the introductory work of unpacking Laruelle's terms. His chapter, and indeed the whole book, should be read alongside this one as a supplement, and I hope that this text may reciprocally supplement his.

33 Brassier, *Nihil Unbound*, p. 133.

34 The method is described by Husserl perhaps most clearly in his *Cartesian Meditations* where he provides this example: "Starting from this table-perception as an example, we vary the perceptual object, table, with a completely free optionalness, yet in such a manner that we keep perception fixed as perception of something, no matter what. Perhaps we begin by fictively changing the shape or the color of the object quite arbitrarily, keeping identical only its perceptual appearing. In other words: Abstaining from acceptance of its being, we change the fact of this perception into a pure possibility, one among other quite 'optional' pure possibilities – but possibilities that are possible perceptions. We, so to speak, shift the

actual perception into the realm of non-actualities, the realm of the as-if, which supplies us with 'pure' possibilities, pure of everything that restricts to this or to any fact whatever.... Thus removed from all factualness, it has become the pure '*eidos*' perception, whose '*ideal*' extension is made up of all ideally possible perceptions, as purely phantisable processes. Analyses of perception are then '*essential*' or '*eidetic*' analyses. All that we have set forth concerning syntheses belonging to the type, perception, concerning horizons of potentiality, and so forth, holds good, as can easily be seen, '*essentially*' for everything formable in this free variation, accordingly for all imaginable perceptions without exception – in other words: with absolute '*essential universality*', and with '*essential necessity*' for every particular case selected, hence for every de facto perception, since every *fact can be thought of merely as exemplifying a pure possibility*" (Edmund Husserl, *Cartesian Meditations: An Introduction to Phenomenology*, trans. Dorion Cairns [Dordrecht: Kluwer Academic Publishers, 1999], pp. 70–1).

35   Brassier, *Nihil Unbound*, p. 134.
36   Ibid., p. 133.
37   On this point Heidegger was perhaps indebted to his former teacher, Husserl, whom he betrayed. Husserl's own relation to Eurocentrism is not straightforward and is made even more complex by his Jewish background – a background, it should be said, that he rejected in his conversion to Protestant Christianity. For a deep but ultimately positive reading of this, see Dermot Moran, *Husserl's Crisis of the European Sciences and Transcendental Phenomenology: An Introduction* (Cambridge: Cambridge University Press, 2012), pp. 178–217.
38   This is a theme that will be taken up at various points in the text around Laruelle's reading of Levinas and Derrida and constituting a "Judaic turn" in European philosophy. This has been the subject of criticism, with accusations of anti-Semitism having been leveled at Laruelle. Most of these accusations live on the internet without much textual engagement, but they have their source in Andrew McGettigan's review of *Philosophies of Difference* and *Future Christ*. See Andrew McGettigan, "Fabrication Defect: François Laruelle's Philosophical Materials" in *Radical Philosophy* 175 (September/October 2012): pp. 33–42. While my remarks throughout this book will in part be a response to those accusations, I will not do so with direct reference to McGettigan, as I have done so elsewhere. See Anthony Paul Smith, "Disempowerment and Mutation:

François Laruelle's Engagement with Religion" in *Religion and European Philosophy: Key Thinkers from Kant to Today*, ed. Philip Goodchild and Hollis D. Phelps (London and New York: Routledge, forthcoming), and Smith, *François Laruelle's Principles of Non-Philosophy*, ch. 5.

39 Brassier, pp. 133–4.

40 DNP, p. 116.

41 This term is a neologism created by Laruelle to more accurately express non-philosophy's relation to its material. In *Philosophie non-standard* he provides this definition: "Directly set against the transcendental, it's symmetrical for radical immanence. A non-relation of immanence (via superposition) to experience, meaning to the particle and more distantly to the corpuscle. Power of under-determination via the Last Instance of double transcendence, which falls in-immanence" (PNS, p. 54). In traditional philosophical terminology, the modifier "transcendental" usually refers to a structure, but it implies a distance between the structure and what is structured. For Laruelle, "immanental" refers to the structure which is lived or inheres in what is structured. He might even write it as "structured-without-structure" to indicate that the immanental structure cannot be understood if thought under the category of distance, since this would be an instance of decision and destroy the nature of its immanence.

42 See also Smith, *François Laruelle's Principles of Non-Philosophy*, pp. 62–84, for a longer exploration.

43 This is true of physics and ecology. See Smith, *Ecologies of Thought*, pp. 39–44.

44 See Smith, *François Laruelle's Principles of Non-Philosophy*, pp. 11–17 for a presentation that is more attentive to this historical development.

45 "Realism" here refers to the philosophical position that transcendental universals (i.e. the *idea* of a chair or goodness and so on) really exist, while nominalism claims that these transcendental universals do not really exist and that universals only exist by virtue of the particular thing existing (*post res*).

2   The Style of Non-Philosophy

1 PD, p. 218 (translation slightly modified).

2 George Bataille, *Theory of Religion*, trans. Robert Hurley (New York: Zone Books, 1989), p. 3.

3   PNP, p. 158.
4   Rocco Gangle, "Translator's Introduction" in François Laru-
    elle, *Philosophies of Difference: A Critical Introduction to Non-
    Philosophy*, trans. Rocco Gangle (London and New York:
    Continuum, 2010), pp. ix–x. See also PD, pp. 202–3.
5   That he claims such practices are themselves transcendental in
    the quote above may be difficult for those schooled in post-
    Kantian philosophy to accept, and indeed he struggles with
    the proper expression of his claim throughout his works. In
    his most recent work, he has come to substitute "immanental"
    for transcendental, yet, as early as *Théorie des identités* (1992),
    he described the transcendental as referring to the "rigorously
    immanent" (TI, p. 56).
6   François Laruelle, "Non-Philosophy, Weapon of Last Defence:
    An Interview with François Laruelle" in *Laruelle and Non-Phi-
    losophy*, ed. John Ó Maoilearca and Anthony Paul Smith, trans.
    Anthony Paul Smith (Edinburgh: Edinburgh University Press,
    2012), p. 239.
7   DNP, p. 15.
8   AB, pp. xxiv–xxv. The original French term is *quantiel*, which
    is a neologism combining *quantique* (quantum) and *logiciel*
    (software). Robin Mackay's translation here is inspired.
9   As Nietzsche and Deleuze were important to Laruelle's early
    philosophical work, it is not surprising to find this Nietzchean
    vision of thought lingering in Laruelle's work. Compare
    Deleuze's description of Nietzsche when he writes, "Never-
    theless Nietzsche is one of the greatest philosophers of the
    nineteenth century. And he alters both the theory and practice
    of philosophy. He compares the thinker to an arrow shot by
    Nature that another thinker picks up where it has fallen so that
    he can shoot it somewhere else" (Gilles Deleuze, *Nietzsche and
    Philosophy*, trans. Hugh Tomlinson [New York: Columbia Uni-
    versity Press, 1983], p. ix).
10 For an introduction to the concepts that recur throughout
    each of the particular interventions that Laruelle has made
    throughout his career, readers should also consult his *Diction-
    ary of Non-Philosophy*. This is an interesting text as it was a
    collaborative project with a number of Laruelle's students and
    others who had picked up on certain tools in non-philosophy
    useful for their own projects. While much of the shape of
    non-philosophy is given – and given alone – in the specificity
    of the field it is conjugating with, this dictionary aims to set

out the central concepts of non-philosophy and is "intended to summarize the theoretical acquisitions, present the essentials of the technique and distinguish the parallel, neighboring or variant thoughts in the midst of which it has developed" (DNP, p. 19).

11   PhNP, p. 79 (translation slightly modified).

12   PhNP, pp. 33–4.

13   PhNP, p. 33. The reference to Lacan likely comes out of a certain reading of Seminar XX which concerns the "impossibility" of the sexual relation in which two attempt to become One. Lacan is clear here about the similarity of his argument to Neo-Platonism and the forms of religious mysticism that often make use of Neo-Platonism. See Jacques Lacan, *The Seminar of Jacques Lacan, Book XX: On Feminine Sexuality, The Limits of Love and Knowledge. Encore 1972–1973*, trans. Bruce Fink (New York: W. W. Norton and Company, 1998), pp. 64–77. My thanks to Marika Rose for discussions on what school this passage likely refers to.

14   The most direct and, perhaps, important of Laruelle's works on the One are *Philosophy and Non-Philosophy* and *Principles of Non-Philosophy*. See PhNP, pp. 33–78, and PNP, pp. 17–36.

15   PhNP, p. 33.

16   PD, p. 218.

17   Brassier, *Nihil Unbound*, p. 128. Brassier had taken Laruelle's summary of axioms concerning the One and presented it as axioms concerning the Real. This is legitimate since Laruelle consistently claims that "the One" and "the Real" are equivalent terms. Brassier's summary is very helpful, but leaving the terms as "the Real" would be confusing in this context.

18   DNP, p. 166 (translation slightly modified).

19   Daniel Colucciello Barber, *On Diaspora: Christianity, Religion, and Secularity* (Eugene, OR: Cascade Books, 2011), pp. 1–11.

20   PhNP, p. 37.

21   See Smith, *François Laruelle's Principles of Non-Philosophy*, ch. 4, for a longer exposition.

22   See DNP, pp. 49–50.

23   DNP, p. 50.

24   DNP, p. 51.

25   DNP, p. 51.

26   PD, p. 221.

27   PNP, p. 46.

28   NM, p. 42.

29	The term was popularized amongst a certain avant-garde of Continental philosophy because of the French philosopher Quentin Meillassoux in his *After Finitude: An Essay on the Necessity of Contingency*, trans. Ray Brassier (London: Continuum, 2008). The problem of correlationism became for some the most cogent problem for philosophy, and their work was couched under the misnomer of "Speculative Realism." For a synoptic account of various responses to this problem, see Louis Morelle, "Speculative Realism: After Finitude, and Beyond? A *vade mecum*," trans. Leah Orth with the assistance of Mark Allan Ohm, Jon Cogburn, and Emily Beck Cogburn, in *Speculations* 3 (2012): 241–72.

30	See Levi R. Bryant's summary of correlationism where he lists "subject, language, and power" as three examples of this subjective content (Levi R. Bryant, "Correlationism" in *The Meillassoux Dictionary*, ed. Peter Gratton and Paul J. Ennis [Edinburgh: Edinburgh University Press, 2015], pp. 46–8). Michael Austin's summary in the same volume provides a quick overview of the various forms correlationism is said to take by Meillassoux (Michael Austin, "Correlationism: Weak and Strong," pp. 48–50).

31	DNP, p. 52 (translation slightly modified).

32	DNP, p. 51.

33	For a longer exposition of FT with special attention to its importance for Laruelle's theory of the Ego and subject, see Smith, *François Laruelle's Principles of Non-Philosophy*, ch. 2.

34	DNP, p. 64.

35	DNP, p. 63.

36	George Jackson, *Soledad Brother: The Prison Letters of George Jackson* (Chicago: Lawrence Hill Books, 1994), p. 328.

37	See Michele Koerner, "Line of Escape: Gilles Deleuze's Encounter with George Jackson" in *Genre* 44.2 (2011): pp. 157–80. As Koerner explains, Jackson's use of the word "stick" was translated in the French edition of his text as "*arme*" or "weapon."

38	DNP, p. 20 (my emphasis).

39	FC, p. xxvi.

40	Cf. DNP, pp. 62–3.

41	DNP, p. 62.

42	FC, p. xxvi.

43	FC, p. xxvi.

44	NM, p. 120.

45	PNP, 176.

46	FC, p. xxviii.

3 Politics, or a Democracy (of) Thought

1 Galloway, p. 186.
2 PNP, p. 33.
3 François Laruelle quoted in Robin Mackay, "Introduction: Laruelle Undivided" in *From Decision to Heresy: Experiments in Non-Standard Thought*, ed. Robin Mackay (Falmouth: Urbanomic, 2012), p. 1.
4 Jacques Derrida, *The Post Card: From Socrates to Freud and Beyond*, trans. Alan Bass (Chicago: University of Chicago Press, 1987), p. 405.
5 Ibid., p. 405 n. 11.
6 Laruelle and Derrida, p. 80.
7 Ibid., p. 76.
8 Ibid., p. 81.
9 Martin Hägglund, *Radical Atheism: Derrida and the Time of Life* (Stanford: Stanford University Press, 2008), ch. 4.
10 Without entering into the debate, I will note that Caputo's own clear commitments to rationalism and Enlightenment values, including the decline of institutional religion through education, is largely ignored by Hägglund, though clearly on display in Caputo's response to Hägglund's reading. See John D. Caputo, "The Return of Anti-Religion: From Radical Atheism to Radical Theology" in *Journal for Cultural and Religious Theory* 11.2 (Spring 2011): pp. 32–125.
11 MT, p. 18. The text in parentheses is a translation of the footnote attached to the sentence. All translations are mine unless otherwise noted.
12 In *Nietzsche contre Heidegger*, Laruelle explains that machinic also refers to a process of production beyond or prior to the split between *physis* and *techne* (NH, pp. 104–5).
13 Gilles Deleuze and Félix Guattari, *Anti-Oedipus: Capitalism and Schizophrenia*, trans. Robert Hurley, Mark Seem, and Helen R. Lane (Minneapolis: University of Minnesota Press, 1983), pp. 1–16.
14 MT, p. 11.
15 MT, p. 103.
16 This materialist reading of Derrida via Deleuze, or the creation of a Delida/Derreuze series, is expanded and made general in Laruelle's *Le Déclin de l'écriture*. There Laruelle deepens his reading of Derrida and Deleuze to create a "minor hermeneutics" that brings in many of the themes from *Nietzsche*

contre Heidegger and *Au-delà du principe de pouvoir*. While *Le Déclin de l'écriture* marks the culmination of Philosophy I, we do not touch on its themes here, but will return to related questions of writing later, in chapter 6.

17   MT, p. 16.

18   This is the focus of the final chapter of the book (MT, pp. 261–91) and the question of the subject comes to be a major theme throughout non-philosophy. See, PNP, ch. 3, and Smith, *François Laruelle's Principles of Non-Philosophy*, ch. 3.

19   This book also sketches out a way of reading that is materialist: "Do not look for the 'meaning' of Nietzsche-thought within a theoretical system, in doctrinal themes, or a scene of writing, look instead within the operation of a process, within the production in the last instance of specifically political effects" (NH, p. 22).

20   NH, p. 17.

21   NH, pp. 11, 15, 145.

22   NH, p. 19.

23   NH, p. 14.

24   NH, p. 31.

25   NH, p. 35.

26   NH, p. 35.

27   NH, p. 31. Already we see the importance of the concept of "determination-in-the-last-instance" that will structure the majority of Laruelle's mature work.

28   For a much longer explication of the force-(of)-thought, see Smith, *François Laruelle's Principles of Non-Philosophy*, ch. 3, and for Laruelle's own presentation, see PNP, ch. 3.

29   BHO, p. 7. The entire quotation by Mao comes from his speech at Stalin's 60th birthday and reads: "Marxism comprises many principles, but in the final analysis they can all be brought back to a single sentence: it is right to rebel against the reactionaries." It came to be a major slogan during the Cultural Revolution in China that influenced communist thinkers in Europe who were not aligned with the Soviet vision of State communism. As a slogan, it appeared to take on a life of its own with Mao writing to revolutionary student groups asking them to give him support in their rebellion, but also urging them to practice restraint as well, saying: "at the same time we ask you to pay attention to uniting with all who can be united with. As for those who have committed serious mistakes, after their mistakes have been pointed out you should offer them a way

out of their difficulties by giving them work to do, and ena-
bling them to correct their mistakes and become new men.
Marx said: the proletariat must emancipate not only itself
but all mankind. If it cannot emancipate all mankind, then
the proletariat itself will not be able to achieve final emancipa-
tion. Will comrades please pay attention to this truth too" (Mao
Tse-Tung, "A Letter to the Red Guards of Tsinghua University
Middle School," https://www.marxists.org/reference/archive/
mao/selected-works/volume-9/mswv9_60.htm).

30   BHO, p. 7.
31   Carl Schmitt, *The Concept of the Political*, trans. George Schwab
     (Chicago and London: University of Chicago Press, 1996), p. 26.
32   This need to distinguish between friend and enemy is dis-
     cussed by many communist and other left-wing theorists, but
     Jodi Dean makes the case very forcefully and does so informed
     by the philosophical tradition. See Jodi Dean, *The Communist
     Horizon* (New York: Verso, 2012).
33   See Alain Badiou, *Saint Paul: The Foundation of Universalism*,
     trans. Ray Brassier (Stanford: Stanford University Press, 2003),
     and Slavoj Žižek, *The Puppet and the Dwarf: The Perverse Core of
     Christianity* (Cambridge, MA: MIT Press, 2003), ch. 5.
34   I will explore this in more detail in chapters 5–7. I recognize
     that the claim made here is not uncontroversial. It is also a
     claim that, in this form, brings together a number of arguments
     in political theory, the study of religion and culture, philoso-
     phy, theology, and other related fields. The literature on this is
     massive but interested readers may want to begin with the
     books listed below. Regarding specifics related to American
     and French forms of liberalism and universalism compare
     Andrew Dilts, *Punishment and Inclusion: Race, Membership, and
     the Limits of American Liberalism* (New York: Fordham Univer-
     sity Press, 2014), and Mayanthi L. Fernando, *The Republic
     Unsettled: Muslim French and the Contradictions of Secularism*
     (Durham: Duke University Press, 2014). Regarding subtraction
     and universalism in St. Paul, see Barber, *On Diaspora*, espe-
     cially chs. 3 and 4. See also Daniel Boyarin, *Border Lines: The
     Partition of Judaeo-Christianity* (Philadelphia: University of
     Pennsylvania Press, 2004), especially chs. 1–3. With regard to
     the specificity of the exclusion of Black and the subsequent
     need to subtract blackness to "belong," one should consult
     Frank B. Wilderson III, *Red, White, and Black: Cinema and the
     Structure of U.S. Antagonisms* (Durham and London: Duke

University Press, 2010), for an abstract investigation, and Khalil Gibran Muhammad, *The Condemnation of Blackness: Race, Crime, and the Making of Modern Urban America* (Cambridge, MA: Harvard University Press, 2010), for a sociological study.

35 TE, pp. 115–16.
36 ITD, p. 237.
37 ITD, p. 229.
38 ITD, p. 230 (translation slightly modified).
39 For the most succinct summary of Badiou's meta-philosophy, see Alain Badiou, *Manifesto for Philosophy*, trans. Norman Madarasz (Albany: State University of New York Press, 1999). There he writes, "philosophy's sole question is indeed that of the truth. Not that it produces any, but because it offers a mode of access to the unity of a moment of truths, a conceptual site in which the generic procedures are thought as compossible" (p. 37).
40 See Alain Badiou, *Logics of Worlds: Being and Event II*, trans. Alberto Toscano (New York and London: Continuum, 2009), pp. 9–33. Here Badiou sketches out how, in his view, the particular truth that "There are only bodies and language; except that there are truths" manifests in the four conditions of philosophy. Of course, this metaphilosophical statement accords with Badiou's particular philosophy and so it is about as surprising to find Badiou claiming this truth is manifest in all four domains as it would be to find Hegel declaring his own religious practice and background (Protestant Christianity) to be the highest form of religion.
41 For Laruelle's remarks about Badiou's "planification" of philosophy, see AB, pp. 29–32
42 ITD, p. 231 (translation slightly modified, and my emphasis).
43 "The Real is not political, but it is, from the start, cause of every democracy for which the political is required" (ITD, p. 232).
44 ITD, p. 236.
45 GS, pp. 98–9.
46 See NM, pp. 10–15.
47 NM, p. 15.
48 NM, p. 65.

4 Science, or Philosophy's Other

1 This ambiguous relationship is witnessed to by Heidegger himself in the very essay in which his infamous declaration

that "science does not think" is found. See Martin Heidegger, "Modern Science, Metaphysics, and Mathematics" in *Basic Writings*, trans. and ed. David Farrell Krell (New York: HarperSanFrancisco, 1993).

2 PNP, p. 257.
3 "No philosophy really escapes this triple division of intellectual labor. No epistemology – empiricist or idealist, positivist or materialist – can free itself from what is an invariant (though generally not recognized as such) of the Greco-philosophical interpretation of science, Anglo-Saxon interpretations included)" (TI, p. 55).
4 TI, p. 54.
5 TI, p. 83.
6 Readers especially interested in Laruelle's engagement with science should be aware that the goal of this chapter is to get an understanding of what the identity of science is for Laruelle and to see how that identity comes to be modeled by non-philosophy in its practice. Elsewhere I have written at length on the history of non-philosophy with special reference to this relationship to science. See Smith, *Ecologies of Thought*, ch. 6. For a full understanding of the non-philosophical conception of science, I would recommend reading the previous citation alongside of Smith, *François Laruelle's Principles of Non-Philosophy*, ch. 2.
7 Laruelle's own stance regarding technology is neither sanguine nor gloomy. This is clear from his remarks on biotechnological cloning. When asked by Philippe Petit if he insists on "cloning" for a concept important to *Principles of Non-Philosophy* and other texts during the same period, Laruelle sees no reason to reject science because of its capture by techno-capitalism. The technological element of science is not the essence of science, as he writes: "The technico-experimental apparatus is a material and a means organized by the essence of science, it is not this essence itself" (TI, p. 73).
8 TI, pp. 54–5. Cf. EU, pp. 122–44. In French, there are two words that can be translated into English as "knowledge": *connaissance* and *savoir*. Science is said to produce knowledge of the first kind, which is, roughly speaking, a kind of "know-how" or "understanding" – not knowledge of the essence of things, not true philosophical knowledge, but mere understanding. The second, *savoir*, is what philosophy aims at, the kind of knowledge that is sure and absolute. Knowledge (as under-

standing) is produced by science, but not philosophical knowledge, not philosophical *thought*.

9   TI, p. 55.
10 For a longer discussion of this non-philosophical reading of
    Latour, see Smith, *Ecologies of Thought*, pp. 157–61.
11 This term is present throughout Laruelle's work and is an
    important concept in *Théorie des identités*, but also in *Principles
    of Non-Philosophy*.
12 See Friedrich Nietzsche, *Thus Spoke Zarathustra: A Book for None
    and All*, trans. Robert B. Pippin, ed. Adrian del Caro (Cam-
    bridge: Cambridge University Press, 2006), pp. 20, 164.
13 EU, p. 52.
14 EU, p. 52.
15 EU, p. 53.
16 PD, p. 217 (translation slightly modified).
17 Gilles Deleuze and Félix Guattari, *What Is Philosophy?*, trans.
    Hugh Tomlinson and Graham Burchell (New York: Columbia
    University Press, 1994), p. 220 n. 5.
18 Ibid., p. 234 n. 16. Laruelle responded in two essays to these
    and other questions that Deleuze posed to Laruelle in private
    correspondence. These have been published in English as
    François Laruelle, "I, the Philosopher, Am Lying: A Reply to
    Deleuze" in *The Non-Philosophy Project: Essays by François Laru-
    elle*, trans. Taylor Adkins, ed. Gabriel Alkon and Boris Gunjevic
    (New York: Telos Press Publishing, 2012), pp. 40–74, and
    François Laruelle, "Letter to Deleuze," trans. Robin Mackay in
    From Decision to Heresy: Experiments in Non-Standard Thought,
    ed. Robin Mackay (Falmouth: Urbanomic, 2012), pp. 393–
    400.
19 Alain Badiou, "Mathematics and Philosophy: The Grand Style
    and the Little Style" in *Theoretical Writings*, trans. and ed. Ray
    Brassier and Alberto Toscano (London and New York: Con-
    tinuum, 2006), p. 17 (my emphasis).
20 TI, p. 100.
21 EU, p. 83.
22 TI, pp. 66–7.
23 TI, p. 105.
24 TI, p. 78.
25 TI, p. 74.
26 TI, p. 74.
27 TI, p. 75.
28 TI, p. 77.

29   TI, p. 92.
30   TI, p. 92.
31   TI, p. 93.
32   TI, p. 96.
33   TI, p. 96.
34   TI, p. 96.
35   See Smith, *François Laruelle's Principles of Non-Philosophy*, ch. 4, for a chapter-length study of Fichte's influence upon Laruelle's *Principles of Non-Philosophy*.
36   It is worth reminding readers of the clearest description of determination-in-the-last-instance found in *Introduction to Non-Marxism* and quoted in ch. 2: "So it is not a matter of 'difference,' of the co-extension of the One and the Two, of the One that is Two and of the Two which is One in some reversible way. It seems, instead, that DLI must be irreversible, the One is only One, even with the Two, and the Two forms a Two with the One only from its point of view as the Two" (NM, p. 42).
37   TI, p. 97.
38   EU, p. 67. Ian James also points out this privileging of science. See James, pp. 170–2.
39   PNP, pp. 33–4.
40   TI, p. 21.
41   TI, p. 22.

5   Ethics, or Universalizing the Stranger-Subject

1   Galloway, p. 187.
2   Frantz Fanon, *Black Skin, White Masks*, trans. Richard Philcox (New York: Grove Press, 2008), p. 76 (translation slightly modified).
3   The description of this work as "pessimistic" is first found in Saidiya V. Hartman, "The Position of the Unthought," an interview with Frank B. Wilderson III in *Qui Parle* 13.2 (Spring/ Summer 2003): pp. 183–201. Also important is the position put forward by the editors of that issue, Jared Sexton and Huey Copeland: "Raw Life: An Introduction," pp. 53–62. This position came to be criticized by Fred Moten in a series of articles, though eventually he came to try and harmonize his thought with that of Afro-pessimism following Jared Sexton's own attempts to harmonize Afro-pessimism with Moten's "Black

optimism." This is discussed in chapter 6. My thanks go to Daniel Colucciello Barber for the introduction to this debate and for pointing me toward the appropriate bibliographical references.

4 IP, p. 19.

5 Martin Heidegger, *Gesamtausgabe*, Vol. XCV (Frankfurt am Main: Vittorio Klostermann, 2014) p. 97. Translation on-line: www.critical-theory.com/7-new-translated-excerpts-on-heideggers-anti-semitism.

6 Martin Heidegger, *Gesamtausgabe*, Vol. XCVI, (Vittorio Klostermann: Frankfurt am Main, 2014), p. 243. Translation on-line <http://www.critical-theory.com/7-new-translated-excerpts-on-heideggers-anti-semitism/>.

7 Jared Sexton, "Unbearable Blackness," keynote lecture of "Terror and the Inhuman," Brown University, Providence, RI, October 25, 2012. The video of the keynote is available on-line: https://vimeo.com/52199779. For the sake of contextualizing his remarks and to join others in disseminating his work, I have transcribed the relevant remarks, excising some verbal tics: "natal alienation has been important to that distinction I have tried to draw. So I assert...that natal alienation, as the kind of signature of enslavement, is not something that is generalizable across a whole field of racial oppressions, colonial or otherwise. But what I am starting to think about more recently is that it's not just that natal alienation characterizes racial blackness, in law and politics, economy and culture, and so forth, but that what the fact of natal alienation, the legal fact, the political fact of it, the economic and cultural fact of it as it were, what it actually demonstrates is not...that there is a class of beings excluded from nativity and excluded from kinship and from genealogy and so on and so forth. But what that exclusion demonstrates is the untenability of kinship as such, of genealogy as such, as any natal occasion whatsoever. So what interests me maybe even more so now than my earlier attempt to try and demonstrate singularity and break out of the 'people of color' subsumption is the ways in which an attention to natal alienation in this way actually might make possible deracination in the most universal sense. For everything. Not just saying we suffer from deracination in ways you don't and so deal with that. That starts a conversation. But what I am interested in is how *we are deracinated, and you can be too.*"

8   IP, pp. 78, 79.
9   I have elsewhere addressed some of the criticisms of Laru-
    elle's work regarding his views on the Judaic turn in philoso-
    phy, and Jewish thought more generally. See Smith, *François
    Laruelle's Principles of Non-Philosophy*, pp. 87–92. Laruelle sees
    the philosophical tradition forming a Greek/Jew dyad. That
    is, while he is able to see the ways in which the dominant
    "Greek" culture (meaning the Europe of paganism baptized
    into Christianity) created a differential identity for itself by
    couching an internal other in "the Jew," he also recognizes
    that some of the greatest ideas in European culture flow from
    Jewish thought. This means, though, that even when the tradi-
    tion of Judaism is weaponized against that dominant culture,
    as in Levinas or Derrida, it still remains within the philosophi-
    cal dyad of Greek/Jew. As he writes: "The Jew is a heretic in
    philosophy, not outside of it. He can interrupt the course of
    philosophy enough to reverse it and to turn it upside down,
    not to seize it in its human identity and its non-sufficiency"
    (FC, pp. 54–5). Here we must understand that he is speaking
    of Judaism as it manifests within philosophy, not as a com-
    munity or a lived tradition. While there may be problems with
    his engagement with Christianity, as Daniel Colucciello Barber
    has argued in "Meditation, Religion, and Non-Consistency
    in-One" (*Angelaki: Journal of the Theoretical Humanities* 19.2
    [2014]: pp. 161–74), Laruelle's writing on Judaism is far from
    an anti-Semitism since he refuses the differential form of iden-
    tity inherent to anti-Semitic thought. If one wanted to engage
    more directly than Laruelle does with Jewish religious thought
    using the methods and concepts of non-philosophy to fashion
    a kind of "non-Judaism," there is nothing inherent to non-
    philosophy to prohibit such an undertaking. I have done this
    elsewhere with Islam to fashion a kind of non-Islam. See
    Anthony Paul Smith "Nature Deserves to Be Side by Side with
    the Angels: Nature and Messianism by way of Non-Islam" in
    Angelaki: Journal of the Theoretical Humanities 19.1 (2014): pp.
    151–69.
10 EE, p. 177. See EE, pp. 177–80, for his fuller argument that
    "ethics is structured as a metaphysics."
11 EE, p. 255.
12 TE, p. 128.
13 TE, p. 129.
14 IP, p. 24.

15 IP, pp. 24–5.
16 FC, p. 107.
17 See Norman Finkelstein, *The Holocaust Industry: Reflections on the Exploitation of Jewish Suffering*, 2nd edition (New York: Verso, 2015).
18 Laruelle is here in accord with Judith Butler's work on similar questions. See Judith Butler, *Frames of War: When Is Life Grievable?* (New York: Verso, 2009), pp. 1–32.
19 FC, pp. 106–7.
20 FC, p. 34.
21 GTV, p. 129.
22 GTV, p. 129 (translation slightly modified).
23 GTV, p. 45.
24 On moving from pity to compassion see GTV, pp. 45–9.
25 See GTV, pp. 106–16.
26 IP, p. 81.
27 AB, p. 231.
28 See Smith, *François Laruelle's Principles of Non-Philosophy*, pp. 68–80, for a fuller explication of this formalism.
29 AB, p. 233.
30 Regarding feminist uses of non-philosophy, see Kolozova, *Cut of the Real*, and for a reading of Laruelle crossed with queer theory, see Michael O'Rourke, "Quantum Queer: Towards a Non-Standard Queer Theory" in *Identities: Journal for Politics, Gender and Culture* 10.1–2 (2013): pp. 123–34.
31 François Laruelle quoted in Mackay, "Introduction: Laruelle Undivided," pp. 11–12.
32 NM, p. 71.
33 See Gilles Deleuze, "Immanence: A Life" in *Pure Immanence: Essays on a Life*, trans. Anne Boyman (New York: Zone Books, 2001), pp. 25–34, for his famous reading of a passage from Charles Dickens' *Our Mutual Friend*. There he describes the denuded character of a singular life as the essence of pure immanence.
34 This argument has been made by many, including Karl Marx in *Capital*, but for a succinct summary of the evidence mixed with personal narratives of enslaved Black people see Edward E. Baptist, *The Half Has Never Been Told: Slavery and the Making of American Capitalism* (New York: Basic Books, 2014).
35 See FC, pp. 101–4. Laruelle writes in this section, "*onto-biological death is already defeated by Man-in-Man*" (p. 103).

36   Fanon, pp. 185, 186. While *comparaison* is a standard French
      term that simply translates to its English cognate "compari-
      son," Fanon's translator recognizes that it is also a Creole term
      with a particular meaning for those in the French Antilles
      where Fanon was born and lived until adulthood. The meaning
      of the term within the linguistic world of Creole carries with
      it the sense of "contemptuousness" and "contemptible." See
      Shu-Mei Shih, "Comparative Racialization: An Introduction"
      in *PMLA* 123.5 (October 2008): pp. 1347–62, for a longer discus-
      sion. In this particular passage from Fanon, this double sense
      of *comparaison* refers to the white/Black philo-racial decision
      that even settles into the colonized mind and creates a disdain
      that a black subject may feel toward other black subjects *qua*
      blackness. But always, as Shu-Mei Shih writes, "Comparison
      is an enactment of contempt" (p. 1349).
37   Fanon, pp. 89, 93–4 (translation slightly modified).
38   Wilderson, pp. 10–11.
39   Ibid., p. 11.
40   John Eligon, "Michael Brown Spent Last Weeks Grappling
      with Problems and Promise," *New York Times*, August 24, 2014.
41   Afro-pessimist understandings of the ontological framing of
      Black people as humans differ from Giorgio Agamben's con-
      ception of bare life and the figure of *Homo sacer*. Agamben's
      analysis is faulted for ignoring the importance of anti-black-
      ness in the construction of the death camps intended to destroy
      European Jews and other Europeans marked as not-quite-
      human and so closer to the Black subject marked as "not-
      human." Such camps were based on designs and experiments
      carried out first in the colonization of Africa, and on the linger-
      ing effects of slavery throughout the West. Furthermore, by
      extending the frame of biopolitics beyond European antago-
      nisms, Afro-pessimist theorists are able to show a deeper
      antagonism within which anti-Semitism functions. This allows
      for a better understanding of anti-Semitism just as much as it
      allows for a better understanding of anti-blackness. See Jared
      Sexton, "The Social Life of Social Death: On Afro-Pessimism
      and Black Optimism" in *Intensions* 5 (Fall/Winter 2011), pp. 12,
      16–19, and Alexander G. Weheliye, *Habeas Viscus: Racializing
      Assemblages, Biopolitics, and Black Feminist Theories of the Human*
      (Durham and London: Duke University Press, 2014), pp. 33–45.
      It is important to note that I am not suggesting an engagement
      between Laruelle and Agamben is not possible, but I find it

more faithful to the strangeness of non-philosophy to put it in dialogue with creative and powerful theorists who are, despite their creativity and power, thrust to the outside of European philosophy proper.

42 PNP, p. 206. For a longer explication of this passage with specific reference to other European philosophers, see Smith, *François Laruelle's Principles of Non-Philosophy*, pp. 94–100.
43 PNP, pp. 207–8.
44 Fanon, p. 197.
45 Galloway, p. 189.
46 Cf. TE, p. 24.

6   Fabulation, or Non-Philosophy as Philo-Fiction

1 Walidah Imarisha, "Introduction" in *Octavia's Brood: Science Fiction from Social Justice Movements*, ed. adrienne maree brown and Walidah Imarisha (Oakland: AK Press, 2015), p. 3.
2 PF, p. 63.
3 Other authors more expert than myself regarding visual artistic practices have written on this subject at great length. For a non-philosophical vision of film, see Ó Maoilearca, *Philosophy and the Moving Image*, ch. 8 and Conclusion; and see Galloway, ch. 8, for a detailed discussion of the way Laruelle's investigations into photography and drawing manifest his understanding of utopia.
4 See John Ó Maoilearca and Anthony Paul Smith, "The Philosophical Inversion: Laruelle's Knowledge Without Domination" in *Laruelle and Non-Philosophy*, ed. John Ó Maoilearca and Anthony Paul Smith (Edinburgh: Edinburgh University Press, 2012), pp. 1–18.
5 Laruelle, "Non-Philosophy, Weapon of Last Defence," p. 247.
6 PF, p. 3.
7 See Badiou, *Manifesto for Philosophy*, pp. 33–40, 61–8, 79–88.
8 Laruelle privileges the example of photography through two long essays. It is clear from those essays, though, that photography provides simply the material for thinking generally about art, and so he is not making an argument about the progress of art through technology or photography's superior place with regard to other forms of art: "Photo-fiction is certainly not an eye equipped with an apparatus reducible to a

technology. It is comprised of technology and the lived but also of the concept and algebra disposed to differentiated places, for example whole numbers that are opened up or fragmented. Photo-fiction cannot be reduced to the photographic act or the taking of a photo that is simply commented upon or provided with some sort of caption. It is a thought that builds itself off the photo without being its metaphor, but which is nonetheless a fiction and an attempt at a generic science of the world" (PF, p. 33).

9   PF, p. 5.
10 PNS, p. 490.
11 PNS, p. 493.
12 PF, p. 28.
13 While Laruelle clearly draws in many ways from various forms of philosophical realism, he also clearly rejects the naive realism present in a great deal of theorizing regarding photography as when he writes, "photo-fiction is lived as art without any bit of realism and it is in this way that it forms an even more intense chaos through the absence of the world or of its own sufficiency" (PF, 20).
14 PF, p. 84 (translation slightly modified).
15 PF, p. 84.
16 Weheliye, p. 4.
17 Ibid., p. 5. Weheliye directs a stinging criticism of the way in which white scholars often engage with Black studies when he points to Judith Butler's mere "passing reference" to the work of Sylvia Wynter and others (ibid., pp. 22–3). In the course of this text, my use of what I have learned from the work of major theorists in Black studies could appear somewhat like a passing reference and indeed, since this is a book aiming to help elucidate the thought of François Laruelle, I do make use of their work to speak about what Laruelle has written. However, without being able to speak to its failure or success, as that is for others to decide, my goal has been precisely to show the ways in which Laruelle's thought is strange to the standard model of (white) European philosophy. That a project like Laruelle's is carried out in similar ways by those cast as minorities according to the logic of the (European) world should not come as a surprise then. But the precise ways in which these projects converge is striking. So, for example, Hortense Spillers is influenced by the Althusserian distinction between the real object and the object of knowledge in the

same way that Laruelle is. Spillers deploys it in her attempt to rethink the human outside of the determinations of philosophy, while also tracing the exact contours of that determining apparatus (ibid., pp. 18–19), just as Laruelle does. Or, to take another example from Weheliye's study, Wynter attempts to rethink the very conception of the human and does so by rejecting all forms of theodicy, including the naturalized form of "biodicy" (ibid., p. 25). Frankly, if Laruelle were just another in a long list of French philosophers who might allow for interesting discussions in the parlor, I would not be interested in his work when there are thinkers to read and think with like Frantz Fanon, Frank B. Wilderson III, Hortense Spillers, Sylvia Wynter, and others. But insofar as the question of human liberation and salvation guides his work and he has given much time to thinking how the house of philosophy may be used against itself by homeless strangers, then his work may offer resources alongside of these thinkers in reframing thought according to a human freed from the philosophical overdetermination of Man.

18 I owe the insight that there is a certain fit between Moten's work and Laruelle's to a conversation with Alex Dubilet. He is working on a study of their work which will likely go deeper into Moten's rich oeuvre to develop other lines of alliance between Moten's notion of the "undercommons" and Laruelle's positive conception of the victim.

19 Fanon, p. 90.

20 Fred Moten, "Blackness and Nothingness (Mysticism in the Flesh)" in *The South Atlantic Quarterly* 112.4 (Fall 2013): p. 749. Again, and especially with regard to this issue, I want to acknowledge and thank Alex Dubilet for discussions regarding Laruelle and Moten.

21 Moten, pp. 749–50.

22 Wilderson, p. 23.

23 See Sexton, "Social Life."

24 Wilderson, p. 23.

25 For an anthropological study of this current conjuncture of racism, see Eduardo Bonilla-Silva, *Racism without Racists: Color-Blind Racism and the Persistence of Racial Inequality in America* (Lanham, MD: Rowman & Littlefield Publishers, 2014). While this study is limited to an American context, it may very likely be applied to European multicultural societies.

26 See Eugene Thacker, Daniel Colucciello Barber, Nicola Masciandaro, and Alexander R. Galloway, *Dark Nights of the Universe* (Miami: [Name], 2013).
27 Instructive here is Alexander R. Galloway's weaving of the
declaration of the Haitian revolution that "all citizens will be
called black regardless of color" (Galloway, p. 145) with this
cosmic *uchronia*. See Galloway, pp. 145–50.
28 GTV, p. 44.

7   Religion, or a Rigorous Heresy

1 Søren Kierkegaard, *Practice in Christianity*, trans. Howard V.
Hong and Edna H. Hong (Princeton: Princeton University
Press: 1991), p. 9. For a materialist reading of Kierkegaard's
work in line with recent French philosophical recoveries of
Hegel, Nietzsche, and others, see Michael O'Neill Burns,
Kierkegaard and the Matter of Philosophy: A Fractured Dialectic
(London: Rowman & Littlefield International, 2015).
2 Kierkegaard, p. 9.
3 See Smith, *Ecologies of Thought*, pp. 95–112.
4 Of course the two philosophers have very different senses
of materialism, and Laruelle's "decline of materialism in the
name of matter" differs from both even more. However,
Henry's recasting of a radical phenomenology has been predicated on directing his analyses away from the *eidos* (essence,
idea, form) and toward the *hyle* (matter, stuff) – see Michel
Henry, *Material Phenomenology*, trans. Scott Davidson (New
York: Fordham University Press, 2008) – while Badiou has
explicitly declared his project to be an attempt to reinvent
dialectical materialism – see Badiou, *Logics of Worlds*.
5 Gilles Deleuze, "Seminar on Spinoza / Cours Vincennes
25/11/1980," www.webdeleuze.com/php/texte.php?cle=17&
groupe=Spinoza&langue=2.
6 My sense of "attention" and the challenge to the smooth
functioning of thought is indebted to Philip Goodchild's
philosophical analysis of piety. See Philip Goodchild, *Capitalism and Religion: The Price of Piety* (London: Routledge,
2002).
7 See Jean-Yves Lacoste, "Foreword to Michel Henry's *Words of
Christ*," trans. Aaron Riches and Peter M. Candler Jr., in Michel

Henry, *Words of Christ* (Grand Rapids: William B. Eerdmans Publishing Company, 2012), p. x, and Michelle Rebidoux, "*C'est moi le principe et la fin*: The Mysterious 'Middle' of Michel Henry's (Christian) Phenomenology of Life" in *Analecta Hermeneutica* 3 (2011): pp. 7–10. A particularly desperate attempt to persuade us that Henry is rigorously and unimpeachably orthodox may also be found in Karl Hefty's "Introduction to the English Edition" of *Words of Christ* (trans. Christina M. Gschwandtner). Throughout his introduction, Hefty goes to great pains to emphasize that Henry's philosophy is completed in an already decided theology.

8   For more on these two tendencies in Continental philosophy of religion, see Anthony Paul Smith and Daniel Whistler, "What is Continental Philosophy of Religion Now?" in *After the Postsecular and the Postmodern: New Essays in Continental Philosophy of Religion* (Newcastle-upon-Tyne: Cambridge Scholars Publishing, 2010), pp. 1–24.

9   Michel Henry, *I Am the Truth: Toward a Philosophy of Christianity*, trans. Susan Emanuel (Stanford: Stanford University Press, 2003), p. 1.

10 Ibid., pp. 1–2.

11 Ibid., pp. 23, 30.

12 These remarks are found throughout *I Am the Truth* but perhaps nowhere is the vitriol so much on display as in *Barbarism*, trans. Scott Davidson (New York and London: Continuum, 2012).

13 Henry, *I Am the Truth*, p. 60 (translation modified).

14 Ibid., p. 104.

15 Ibid., p. 260.

16 On the hidden and invisible in Islam and a philosophical interpretation of those themes there, see Christian Jambet, *Le Caché et l'apparent* (Paris: Herne, 2003).

17 Henry, *I Am the Truth*, p. 171.

18 While the obsession with messianism is well known in Continental philosophy of religion, largely dominated by Christian concerns with some important Jewish thinkers also finding a certain pride of place, the particular form this takes in Islam is all but unknown, especially in the Anglophone literature. Christian Jambet's *La Grande Resurrection d'Alamût. Les formes de la liberté dans le shî'isme ismaélien* (Lagresse: Verdier, 1990) should be a classic in this regard, but has been mostly passed over in the Anglophone world.

19　See Slavoj Žižek, *The Ticklish Subject: The Absent Centre of Political Ontology* (London and New York: Verso, 2008), ch. 3, as well as Bruno Bosteels' remarks in his translator's introduction to Alain Badiou, *Theory of the Subject* (London and New York: Continuum, 2009), p. x.

20　Badiou, *Saint Paul*, p. 1.

21　Ibid., p. 4.

22　Ibid., p. 5.

23　Ibid.

24　Ibid.

25　For Badiou's mature theory of the subject and the different figures in which a subject may be expressed as a mode of the event (faithful, reactive, and obscure), see Badiou, *Logics of Worlds*, pp. 43–78.

26　Badiou, *Theory of the Subject*, p. 15.

27　Ibid, pp. 17, 16.

28　Ibid., p. 17.

29　Ibid.

30　Badiou, *Logics of Worlds*, p. 428.

31　Badiou, *Theory of the Subject*, p. 16.

32　Kierkegaard, p. 174.

33　FC, p. 113.

34　FC, p. 114.

35　Gabriel Alkon and Boris Gunjevic, "Theology and Non-Philosophy" in *The Non-Philosophy Project: Essays by François Laruelle*, ed. Gabriel Alkon and Boris Gunjevic (New York: Telos Press Publishing, 2012), p. 238.

36　Alkon and Gunjevic, p. 240.

37　MNP, p. 104.

38　Alkon and Gunjevic, pp. 241–2.

39　FC, p. 102.

40　FC, p. 103.

41　AB, pp. 111–46.

42　On Christianity and European colonialism, see Barber, *On Diaspora*, pp. 88–114.

43　FC, p. 46.

44　FC, p. 115.

45　FC, p. 116.

46　FC, p. 117.

47　Christian Jambet and Guy Lardreau, *L'Ange. Pour une cynégétique du semblant, Ontologie de la révolution 1* (Paris: Grasset, 1976). Again, this work is an important reference point for

Laruelle's *Nietzsche contre Heidegger* as it is often cited, and some of the themes regarding dualism in politics are derived in dialogue with this text.

48 Christian Jambet and Guy Lardreau, *Le Monde. Réponse à la question: qu'est-ce que les droits de l'homme?* (Paris: Grasset, 1978).

49 BHO, p. 7.

50 FC, pp. 38–9.

51 FC, p. xxviii.

52 FC, p. xxviii.

53 FC, p. xxviii.

54 FC, p. 39.

55 FC, p. 41 (my emphasis).

56 Ibid.

57 In always referring to this as the Shoah we bring attention to the fact that, while we are entreated to never forget, we do often forget the 5 million non-Jewish people murdered during the Holocaust; we forget that the measure of such a crime has not yet truly been taken.

58 FC, p. 4.

59 SU, p. 3.

60 SU, p. 192.

61 PNP, pp. 55–6. As Nicola Rubczak and I explain in our translators' note, Laruelle here marks a difference between *la mystique* and *le mystique*, the latter taking the male definite article, which has the effect of forming a neologism in French. The difference follows that of *la politique* and *le politique* in French, which marks the philosophical difference between "politics" and "the political." We have tried to capture this by translating *la mystique* as "mystique" – since Laruelle also distinguishes this from what we would call "mysticism" (*le mysticisme*, another French neologism) – and *le mystique* as "the mystical."

62 MNP, p. 8.

63 Meister Eckhart, "On Detachment" in *The Complete Mystical Works of Meister Eckhart*, trans. and ed. Maurice O'C. Walshe (New York: The Crossroad Publishing Company, 2009), p. 566.

64 Ibid.

65 Bernard McGinn, "Three Forms of Negativity in Christian Mysticism" in *Knowing the Unknowable: Science and Religions on God and the Universe*, ed. John W. Bowker (London: I. B. Tauris, 2008), p. 110.

66 MNP, p. 231.

67 MNP, p. 109.
68 MNP, p. 85.
69 MNP, p. 27.
70 MNP, p. 174.
71 PNS, p. 440.
72 See H. Peter Steeves, "Mars Attacked! Interplanetary Environ-
    mental Ethics and the Science of Life" in *The Things Themselves:
    Phenomenology and the Return to the Everyday* (Albany: SUNY
    Press, 2006), pp. 127–45, and Lee Smolin, *The Life of the Cosmos*
    (Oxford: Oxford University Press, 1997).
73 PNS, p. 440.
74 PNS, p. 450.
75 FC, p. 113.

Conclusion: The Future of Non-Philosophy

1   FC, p. 121.
2   IP, p. 50.
3   IP, p. 25.
4   By way of a reminder, the locution *penser victime* is translated
    in IP as "victim-thinking," and I explain there that the original
    term shares many of the same difficulties found in translating
    Luce Irigaray's "parler femme."
5   IP, p. 50.
6   IP, p. 80.
7   This is what Laruelle gets at in his discussion with Philippe
    Petit when they discuss the issue of homelessness. See IP,
    pp. 87–8.
8   IP, p. 80.
9   FC, pp. 121–2.
10 FC, p. 77.
11 FC, p. 123.
12 PNS, pp. 437–9.
13 PNS, p. 437.
14 Fanon, p. 76.
15 See Daniel Colucciello Barber, "Whylessness: The Universe
    Deaf and Blind" in *Dark Nights of the Universe* (Miami: [Name],
    2013), pp. 21–44. There he writes, "What Laruelle is telling us,
    or what we may find Laruelle's departure from Eckhart, is that
    life [a transcendental hallucination produced by philosophy],
    if it is something communicable, is not the universe [a first

name for the One]. Life divides the universe, it gives the Universe an aim, the aim of achieving life. Life subjects the Universe to survival.... They [the philosopher and the theologian] constantly seek to make sure that life begins, that there is survival. But in the beginning there is not light, there is not life, there is the black Universe. Survival is the denial of the Universe" (pp. 37, 38).

Bibliography

Alkon, Gabriel, and Boris Gunjevic. "Theology and Non-Philosophy" in *The Non-Philosophy Project: Essays by François Laruelle.* Edited by Gabriel Alkon and Boris Gunjevic. New York: Telos Press Publishing, 2012. 232–42.

Austin, Michael. "Correlationism: Weak and Strong" in *The Meillassoux Dictionary.* Edited by Peter Gratton and Paul J. Ennis. Edinburgh: Edinburgh University Press, 2015. 48–50.

Badiou, Alain. "Interview with Ben Woodard" in *The Speculative Turn: Continental Materialism and Realism.* Edited by Levi Bryant, Nick Srnicek, and Graham Harman. Melbourne: re:press, 2011. 19–20.

—— *Logics of Worlds: Being and Event II.* Translated by Alberto Toscano. New York and London: Continuum, 2009.

—— *Manifesto for Philosophy.* Translated by Norman Madarasz. Albany: State University of New York Press, 1999.

—— "Mathematics and Philosophy: The Grand Style and the Little Style" in *Theoretical Writings.* Edited and translated by Ray Brassier and Alberto Toscano. London and New York: Continuum, 2004.

—— *Saint Paul: The Foundation of Universalism.* Translated by Ray Brassier. Stanford: Stanford University Press, 2003.

—— *Theory of the Subject.* Translated by Bruno Bosteels. London and New York: Continuum, 2009.

Baptist, Edward E. *The Half Has Never Been Told: Slavery and the Making of American Capitalism.* New York: Basic Books, 2014.

Barber, Daniel Colucciello. "Meditation, Religion, and Non-Consistency in-One" in *Angelaki: Journal of the Theoretical Humanities* 19.2 (2014): 161–74.

—— *On Diaspora: Christianity, Religion, and Secularity.* Eugene, OR: Cascade Books, 2011.

—— "Whylessness: The Universe Deaf and Blind" in *Dark Nights of the Universe*. Miami: [Name], 2013. 21–44.

Bataille, Georges. *Theory of Religion.* Translated by Robert Hurley. New York: Zone Books, 1989.

Bonilla-Silva, Eduardo. *Racism without Racists: Color-Blind Racism and the Persistence of Racial Inequality in America.* Lanham, MD: Rowman and Littlefield Publishers, 2014.

Boyarin, Daniel. *Border Lines: The Partition of Judaeo-Christianity.* Philadelphia: University of Pennsylvania Press, 2004.

Brassier, Ray. "Laruelle and the Reality of Abstraction" in *Laruelle and Non-Philosophy*. Edited by John Ó Maoilearca and Anthony Paul Smith. Edinburgh: Edinburgh University Press, 2012. 100–21.

—— *Nihil Unbound: Enlightenment and Extinction.* Basingstoke: Palgrave, 2007.

Burns, Michael O'Neill. *Kierkegaard and the Matter of Philosophy: A Fractured Dialectic.* London: Rowman & Littlefield International, 2015.

Butler, Judith. *Frames of War: When Is Life Grievable?* New York: Verso, 2009.

Byrant, Levi R. "Correlationism" in *The Meillassoux Dictionary*. Edited by Peter Gratton and Paul J. Ennis. Edinburgh: Edinburgh University Press, 2015. 46–8.

Caputo, John D. "The Return of Anti-Religion: From Radical Atheism to Radical Theology" in *Journal for Cultural and Religious Theory* 11.2 (Spring 2011): 32–125.

Césaire, Aimé. *Discourse on Colonialism.* Translated by Joan Pinkham. New York: Monthly Review Press, 2000.

Dean, Jodi. *The Communist Horizon.* New York: Verso, 2012.

Deleuze, Gilles. "Immanence: A Life" in *Pure Immanence: Essay on a Life*. Translated by Anne Boyman. New York: Zone Books, 2001. 25–34.

—— *Nietzsche and Philosophy.* Translated by Hugh Tomlinson. New York: Columbia University Press, 1983.

—— "Seminar on Spinoza / Cours Vincennes 25/11/1980." www.webdeleuze.com/php/texte.php?cle=17&groupe=Spinoza&langue=2.

Deleuze, Gilles, and Félix Guattari. *Anti-Oedipus: Capitalism and Schizophrenia*. Translated by Robert Hurley, Mark Seem, and Helen R. Lane. Minneapolis: University of Minnesota Press, 1983.

—— *What Is Philosophy?* Translated by Hugh Tomlinson and Graham Burchell. New York: Columbia University Press, 1994.

Derrida, Jacques. *The Post Card: From Socrates to Freud and Beyond*. Translated by Alan Bass. Chicago: University of Chicago Press, 1987.

Dilts, Andrew. *Punishment and Inclusion: Race, Membership, and the Limits of American Liberalism*. New York: Fordham University Press, 2014.

Eckhart, "On Detachment" in *The Complete Mystical Works of Meister Eckhart*. Edited and translated by Maurice O'C. Walshe. New York: The Crossroad Publishing Company, 2009. 566–75.

Eligon, John. "Michael Brown Spent Last Weeks Grappling with Problems and Promise." *New York Times*, August 24, 2014.

Fanon, Frantz. *Black Skin, White Masks*. Translated by Richard Philcox. New York: Grove Press, 2008.

Fernando, Mayanthi L. *The Republic Unsettled: Muslim French and the Contradictions of Secularism*. Durham: Duke University Press, 2014.

Finkelstein, Norman. *The Holocaust Industry: Reflections on the Exploitation of Jewish Suffering*, 2nd edition. New York: Verso, 2015.

Foucault, Michel. *The Order of Things: An Archeology of the Human Sciences*. London: Routledge, 2002.

Galloway, Alexander R. *Laruelle: Against the Digital*. Minneapolis: University of Minnesota Press, 2014.

Gangle, Rocco. *François Laruelle's Philosophies of Difference: A Critical Introduction and Guide*. Edinburgh: Edinburgh University Press, 2013.

—— "Translator's Introduction" in *Philosophies of Difference: A Critical Introduction to Non-Philosophy*. London and New York: Continuum, 2010. vi–xii.

Goodchild, Philip. *Capitalism and Religion: The Price of Piety*. London: Routledge, 2002.

Hägglund, Martin. *Radical Atheism: Derrida and the Time of Life*. Stanford: Stanford University Press, 2008.

Hartman, Saidiya V. "The Position of the Unthought." Interview with Frank B. Wilderson III in *Qui Parle* 13.2 (Spring/Summer 2003): 183–201.

Heidegger, Martin. "Modern Science, Metaphysics, and Mathematics" in *Basic Writings*. Edited and translated by David Farrell Krell. New York: HarperSanFrancisco, 1993. 247–82.

Henry, Michel. *Barbarism*. Translated by Scott Davidson. New York and London: Continuum, 2012.

—— *I Am the Truth: Toward a Philosophy of Christianity*. Translated by Susan Emanuel. Stanford: Stanford University Press, 2003.

—— *Material Phenomenology*. Translated by Scott Davidson. New York: Fordham University Press, 2008.

Husserl, Edmund. *Cartesian Meditations: An Introduction to Phenomenology*. Translated by Dorion Cairns. Dordrecht: Kluwer Academic Publishers, 1999.

Imarisha, Walidah. "Introduction" in *Octavia's Brood: Science Fiction from Social Justice Movements*. Edited by adrienne maree brown and Walidah Imarisha. Oakland: AK Press, 2015. 3–5.

Jackson, George. *Soledad Brother: The Prison Letters of George Jackson*. Chicago: Lawrence Hill Books, 1994.

Jambet, Christian. *La Grande Résurrection d'Alamût. Les formes de la liberté dans le shî'isme ismaélien*. Lagresse: Verdier, 1990.

—— *Le Caché et l'apparent*. Paris: Herne, 2003.

Jambet, Christian, and Guy Lardreau. *L'Ange. Pour une cynégétique du semblant, ontologie de la révolution 1*. Paris: Grasset, 1976.

—— *Le Monde. Réponse à la question: qu'est-ce que les droits de l'homme?* Paris: Grasset, 1978.

James, Ian. *The New French Philosophy*. Cambridge: Polity, 2012.

Kant, Immanuel. *Critique of Pure Reason*. Edited and translated by Paul Guyer and Allen W. Wood. Cambridge: Cambridge University Press, 1998.

Kierkegaard, Søren. *Practice in Christianity*. Translated by Howard V. Hong and Edna H. Hong. Princeton: Princeton University Press, 1991.

Koerner, Michele. "Line of Escape: Gilles Deleuze's Encounter with George Jackson" in *Genre* 44.2 (2011): 157–80.

Kolozova, Katerina. *Cut of the Real: Subjectivity in Poststructuralist Philosophy*. New York: Columbia University Press, 2014.

Lacan, Jacques. *The Seminar of Jacques Lacan, Book XVII: The Other Side of Psychoanalysis*. Translated by Russell Grigg. New York: W. W. Norton & Company, 2007.

—— *The Seminar of Jacques Lacan, Book XX: On Feminine Sexuality, The Limits of Love and Knowledge. Encore 1972–1973*. Translated by Bruce Fink. New York: W. W. Norton and Company, 1998.

Lacoste, Jean-Yves. "Foreword to Michel Henry's Words of Christ." Translated by Aaron Riches and Peter M. Candler Jr. In Michel Henry, *Words of Christ*. Grand Rapids: William B. Eerdmans Publishing Company, 2012. ix–x.

Lardreau, Guy. *La véracité. Essai d'une philosophie négative*. Paris: Verdier, 1993.

—— *Vive le materialisme!* Paris: Verdier, 2001.

Laruelle, François. *Anti-Badiou: On the Introduction of Maoism into Philosophy*. Translated by Robin Mackay. London: Bloomsbury, 2013.

—— *Au-delà du principe de pouvoir*. Paris: Payot, 1978.

—— *En tant qu'Un. La "non-philosophie" expliquée aux philosophes*. Paris: Aubier, 1991.

—— *Éthique de l'étranger. Du crime contre l'humanité*. Paris: Kimé, 2000.

—— *Future Christ: A Lesson in Heresy*. Translated by Anthony Paul Smith. London: Continuum, 2010.

—— *General Theory of Victims*. Translated by Jessie Hock and Alex Dubilet. Cambridge: Polity, 2015.

—— "I, the Philosopher, Am Lying: A Reply to Deleuze." Translated by Taylor Adkins. In *The Non-Philosophy Project: Essays by François Laruelle*. Edited by Gabriel Alkon and Boris Gunjevic. New York: Telos Press Publishing, 2012. 40–74.

—— *Intellectuals and Power: The Insurrection of the Victim*. In conversation with Philippe Petit. Translated by Anthony Paul Smith. Cambridge: Polity, 2014.

—— *Introduction aux sciences génériques*. Paris: Pétra, 2008.

—— *Introduction to Non-Marxism*. Translated by Anthony Paul Smith. Minneapolis: Univocal Publishing, 2015.

—— "Is Thinking Democratic? Or, How to Introduce Theory into Democracy." Translated by Anthony Paul Smith. In *Laruelle and Non-Philosophy*. Edited by John Ó Maoilearca and Anthony Paul Smith. Edinburgh: Edinburgh University Press, 2012. 227–37.

—— *Le Déclin de l'écriture*. Paris: Aubier-Flammarion, 1977.

—— *Le Principe de minorité*. Paris: Aubier Montaigne, 1981.

—— "Letter to Deleuze" Translated by Robin Mackay. In *From Decision to Heresy: Experiments in Non-Standard Thought*. Edited by Robin Mackay. Falmouth: Urbanomic, 2012. 393–400.

—— *Machines textuelles. Déconstruction et libido d'écriture*. Paris: Éditions du Seuil, 1976.

—— *Mystique non-philosophique à l'usage des contemporains*. Paris: L'Harmattan, 2007.

——*Nietzsche contre Heidegger. Thèses pour une politique nietzschéenne.* Paris: Payot, 1977.

—— "Non-Philosophy, Weapon of Last Defence: An Interview with François Laruelle." Translated by Anthony Paul Smith. In *Laruelle and Non-Philosophy*. Edited by John Ó Maoilearca and Anthony Paul Smith. Edinburgh: Edinburgh University Press, 2012. 238–51.

—— *Philosophie non-standard. Générique, quantique, Philo-Fiction.* Paris: Kimé, 2010.

—— *Philosophies of Difference: A Critical Introduction to Non-Philosophy.* Translated by Rocco Gangle. London and New York: Continuum, 2010.

—— *Philosophy and Non-Philosophy.* Translated by Taylor Adkins. Minneapolis: Univocal Publishing, 2013.

—— *Photo-Fiction, a Non-Standard Aesthetics.* Translated by Drew S. Burk. Minneapolis: Univocal Publishing, 2012.

—— "Principles for a Generic Ethics." Translated by Anthony Paul Smith. In *Angelaki: Journal of the Theoretical Humanities* 19.2 (2014): 12–23.

—— *Principles of Non-Philosophy.* Translated by Nicola Rubczak and Anthony Paul Smith. London and New York: Bloomsbury, 2013.

—— *Struggle and Utopia at the End Times of Philosophy.* Translated by Drew S. Burk and Anthony Paul Smith. Minneapolis: Univocal Publishing, 2012.

—— "The Transcendental Method." Translated by Christopher Eby. In *From Decision to Heresy: Experiments in Non-Standard Thought*. Edited by Robin Mackay. Falmouth: Urbanomic, 2012. 135–71.

—— *Théorie des étrangers. Science des hommes, démocratie, non-psychanalyse.* Paris: Kimé, 1995.

—— *Théorie des identités. Fractalité généralisée et philosophie artificielle.* Paris: PUF, 1992.

—— *Une biographie de l'homme ordinaire. Des autorités et des minorités.* Paris: Aubier, 1985.

—— "What Is Non-Philosophy?" Translated by Taylor Adkins. In *From Decision to Heresy: Experiments in Non-Standard Thought.* Edited by Robin Mackay. Falmouth: Urbanomic, 2012. 185–244.

Laruelle, François, and Jacques Derrida. "Controversy Over the Possibility of a Science of Philosophy." Translated by Ray Brassier and Robin Mackay. In *The Non-Philosophy Project: Essays by François Laruelle*. Edited by Gabriel Alkon and Boris Gunjevic. New York: Telos Press Publishing, 2012. 75–93.

Laruelle, François, Tony Brachet, Gilbert Kieffer, et al. *Dictionary of Non-Philosophy*. Translated by Taylor Adkins. Minneapolis: Univocal Publishing, 2013.

Mackay, Robin. "Introduction: Laruelle Undivided" in *From Decision to Heresy: Experiments in Non-Standard Thought*. Edited by Robin Mackay. Falmouth: Urbanomic, 2012. 1–32.

McGinn, Bernard. "Three Forms of Negativity in Christian Mysticism" in *Knowing the Unknowable: Science and Religions on God and the Universe*. Edited by John W. Bowker. London: I. B. Tauris, 2008. 99–121.

Meillassoux, Quentin. *After Finitude: An Essay on the Necessity of Contingency*. Translated by Ray Brassier. London: Continuum, 2008.

Moran, Dermot. *Husserl's Crisis of the European Sciences and Transcendental Phenomenology: An Introduction*. Cambridge: Cambridge University Press, 2012.

Morelle, Louis. "Speculative Realism: After Finitude, and Beyond? A *vade mecum*." Translated by Leah Orth with the assistance of Mark Allan Ohm, Jon Cogburn, and Emily Beck Cogburn. *Speculations* 3 (2012): 241–72.

Moten, Fred. "Blackness and Nothingness (Mysticism in the Flesh)" in *The South Atlantic Quarterly* 112.4 (Fall 2013): 737–80.

Muhammad, Khalil Gibran. *The Condemnation of Blackness: Race, Crime, and the Making of Modern Urban America*. Cambridge, MA: Harvard University Press, 2010.

Nietzsche, Friedrich. *Thus Spoke Zarathustra: A Book for None and All*. Edited by Adrian del Caro. Translated by Robert B. Pippin. Cambridge: Cambridge University Press, 2006.

Ó Maoilearca, John. *All Thoughts Are Equal: Laruelle and Nonhuman Philosophy*. Minneapolis: University of Minnesota Press, 2015.

—— *Philosophy and the Moving Image: Refractions of Reality*. Basingstoke: Palgrave Macmillan, 2010.

—— *Post-Continental Philosophy: An Outline*. London and New York: Routledge, 2006.

Ó Maoilearca, John, and Anthony Paul Smith. "The Philosophical Inversion: Laruelle's Knowledge Without Domination" in *Laruelle and Non-Philosophy*. Edited by John Ó Maoilearca and Anthony Paul Smith. Edinburgh: Edinburgh University Press, 2012. 1–18.

O'Rourke, Michael. "Quantum Queer: Towards a Non-Standard Queer Theory" in *Identities: Journal for Politics, Gender and Culture* 10.1–2 (2013): 123–34.

Plato, *Epistles*. Translated by R. G. Bury. Cambridge, MA: Harvard University Press, 1999.

Rebidoux, Michelle. *"C'est moi le principe et la fin*: The Mysterious 'Middle' of Michel Henry's (Christian) Phenomenology of Life" in *Analecta Hermeneutica* 3 (2011): 1–14.

Schmitt, Carl. *The Concept of the Political*. Translated by George Schwab. Chicago and London: University of Chicago Press, 1996.

Sexton, Jared. "The Social Life of Social Death: On Afro-Pessimism and Black Optimism" in *Intensions* 5 (Fall/Winter 2011): 1–47.

—— "Unbearable Blackness," keynote lecture of "Terror and the Inhuman," Brown University, Providence, RI, October 25, 2012.

Sexton, Jared, and Huey Copeland. "Raw Life: An Introduction" in *Qui Parle* 13.2 (Spring/Summer 2003): 53–62.

Shih, Shu-Mei. "Comparative Racialization: An Introduction" in *PMLA* 123.5 (October 2008): 1347–62.

Smith, Anthony Paul. *A Non-Philosophical Theory of Nature: Ecologies of Thought*. New York and London: Palgrave Macmillan, 2013.

—— "Disempowerment and Mutation: François Laruelle's Engagement with Religion" in *Religion and European Philosophy: Key Thinkers from Kant to Today*. Edited by Philip Goodchild and Hollis D. Phelps. London and New York: Routledge, forthcoming.

—— "Editorial Introduction: Laruelle Does Not Exist" in *Angelaki: Journal of the Theoretical Humanities* 19.2 (2014): 1–11.

—— *François Laruelle's Principles of Non-Philosophy: A Critical Introduction and Guide*. Edinburgh: Edinburgh University Press, 2016.

—— "Nature Deserves to Be Side by Side with the Angels: Nature and Messianism by Way of Non-Islam" in *Angelaki: Journal of the Theoretical Humanities* 19.1 (2014): 151–69.

Smith, Anthony Paul, and Daniel Whistler. "What is Continental Philosophy of Religion Now?" in *After the Postsecular and the Postmodern: New Essays in Continental Philosophy of Religion*. Newcastle-upon-Tyne: Cambridge Scholars Publishing, 2010. 1–24.

Smolin, Lee. *The Life of the Cosmos*. Oxford: Oxford University Press, 1997.

Steeves, H. Peter. "Mars Attacked! Interplanetary Environmental Ethics and the Science of Life" in *The Things Themselves: Phenomenology and the Return to the Everyday*. Albany: SUNY Press, 2006. 127–45.

Thacker, Eugene, Daniel Colucciello Barber, Nicola Masciandaro, and Alexander R. Galloway. *Dark Nights of the Universe*. Miami: [Name], 2013.

Weheliye, Alexander G. *Habeas Viscus: Racializing Assemblages, Biopolitics, and Black Feminist Theories of the Human*. Durham and London: Duke University Press, 2014.

Wilderson III, Frank B. *Red, White, and Black: Cinema and the Structure of U.S. Antagonisms*. Durham and London: Duke University Press, 2010.

Wolfendale, Peter. *Object-Oriented Philosophy: The Noumenon's New Clothes*. Falmouth: Urbanomic, 2014.

Žižek, Slavoj. *The Puppet and the Dwarf: The Perverse Core of Christianity*. Cambridge, MA: MIT Press, 2003.

—— *The Ticklish Subject: The Absent Centre of Political Ontology*. London and New York: Verso, 2008.

Index